STOKE CITY FOOTBALL CLUB
THE OFFICIAL YEARBOOK 2006/07

Editorial
Ian Bayley
Chris Alcock

Sidan Press Team
Simon Rosen, Julian Hill-Wood, Marc Fiszman, Mark Peters, Karim Biria, Rob Cubbon,
Anette Lundebye, Marina Kravchenko, Gareth Peters, Janet Calcott, Trevor Scimes, John Fitzroy,
Jenny Middlemarch, Anders Rasmussen, Lim Wai-Lee, Emma Turner, Charles Grove, Tim Ryman

Photography
Action Images

Copyright © 2006 Stoke City Football Club

Sidan Press, 63-64 Margaret St, London W1W 8SW
Tel: 020 7580 0200
Email: info@sidanpress.com

sidanpress.com

Club Directory

Who's Who

Chairman
Peter Coates
President
Gordon Banks
Vice President
Alex Humphreys
Directors
Keith Humphreys, Phil Rawlins
Chief Executive
Tony Scholes
Manager
Tony Pulis
Director of Football
John Rudge
Academy Administration Director
Gordon Bennett
Academy Manager/U18 Coach
Noel Blake
Academy U9/U16 Assistant Director
Ronnie Sinclair
Physiotherapist
Dave Watson
Kit Manager
Winnie Hudson
Retail Manager
Wayne Cowen
Financial Controller
Ian Bailey
Club Secretary
Diane Richardson
Stadium and Safety Manager
John Alcock
Commercial Manager
John Booth
Ticket Office Manager
Richard Potts
Media and Communications Manager
Ian Bayley
Football in the Community Officer
Adrian Hurst

Contacts

Ticket Office
Tel: (01782) 592204
Fax: (01782) 592201

Ticket Information Line
(01782) 592200

Hospitality, Sales & Marketing
Tel: (01782) 592211
Fax: (01782) 592210
email: matchday@stokecityfc.com

Media and Communications
Tel: (01782) 592123/592260

Britannia Stadium Superstore
Tel: (01782) 592242
Fax: (01782) 592243
email: scfcshop@stokecityfc.com

The Stoke City Shop (Stafford Street, Hanley)
Tel: (01782) 201863
Fax: (01782) 286667

Football in the Community
Tel: (01782) 592252
Fax: (01782) 592220
email: community@stokecityfc.com

Safety and Maintenance
Tel: (01782) 592271

Conference and Banqueting
Tel: (01782) 592233
Fax: (01782) 592232

Accounts
Tel: (01782) 592266
Fax: (01782) 592221

Lotteries
Tel: (01782) 592288
email: lottery@stokecityfc.com

Academy
Tel: (01782) 592101
Fax: (01782) 592201

Club Honours

Division Two Champions
1932/33, 1962/63, 1992/93
Division Two Runners-Up
1921/22
Division Three (North) Champions
1926/27
Football League Cup Winners
1971/72
Football League Cup Runners-Up
1963/64
Autoglass Trophy Winners
1991/92
Auto Windscreens Shield Winners
1999/2000

Stoke City Football Club
Britannia Stadium
Stanley Matthews Way
Stoke-on-Trent
Staffs ST4 4EG

Official Website: www.stokecityfc.com
Telephone: (01782) 592222 – Main Switchboard
email: info@stokecityfc.com

Contents

Stoke City FC
Save and Support Account

EXCLUSIVELY FOR STOKE CITY FC SUPPORTERS

Great bonus from the Stoke City FC Save and Support Account

Pay

£846,117
2005 - 2006 season bonus

Thanks to over 13,600 SCFC fans, Britannia has given SCFC over

£4.1 million
from the Stoke City FC Save and Support Account since 1999

Britannia Where membership means a great deal

Stoke City FC Save and Support Account

What's in it for City fans?

- 🔵 Attractive interest rates with instant access.
- 🔵 Fantastic Stoke City FC offers including 10% discount at the club shop.
- 🔵 Special Edition Stoke City FC passbook.
- 🔵 An annual share of profits through Britannia Membership Reward. Subject to scheme rules and qualifying period.

What's in it for Stoke City FC?

- 🔵 Britannia gives Stoke City FC an annual bonus of up to 1% of the value in all savings accounts, so every pound you invest supports the future development and success of Stoke City FC.

To find out more
Call free on **0800 132 304**
Visit **britannia.co.uk/scfc**
Talk to **Britannia branch staff**

*Lines are open Mon-Fri 8am-8pm and Sat 9am-12 noon. Telephone calls may be recorded and/or monitored.
Calls from landline phones are free however, mobile providers may charge.

Britannia Building Society,
Britannia House, Leek,
Staffordshire Moorlands ST13 5RG

Britannia undertakes to comply with The Banking Code.
Copies of this Code are available on request from any of
the Society's branches or by calling free on 0800 132 304

Foreword

From Stoke City chairman Peter Coates

Welcome to the 2006/07 official Stoke City yearbook.

We are delighted to have teamed up with Sidan Press to bring you this new publication, which we hope will become your indispensable guide for the next nine months.

It includes vital information on all our Championship opponents, plus ground guides, player biographies, match reports, and a wealth of other statistics.

We are all looking forward to the new season, and with very good reason.

With the club under new ownership, and with a new manager, 2006/07 represents an exciting fresh start.

The club's financial position has been considerably improved since the summer takeover and we have a united Board of Directors and management team all working with one purpose and towards one aim – Premiership football.

Of course, the united front must also include supporters and I would like to take this opportunity to thank you for your continued support and to say we look forward to seeing you at the Britannia Stadium many times during the coming season.

The club is moving forward both on and off the field. Progress must be long-term as well as medium and short-term and this means there has been and will continue to be investment in the infrastructure of the club.

We have a lot of work to do at the club to achieve the success we desire. I firmly believe that together we can do it. I for one cannot wait for August 5th and the start of the new season.

Manager's Message
Tony Pulis

First of all, let me tell you how delighted I am to once again be the manager of Stoke City.

I didn't want to leave the club last year, and the opportunity to return and work with new chairman Peter Coates was what enticed me back.

My aim now is to help bring stability to the club and to make progress on and off the field by working closely with the chairman and the Board of Directors.

The new season is a fresh start for everyone – for the Board, for me, for the players, for the staff and of course for every supporter of Stoke City.

For the first time in a long while I feel we have a togetherness at the Britannia Stadium and I want to build on that because you need it at any club.

One of the most important factors critical for success is a good relationship between manager and chairman.

With that established, we need to build a team fans can be proud of and a team everyone wants to support.

When all that is in place, and it is being put in place, then we have a great chance of pushing forward.

One thing I can promise you this season is that the team will be very well-organised and very committed.

But we also want to use players, especially in wide positions, who have flair and, of course, players who can score goals.

I am confident that I and my management team can identify those players and then, working closely with the Board of Directors, get them in.

I am terrifically excited by the season ahead and looking forward to it immensely.

We have an interesting start, with an opening day trip to Southend followed by two big Midlands derbies at home, and hopefully we can use those matches as a launch pad for a great campaign.

How to Read the Stats

This year's review is better than ever, packed with the sort of in-depth stats which really get you close to the action. If you'd like to know why a particular match turned out the way it did, how a player's form varied over the course of the season, or how City have fared against their biggest rivals, you'll find all the info inside.

To make sure you're getting the most out of the stats, we're including this section to highlight the information presented by some of the charts and tables.

Colours

City vs Opposition

There are lots of comparisons between City and our opponents throughout the book. City stats are shown in red; opponents are shown in grey:

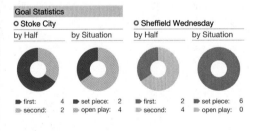

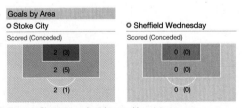

Figure 1: City stats are in red; opposition stats are grey.

WDL, Scored, Conceded

When reviewing match results, wins, draws and losses are indicated by green, grey and orange blocks, respectively. For goals, green blocks indicate goals scored; orange blocks show goals conceded:

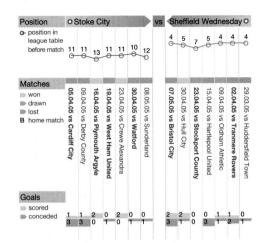

Figure 2: Wins, draws, losses and goals are clearly colour-coded.

Match Reports

The Match Report section contains reports, quotes, facts and stats from every City match of the 2005/06 season.

Stats Order (Home and Away)

The order of the stats varies depending on whether a match was home or away: for home matches, City stats are shown on the left, for away matches they're on the right:

Championship Totals	o Stoke	Sheff Wed o
Championship Appearances	311	46
Team Appearances	231	0
Goals Scored	8	1
Assists	23	4
Clean Sheets (goalkeepers)	14	0
Yellow Cards	41	7
Red Cards	2	0
Full Internationals	3	1

Figure 3: For home matches, City stats appear on the left.

Championship Totals	○Leicester	Stoke○
Championship Appearances	221	294
Team Appearances	183	176
Goals Scored	21	15
Assists	15	20
Clean Sheets (goalkeepers)	0	15
Yellow Cards	33	29
Red Cards	1	3
Full Internationals	8	2

Figure 4: For away matches, City stats appear on the right.

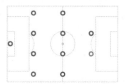

Figure 6: Major positions are shown in dark red; minor positions are shown in light red.

Form Coming into Fixture

Stats are from the previous seven league games. For the first few matches, these stats include games from the end of the previous season.

Team Statistics

Stats are for starters and playing subs. The "Championship Totals" chart measures performance within the Championship (with the exception of "Full Internationals").

Championship Totals	○Stoke	Sheff Wed○
Championship Appearances	311	46
Team Appearances	231	0
Goals Scored	8	1
Assists	23	4
Clean Sheets (goalkeepers)	14	0
Yellow Cards	41	7
Red Cards	2	0
Full Internationals	3	1

Age/Height

Stoke City Age	Sheffield Wednesday Age
▶ 26 yrs	▶ 23 yrs, 6 mo
Stoke City Height	Sheffield Wednesday Height
▶ 6'	▶ 6'

Figure 5: Team statistics are for starters and playing subs.

Player Profiles

The Player Profile section provides season reviews and comprehensive stats for City's players. The section is organised by position, starting with goalkeepers.

Pitch Diagram

The diagram shows all positions the player played during 2005/06. The main position is denoted by a dark red circle; alternative positions are denoted by light red circles:

Player Performance

All stats show league performance, with the exception of the "Cup Games" table. The "League Performance" chart provides an excellent overview of the player's performance over the course of the season. At a glance, you can see when and how much he played, and how he contributed to the team's overall performance at different stages of the season.

Career History

Due to the difficulties involved in obtaining reliable stats for international clubs, the "Clubs" table is incomplete for players who have played for non-English clubs. The names of all clubs have been included for the reader's interest, but international stats have been left blank.

The Opposition

The Opposition section shows how City sizes up against the other 23 teams in the Championship.

Points / Position

The points / position chart is a snapshot of the last 10 years' league performance of City and the opponent. For any season when the two teams met in the league, the results of their clashes are shown at the bottom of the chart.

Championship Head-to-Head

Stats are only for the two teams' meetings in the Championship.

Make recycling your goal this summer

GLASS **2** PLASTIC **0** CANS **0** PAPER **6**

the **BIG** recycle

the **BIG** recycle 2006

"Over half of the rubbish we put in our bins can be recycled or composted. Don't forget to support recycling this summer!"

Gabby Logan

STOKE CITY · 1863 · THE POTTERS

the **BIG** recycle

www.recyclenow.com

0-0

Stoke City ○
Sheffield Wednesday ○

▶ Kevin Harper battles to keep possession

Event Line

3 ○ ■	Simek	
13 ○ ■	Taggart	
	Foul	
14 ○ ⇄	Buxton > Russell	
Half time 0-0		
70 ○ ■	Lee	
72 ○ ⇄	Harper > Kolar	
73 ○ ⇄	Proudlock > Best	
78 ○ ⇄	Partridge > Eagles	
85 ○ ■	Rocastle	
90 ○ ⇄	Henry > Junior	
Full time 0-0		

Johan Boskamp endured a frustrating start to his reign in an opening-day stalemate against newly-promoted Sheffield Wednesday.

Despite playing most of the game with ten men after Gerry Taggart saw red, sub Kevin Harper missed a second-half penalty to complete a luckless afternoon.

Referee Mark Clattenburg sent Taggart off for a late challenge on Wednesday's Leon Best after 13 minutes.

Wednesday withstood heavy pressure, with debutants Junior firing over and Carl Hoefkens heading inches over before Mamady Sidibe's header went equally close.

Martin Kolar forced a superb save from David Lucas before Steve Simonsen equalled that with a stunning stop to keep out Chris Brunt's powerful free-kick. The visitors had their moments and thought they'd grabbed the lead when Lee Peacock met Best's overhead kick and turned the ball home from close range, but he was offside.

John Hills' trip on Hoefkens led to the late penalty, which Harper blazed over and Sidibe missed a late chance.

Quote	Championship Milestone
● **Johan Boskamp**	▶ **Debut**
I guess 0-0 after having a player sent-off so early does not seem such a bad result, but when you have missed a penalty it becomes disappointing.	Martin Kolar, Junior and Carl Hoefkens all made their Championship debuts.

Venue:	Britannia Stadium	Referee:	M.Clattenburg - 05/06
Attendance:	18,744	Matches:	0
Capacity:	28,218	Yellow Cards:	0
Occupancy:	66%	Red Cards:	0

Stoke City
Sheffield Wednesday

Form Coming into Fixture

▶ Martin Kolar runs at the defence

Team Statistics

Starting Line-Ups

Stoke City

Simonsen

Halls — Chadwick

Hoefkens — Junior Henry — Russell Buxton — Peacock

Taggart — Brammer — Sidibe — Best Proudlock

Broomes — Kolar Harper

Sheffield Wednesday

Lucas

Wood — Hills

Rocastle — Brunt

Whelan — Lee

Eagles Partridge — Simek

▶ 4/4/1/1   ▶ 4/4/2

Unused Sub: de Goey, Dyer

Unused Sub: Heckingbottom, Adams, O'Brien

Championship Totals	○Stoke	Sheff Wed○
Championship Appearances	311	46
Team Appearances	231	0
Goals Scored	8	1
Assists	23	4
Clean Sheets (goalkeepers)	14	0
Yellow Cards	41	7
Red Cards	2	0
Full Internationals	3	1

Age/Height

Stoke City Age

▶ **26 yrs**

Sheffield Wednesday Age

▶ **23 yrs, 6 mo**

Stoke City Height

▶ **6'**

Sheffield Wednesday Height

▶ **6'**

Match Statistics

League Table after Fixture

	Played	Won	Drawn	Lost	For	Against	Pts
13 Sheff Wed	1	0	1	0	0	0	1
14 Southampton	1	0	1	0	0	0	1
15 Stoke	1	0	1	0	0	0	1
16 Wolverhampton	1	0	1	0	0	0	1
17 Leeds	0	0	0	0	0	0	0
18 Millwall	0	0	0	0	0	0	0
19 Burnley	1	0	0	1	1	2	0
20 Crystal Palace	1	0	0	1	1	2	0
21 Reading	1	0	0	1	1	2	0

Statistics	○Stoke	Sheff Wed○
Goals	0	0
Shots on Target	4	5
Shots off Target	5	4
Hit Woodwork	0	0
Possession %	48	52
Corners	4	3
Offsides	1	7
Fouls	10	16
Disciplinary Points	12	12

4-2

Leicester City ○
Stoke City ○

► Michael Duberry attempts to win the race for the ball

Event Line	
3 ○ ■	McCarthy
14 ○ ⊕	de Vries / RF / OP / IA
	Assist: Wilcox
40 ○ ⇄	Dyer > Russell
Half time 1-0	
61 ○ ■	Junior
	Violent Conduct
64 ○ ⊕	Broomes / LF / C / IA
	Assist: Hoefkens
66 ○ ⊕	Connolly / LF / IFK / IA
	Assist: Gudjonsson
66 ○ ■	Simonsen
71 ○ ■	de Vries
71 ○ ⇄	Hammond > Sylla
82 ○ ⊕	Connolly / LF / OP / IA
	Assist: Williams
89 ○ ⊕	Halls / RF / OP / IA
	Assist: Chadwick
90 ○ ⊕	Connolly / RF / OP / IA
Full time 4-2	

There were goals galore at the Walker's Stadium as Leicester and City served up an early-season feast of entertaining football.

Mark De Vries' 14th minute goal gave the home side the edge, but the game's major turning point came in the second-half when Potters' midfielder Junior was dismissed following an off-the-ball incident with Joey Gudjonsson.

Junior's red card was the second in two games following Gerry Taggart's sending-off at home to Sheffield Wednesday four days earlier.

Even so, the ten men immediately drew level when Marlon Broomes scored his first goal for the club, only for David Connolly to restore home advantage within two minutes with the first of his hat-trick of strikes.

End-to-end thrills continued and Leicester looked to have the match won when Connolly struck again nine minutes from time, only for John Halls to spark off home jitters when he netted with a minute to go.

The drama continued right to the end when, with boss Johan Boskamp urging his players forward in search of an equaliser, Connolly grabbed his third.

Quote

● **Johan Boskamp**

The players showed a lot of character, but we gave the game away at the end when we were chasing a 3-3.

Championship Milestone

► **First Goal**

Both Marlon Broomes and John Halls netted their first goals in the Championship.

Venue:	Walkers Stadium	Referee:	P.Taylor - 05/06		Leicester City
Attendance:	20,519	Matches:	1		Stoke City
Capacity:	32,500	Yellow Cards:	3		
Occupancy:	63%	Red Cards:	0		

Form Coming into Fixture

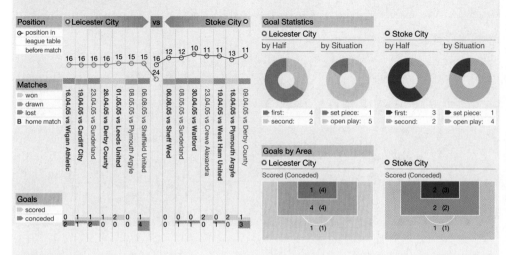

Team Statistics

Starting Line-Ups

Leicester City: Douglas; Gilbert, Wilcox, Johansson, Williams, de Vries, Russell Dyer, Connolly, Sidibe, McCarthy, Gudjonsson, Maybury, Sylla, Hammond

Stoke City: Simonsen; Chadwick, Halls, Junior, Hoefkens, Brammer, Duberry, Kolar, Broomes

4/4/2

4/4/1/1

Unused Sub: Henderson, Stearman, Gerrbrand, Wright

Unused Sub: de Goey, Taggart, Buxton, Henry

Championship Totals

Championship Totals	Leicester	Stoke
Championship Appearances	221	294
Team Appearances	183	176
Goals Scored	21	15
Assists	15	20
Clean Sheets (goalkeepers)	0	15
Yellow Cards	33	29
Red Cards	1	3
Full Internationals	8	2

Age/Height

Leicester City Age **27 yrs**

Stoke City Age **26 yrs, 3 mo**

Leicester City Height **5'11"**

Stoke City Height **6'**

Match Statistics

League Table after Fixture

	Played	Won	Drawn	Lost	For	Against	Pts
↑ 12 Leicester	2	1	0	1	5	6	3
...	...	...	...	...	...	...	...
↑ 18 Watford	2	0	1	1	4	5	1
↓ 19 Southampton	2	0	1	1	2	3	1
● 20 Millwall	2	0	1	1	1	2	1
↓ 21 Stoke	2	0	1	1	2	4	1
↓ 22 Brighton	2	0	1	1	1	3	1
↓ 23 Burnley	2	0	0	2	2	4	0
↓ 24 Crystal Palace	2	0	0	2	2	4	0

Statistics

Statistics	Leicester	Stoke
Goals	4	2
Shots on Target	7	3
Shots off Target	7	11
Hit Woodwork	0	1
Possession %	57	43
Corners	6	4
Offsides	2	1
Fouls	18	16
Disciplinary Points	8	16

0-1

Millwall ○
Stoke City ○

▶ Martin Kolar puts Don Hutchison under pressure

Event Line	
38 ○ ⊕ Halls / RF / OP / IA	
	Assist: Dyer
44 ○ ⇄ Fangueiro > Simpson	
45 ○ ▪ Broomes	
Half time 0-1	
56 ○ ⇄ Peeters > Elliott	
62 ○ Dyer	
75 ○ Morris	
78 ○ ⇄ Harper > Dyer	
85 ○ ⇄ Igoe > Hutchison	
Full time 0-1	

Two teams looking for their first win of the season went into this clash – and afterwards there was only one.

Millwall, who had made an unconvincing start to their campaign after a troubled summer at The New Den, looked ripe for the taking and that's how it proved as John Halls' 38th minute goal – his second in two games - clinched an inaugural Championship victory for Johan Boskamp. It was enough to separate the sides and leave the Lions licking their wounds at the foot of the table. There were other chances, although the match never matched the drama of City's trip to Leicester's Walker's Stadium four days earlier.

Millwall made a flying start and Barry Hayles nearly gave them a first-minute lead when he guided Josh Simpson's cross wide before Bruce Dyer – later to join the Lions on loan - had an effort disallowed for offside from Mamady Sidibe's quickly-taken free-kick

Martin Kolar and Luke Chadwick brought the best out of home `keeper Andy Marshall in the second-half, and there was late pressure to be weathered, with Steve Simonsen keeping out Jody Morris and Bob Peeters before Karl Henry cleared Mark Phillips' header off the line.

Quote	Championship Milestone
● **Johan Boskamp**	▶ **25**
A first win is always pleasing and will settle us down. We could have killed the game off, but didn't, and that allowed Millwall to come back at us.	John Halls made his 25th appearance in the Championship.

Venue:	The New Den	
Attendance:	8,668	
Capacity:	20,146	
Occupancy:	43%	

Referee:	P.Walton - 05/06
Matches:	0
Yellow Cards:	0
Red Cards:	0

Millwall
Stoke City

Form Coming into Fixture

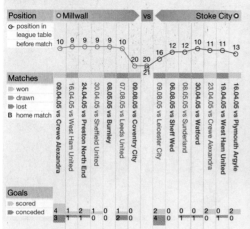

Position ○ Millwall vs Stoke City ○

○- position in league table before match

Matches
- won
- drawn
- lost
B home match

Goals
- scored
- conceded

Goal Statistics

○ Millwall — by Half / by Situation

first:	4	set piece:	2
second:	5	open play:	7

○ Stoke City — by Half / by Situation

first:	2	set piece:	1
second:	4	open play:	5

Goals by Area

○ Millwall — Scored (Conceded)

| 1 (1) |
| 8 (5) |
| 0 (1) |

○ Stoke City — Scored (Conceded)

| 2 (0) |
| 3 (5) |
| 1 (0) |

Team Statistics

Starting Line-Ups

4/5/1   4/4/2

Unused Sub: Robinson P, May

Unused Sub: de Goey, Taggart, Buxton, Gudjonsson

Championship Totals	○ Millwall	Stoke ○
Championship Appearances	341	304
Team Appearances	317	184
Goals Scored	27	15
Assists	20	28
Clean Sheets (goalkeepers)	7	15
Yellow Cards	45	27
Red Cards	5	3
Full Internationals	4	2

Age/Height

Millwall Age	Stoke City Age
27 yrs, 11 mo	26 yrs, 8 mo
Millwall Height	Stoke City Height
5'11"	6'

Match Statistics

League Table after Fixture

		Played	Won	Drawn	Lost	For	Against	Pts
↓ 8	Watford	3	1	1	1	7	6	4
↑ 9	Leeds	3	1	1	1	3	3	4
↑ 10	Southampton	3	1	1	1	3	3	4
• 11	Ipswich	3	1	1	1	2	2	4
• 12	Leicester	3	1	1	1	5	6	4
↓ 13	Plymouth	3	1	1	1	5	6	4
↑ 14	Stoke	3	1	1	1	3	4	4
...	...	...	...	...	...	...	...	...
↓ 24	Millwall	3	0	1	2	1	3	1

Statistics	○ Millwall	Stoke ○
Goals	0	1
Shots on Target	4	1
Shots off Target	1	7
Hit Woodwork	0	0
Possession %	46	54
Corners	3	5
Offsides	3	2
Fouls	17	20
Disciplinary Points	4	8

2-1

Stoke City ○
Luton Town ○

▶ Kevin Harper makes forward progress

Event Line

9	○ ⊕	Morgan / LF / OP / IA
26	○ ■	Howard
		Violent Conduct
Half time 0-1		
46	○ ⇄	Davis > Morgan
60	○ ⇄	Harper > Kolar
63	○ ⊕	Broomes / RF / OP / IA
		Assist: Sidibe
64	○ ⇄	Showunmi > Feeney
70	○ ⇄	Edwards > Brkovic
79	○ ■	Heikkinen
90	○ ⊕	Brammer / RF / OP / OA
		Assist: Henry
Full time 2-1		

Dave Brammer notched an early contender for goal of the season in the dying seconds in a dramatic victory over newly-promoted Luton.

The midfielder's scorching effort from twenty-five yards added to Marlon Broomes' second-half equaliser, which had cancelled out Dean Morgan's early opener.

Luton began strongly but were knocked out of their stride when striker Steve Howard was sent off after an off-the-ball clash with Carl Hoefkens midway through the first-half, continuing the trend of red cards in City's early-season games.

They already led through Morgan, who seized on a loose to fire past Steve Simonsen from twelve yards after just eight minutes and continued to threaten with ten men as Warren Feeney crashed a shot against the post.

The equaliser arrived on the hour when Broomes' powerful volley squirmed under Town 'keeper Marlon Beresford. It was all-out attack after that, and Brammer smashed a shot against the post before the Luton defence was finally breached in injury time with Brammer's sensational strike.

Quote

● Dave Brammer

Sometimes the best way to win the game is in the last minute because it gives the opposition no chance to get back in the game and luckily that's what we did.

Form Coming into Fixture

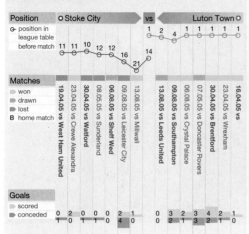

▶ Dave Brammer celebrates his late winner

Team Statistics

Starting Line-Ups

Stoke City: Simonsen; Broomes, Kolar, Harper, Duberry, Brammer, Hoefkens, Henry, Halls, Chadwick, Sidibe, Feeney, Showunmi, Dyer, Howard

Luton Town: Brkovic, Foley, Edwards, Robinson, Heikkinen, Beresford, Nicholls, Davies C, Morgan, Davis, Underwood

▶ 4/4/2   ▶ 4/4/2

Unused Sub: de Goey, Taggart, Buxton, Gudjonsson

Unused Sub: Brill, Perrett

Championship Totals	○ Stoke	Luton ○
Championship Appearances	316	52
Team Appearances	196	34
Goals Scored	16	7
Assists	29	6
Clean Sheets (goalkeepers)	16	0
Yellow Cards	29	5
Red Cards	3	0
Full Internationals	2	5

Age/Height

Stoke City Age	Luton Town Age
▶ 26 yrs, 8 mo	▶ 26 yrs, 10 mo
Stoke City Height	Luton Town Height
▶ 6'	▶ 5'11"

Match Statistics

League Table after Fixture

		Played	Won	Drawn	Lost	For	Against	Pts
↓ 6	Luton	4	2	1	1	6	5	7
↑ 7	Ipswich	4	2	1	1	4	3	7
↑ 8	Southampton	4	2	1	1	4	3	7
↑ 9	Stoke	4	2	1	1	5	5	7
↓ 10	Wolverhampton	4	2	1	1	3	3	7
↓ 11	QPR	4	2	1	1	4	5	7
↓ 12	Crewe	4	1	3	0	7	6	6
↑ 13	Hull	4	1	2	1	3	2	5
↓ 14	Leicester	4	1	2	1	7	8	5

Statistics	○ Stoke	Luton ○
Goals	2	1
Shots on Target	8	7
Shots off Target	4	4
Hit Woodwork	1	0
Possession %	56	44
Corners	6	4
Offsides	3	3
Fouls	16	8
Disciplinary Points	0	16

1-1 a.e.t

Mansfield Town ○
Stoke City ○

➡ Marlon Broomes challenges Richie Barker

Event Line

8 ○ ▦	Sidibe
11 ○ ⊕	Brammer / RF / P / IA
	Assist: Sidibe
16 ○ ⊕	Jelleyman / H / OP / IA
	Assist: Baptiste
Half time 1-1	
46 ○ ⇄	Buxton > Halls
46 ○ ⇄	Gudjonsson > Kolar
66 ○ ⇄	Dawson > Coke
67 ○ ▦	Buxton
69 ○ ⇄	Brown > Beardsley
77 ○ ⇄	Russell > Dyer
106 ○ ⇄	Birchall > Talbot
111 ○ ▦	Birchall
Full time 1-1	

City made a dramatic exit from the Carling Cup after losing a nail-biting penalty shootout at Field Mill.

Richard Barker, Rhys Day and Gareth Jelleyman all converted from the spot for the Stags while Dave Brammer, Carl Hoefkens and Michael Duberry all missed to gift the League Two side a place in the second round.

It had all looked so different after just eleven minutes, when Brammer netted, ironically from the penalty spot.

The midfielder, fresh from signing a new deal with the club, easily stroked home from twelve yards after a foul on Mamady Sidibe, to bag his second in successive outings.

The lead was short-lived, though, as five minutes later, Jelleyman's towering header from the edge of the area left Steve Simonsen stranded.

Sidibe flashed a header wide in a lively opening thirty minutes and Brammer blazed over from a set-piece.

Neither side created much in the second-half, with the only chance of note falling to Kevin Harper who, making his first start of the season, ran at the home defence before unleashing a long-range effort which curled inches wide.

The tie went into extra-time with substitute Darel Russell going close on two separate occasions, before the drama from the penalty spot unfolded.

Venue:	Field Mill	Referee:	G.Salisbury - 05/06

Attendance:	2,799	Matches:	2
Capacity:	10,000	Yellow Cards:	4
Occupancy:	28%	Red Cards:	0

Mansfield Town
Stoke City

➤ Thordur Gudjonsson tries to find a way through

Match Statistics

Starting Line-Ups

Talbot   Jelleyman
Birchall

Day   Coke
        Dawson
    Beardsley   Dyer
    Brown   Russell

White

        Barker — Sidibe
Buxton   Baptiste

Peers   Uhlenbeek

Harper   Halls
          Buxton

Henry   Hoefkens

                Simonsen

Brammer   Duberry

Kolar   Broomes
Gudjonsson

➤ 4/4/2   ➤ 4/4/2

Unused Sub: Jacobs, McLachlan   Unused Sub: de Goey, Taggart

Statistics	○ Mansfield	Stoke ○
Goals	1	1
Shots on Target	5	1
Shots off Target	8	8
Hit Woodwork	0	0
Possession %	55	45
Corners	6	5
Offsides	1	3
Fouls	10	11
Disciplinary Points	4	8

Age/Height

Mansfield Town Age
➤ **22 yrs, 6 mo**

Stoke City Age
➤ **26 yrs, 8 mo**

Mansfield Town Height
➤ **5'10"**

Stoke City Height
➤ **6'**

Quote

● **Johan Boskamp**

Everyone is down. We put out a strong team and this is not the result we wanted.

21

2-0

Crystal Palace o
Stoke City o

▶ Luke Chadwick is a picture of concentration

Event Line

35 O ▨	Broomes	
44 O ⊕	Johnson / RF / OP / OA	
	Assist: Macken	
Half time 1-0		
46 O ⇄	Harper > Kolar	
71 O ⇄	Hughes > Watson	
75 O ⇄	Morrison > Macken	
75 O ⇄	Riihilahti > McAnuff	
78 O ⇄	Dyer > Junior	
85 O ⊕	Johnson / RF / OP / IA	
	Assist: Morrison	
86 O ⇄	Wilkinson > Chadwick	
Full time 2-0		

Andy Johnson scored late in each half to condemn City to defeat at Selhurst Park.

There was little else between the two sides other than the quality marksmanship of the Eagles striker, but it was enough on the day and sealed what in the end turned out to be a relatively comfortable home win.

Johnson might have had a hat-trick but also hit the post in the first-half.
City always competed, and had chances to get on the scoresheet.

The best opportunities came from a Mamady Sidibe header just wide after 22 minutes, a Martin Kolar shot into the side netting seven minutes later and a Carl Hoefkens header which sailed over.

But Palace were more incisive when it counted. Johnson cannoned a shot against the post from six yards after being set up by Emmerson Boyce after 28 minutes but made no mistake after being teed up by Jon Macken a minute before the break, swivelling to strike a powerful shot from 20 yards beyond Steve Simonsen's dive.

His second goal came five minutes from time, swapping passes with substitute Clinton Morrison before darting through to skilfully lift his shot over Simonsen.

Quote

● Johan Boskamp

I want us to continue playing the football because if we can get the right person to put the ball in the net then I think our fans are going to be very happy.

Venue:	Selhurst Park	Referee:	M.Atkinson - 05/06		Crystal Palace
Attendance:	17,637	Matches:	2		Stoke City
Capacity:	26,309	Yellow Cards:	7		
Occupancy:	67%	Red Cards:	0		

Form Coming into Fixture

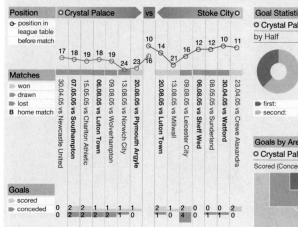

Position
- position in league table before match

Crystal Palace vs **Stoke City**

Crystal Palace positions: 17, 18, 19, 18, 19, 24, 23, 16
Stoke City positions: 10, 14, 16, 12, 12, 21, 10, 11

Matches
- won
- drawn
- lost
- B home match

Crystal Palace fixtures:
30.04.05 vs Newcastle United
07.05.05 vs Southampton
15.08.05 vs Charlton Athletic
06.08.05 vs Luton Town
09.08.05 vs Wolverhampton
13.08.05 vs Norwich City
20.08.05 vs Plymouth Argyle

Stoke City fixtures:
20.08.05 vs Luton Town
13.08.05 vs Millwall
09.08.05 vs Leicester City
06.08.05 vs Sheff Wed
08.05.05 vs Sunderland
30.04.05 vs Watford
23.04.05 vs Crewe Alexandra

Goals
- scored
- conceded

Crystal Palace: scored 0 2 2 1 1 1 | 2 1 2 0 0 0 2 conceded 0 2 2 2 2 1 0 | 1 0 4 0 1 1 0

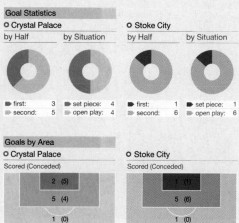

Goal Statistics

Crystal Palace
by Half — first: 3, second: 5
by Situation — set piece: 4, open play: 4

Stoke City
by Half — first: 1, second: 6
by Situation — set piece: 1, open play: 6

Goals by Area

Crystal Palace
Scored (Conceded)
2 (5)
5 (4)
1 (0)

Stoke City
Scored (Conceded)
1 (1)
5 (6)
1 (0)

Team Statistics

Starting Line-Ups

Crystal Palace: Kiraly; Borrowdale, McAnuff/Riihilahti, Ward, Watson/Hughes, Macken/Morrison, Junior/Dyer, Johnson, Sidibe, Hall F, Leigertwood, Boyce, Soares
Stoke City: Simonsen; Chadwick/Wilkinson, Buxton, Brammer, Hoefkens, Henry, Duberry, Kolar/Harper, Broomes

4/4/2

Unused Sub: Speroni, Andrews

4/4/1/1

Unused Sub: de Goey, Taggart

Championship Totals	C. Palace	Stoke
Championship Appearances	130	322
Team Appearances	43	202
Goals Scored	6	16
Assists	6	31
Clean Sheets (goalkeepers)	1	16
Yellow Cards	16	30
Red Cards	0	3
Full Internationals	7	2

Age/Height

	Crystal Palace	Stoke City
Age	25 yrs, 4 mo	25 yrs, 11 mo
Height	5'11"	6'

Match Statistics

League Table after Fixture

		Played	Won	Drawn	Lost	For	Against	Pts
↑	12 Crystal Palace	5	2	1	2	6	5	7
↓	13 Stoke	5	2	1	2	5	7	7
↓	14 Crewe	5	1	3	1	7	8	6
●	15 Coventry	5	1	2	2	5	7	5
↓	16 Leicester	5	1	2	2	7	10	5
↑	17 Preston	5	1	2	2	4	7	5
↑	18 Burnley	5	1	1	3	9	9	4
↑	19 Cardiff	5	1	1	3	6	9	4
↓	20 Plymouth	5	1	1	3	5	8	4

Statistics

Statistics	C. Palace	Stoke
Goals	2	0
Shots on Target	5	2
Shots off Target	4	8
Hit Woodwork	1	0
Possession %	52	48
Corners	1	6
Offsides	2	4
Fouls	12	13
Disciplinary Points	0	4

3-1

Stoke City ○
Norwich City ○

▶ Martin Kolar celebrates opening the scoring

Event Line

9 ○ ⊕	Kolar / RF / OP / IA
	Assist: Sidibe
38 ○ ⊕	Ashton / RF / OP / IA
	Assist: Brennan
45 ○ ⊕	Harper / LF / OP / IA
	Assist: Junior
Half time 2-1	
52 ○ ■	Huckerby
	Disent
60 ○ ⇄	McVeigh > McKenzie
61 ○ ⇄	Henry > Junior
63 ○	Duberry
69 ○ ⊕	Sidibe / RF / C / IA
79 ○ ⇄	Gallagher > Harper
83 ○	Hoefkens
85 ○	Charlton
86 ○ ⇄	Doherty > Ashton
90 ○ ⇄	Dyer > Sidibe
Full time 3-1	

A tough Bank Holiday weekend was rounded off with a superb victory over promotion favourites Norwich City at the Britannia Stadium.

Martin Kolar, Kevin Harper and Mamady Sidibe all grabbed their first goals for City as the Canaries suffered an early-season setback. Former Crewe man Dean Ashton hauled the visitors back into the match, but they wilted after Darren Huckerby saw red early in the second-half.

Kolar got the ball rolling after ten minutes, reacting quickest to a rebound after Sidibe was foiled at point-blank range by Robert Green. Sidibe and Kolar then both had headers saved before Ashton levelled matters after 36 minutes, guiding Jim Brennan's low cross past Steve Simonsen. City restored the advantage on the stroke of half-time when Harper wrong-footed Green and found the top corner of the net with a fine curling effort from 16 yards.

Norwich's task was made all the harder six minutes after the break when Huckerby was dismissed for foul and abusive language after reacting to a tackle from Marlon Broomes. Sidibe put the outcome beyond doubt on 68 minutes, swivelling to fire home from 12 yards after a Dave Brammer corner was half-cleared.

Quote

● **Johan Boskamp**

The sending-off no doubt helped us, but our ball circulation was very good and the players took their goals very well.

Championship Milestone

▶ **First Goal**

Both Martin Kolar and Kevin Harper netted their first goals in the Championship.

Venue:	Britannia Stadium	Referee:	M.S.Pike - 05/06		**Stoke City**
Attendance:	14,249	Matches:	4		**Norwich City**
Capacity:	28,218	Yellow Cards:	5		
Occupancy:	50%	Red Cards:	1		

Form Coming into Fixture

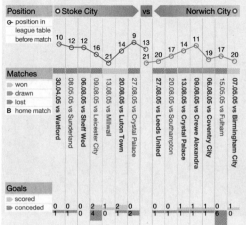

Position
- o position in league table before match

Matches
- won
- drawn
- lost
- B home match

Goals
- scored
- conceded

	vs Watford 30.04.05	vs Sunderland 08.05.05	vs Sheff Wed 06.08.05	vs Leicester City 09.08.05	vs Millwall 13.08.05	vs Luton Town 20.08.05	vs Crystal Palace 27.08.05	vs Leeds United 27.08.05	vs Southampton 20.08.05	vs Crystal Palace 13.08.05	vs Crewe Alexandra 09.08.05	vs Coventry City 06.08.05	vs Fulham 15.05.05	vs Birmingham City 07.05.05
scored	0	0	0	2	1	2	0	0	1	1	1	0		1
conceded	1	1	0	4	0	1	2	1	1	1	1	6		0

Goal Statistics

o Stoke City

by Half

| | first: | 1 | | set piece: | 1 |
| | second: | 4 | | open play: | 4 |

o Norwich City

by Half | by Situation

| | first: | 3 | | set piece: | 2 |
| | second: | 1 | | open play: | 2 |

Goals by Area

o Stoke City

Scored (Conceded)

| 0 (1) |
| 4 (7) |
| 1 (1) |

o Norwich City

Scored (Conceded)

| 2 (3) |
| 2 (6) |
| 0 (2) |

Team Statistics

Starting Line-Ups

Broomes, Kolar, Duberry, Brammer, Sidibe, Dyer, Ashton, Doherty, Chadwick, McKenzie, McVeigh, Hoefkens, Junior, Henry, Buxton, Harper, Gallagher, Simonsen

Huckerby, Colin, Marney, Fleming, Safri, Shackell, Brennan, Charlton, Green

▶ 4/4/1/1   ▶ 4/4/2

Unused Sub: de Goey, Taggart

Unused Sub: Ward, Drury, Jarrett

Championship Totals	o Stoke	Norwich o
Championship Appearances	334	77
Team Appearances	214	50
Goals Scored	16	21
Assists	31	9
Clean Sheets (goalkeepers)	16	0
Yellow Cards	31	6
Red Cards	3	0
Full Internationals	3	5

Age/Height

Stoke City Age	Norwich City Age
▶ **25 yrs, 11 mo**	▶ **26 yrs, 11 mo**
Stoke City Height	Norwich City Height
▶ **6'**	▶ **6'**

Match Statistics

League Table after Fixture

		Played	Won	Drawn	Lost	For	Against	Pts
●	1 Sheff Utd	6	5	0	1	14	7	15
●	2 Reading	6	4	1	1	13	3	13
●	3 Luton	6	4	1	1	10	6	13
↑	4 Watford	6	3	2	1	12	8	11
●	5 Southampton	6	3	2	1	7	4	11
↓	6 Leeds	5	3	1	1	6	3	10
↑	7 Stoke	6	3	1	2	8	8	10
...	...	...	...	...	...	...	...	...
↓	23 Norwich	6	0	3	3	4	8	3

Statistics	o Stoke	Norwich o
Goals	3	1
Shots on Target	6	3
Shots off Target	2	2
Hit Woodwork	0	0
Possession %	55	45
Corners	9	2
Offsides	0	2
Fouls	6	7
Disciplinary Points	8	16

0-3

Stoke City ○
Watford ○

▶ Lewis Buxton outjumps Marlon King

Event Line

24 ○ ⊕	Devlin / H / OP / IA	
	Assist: McNamee	
41 ○ ▨	Stewart	
Half time 0-1		
58 ○ ▨	Hoefkens	
60 ○ ⇄	Gallagher > Harper	
65 ○ ▨	Duberry	
66 ○ ⇄	Doyley > Devlin	
67 ○ ⊕	Young / RF / DFK / OA	
	Assist: Young	
70 ○ ▨	Simonsen	
	Foul	
71 ○ ⇄	de Goey > Kolar	
72 ○ ⊕	King / RF / P / IA	
	Assist: Young	
77 ○ ⇄	Bouazza > Stewart	
83 ○ ⇄	Bangura > Blizzard	
84 ○ ⇄	Dyer > Chadwick	
85 ○ ▨	Brammer	
Full time 0-3		

Watford pulled off a smash-and-grab victory at the Britannia Stadium in another game marred by a sending-off.

This time it was Steve Simonsen who saw red midway through the second-half with the Hornets already buzzing after sweeping into a 2-0 lead. The City 'keeper got his marching orders after pulling down Ashley Young inside the penalty area and Marlon King tucked his spot-kick past substitute Ed De Goey to put the game firmly beyond reach.

It should have been different, though, because a spate of missed chances handed the game to the visitors after they nicked the lead against the run of play through Paul Devlin after 26 minutes.

Lewis Buxton was denied an equaliser by the woodwork while ex-City 'keeper Ben Foster saved from Mamady Sidibe and Junior. Martin Kolar twice fired wide as the Watford defence creaked, but didn't buckle, and they had breathing space after 67 minutes when Ashley Young's free-kick made it 2-0.

A minute later the game was over amid the controversy of the red card and the penalty and it meant a first home league defeat for City.

Quote

● **Johan Boskamp**

I don't know how we lost that 3-0 after the chances we had, the result was crazy. Steve Simonsen said he didn't touch their player and we will appeal against his red card.

Championship Milestone

▶ **50**

Dave Brammer made his 50th appearance in the Championship.

Venue:	Britannia Stadium	Referee:	N.Miller - 05/06		**Stoke City**
Attendance:	14,565	Matches:	7		**Watford**
Capacity:	28,218	Yellow Cards:	17		
Occupancy:	52%	Red Cards:	2		

Form Coming into Fixture

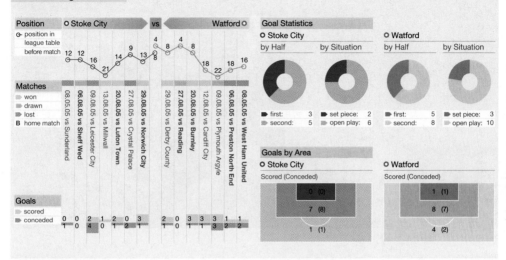

Position
- position in league table before match

Stoke City: 12 12 16 21 14 9 13 8 4
Watford: 4 8 4 8 18 22 18 16

Matches
- won
- drawn
- lost
- B home match

Stoke City matches: 08.05.05 vs Sunderland, 06.08.05 vs Sheff Wed, 09.08.05 vs Leicester City, 13.08.05 vs Millwall, 20.08.05 vs Luton Town, 27.08.05 vs Crystal Palace, 29.08.05 vs Norwich City

Watford matches: 29.08.05 vs Derby County, 27.08.05 vs Reading, 20.08.05 vs Burnley, 12.08.05 vs Cardiff City, 09.08.05 vs Plymouth Argyle, 06.08.05 vs Preston North End, 08.05.05 vs West Ham United

Goals
	scored														
scored	0	0	2	1	2	0	3		2	0	3	3	3	1	1
conceded	1	0	4	0	1	2	1		1	0	1	1	3	2	2

Goal Statistics

Stoke City
by Half | by Situation

| | first: | 3 | set piece: | 2 |
| | second: | 5 | open play: | 6 |

Watford
by Half | by Situation

| | first: | 5 | set piece: | 3 |
| | second: | 8 | open play: | 10 |

Goals by Area

Stoke City — Scored (Conceded)
0 (0)
7 (8)
1 (1)

Watford — Scored (Conceded)
1 (1)
8 (7)
4 (2)

Team Statistics

Starting Line-Ups

Stoke City (4/4/1/1)
Simonsen
Broomes, Kolar de Goey
Duberry, Junior, Sidibe, Young
Hoefkens, Brammer, Chadwick Dyer, King
Buxton, Harper Gallagher

Unused Sub: Taggart, Henry

Watford (4/4/2)
Foster
Devlin Doyley, Chambers
Spring, Carlisle
Blizzard Bangura, Mackay
McNamee, Stewart Bouazza

Unused Sub: Chamberlain, DeMerit

Championship Totals

	Stoke	Watford
Championship Appearances	326	384
Team Appearances	206	248
Goals Scored	19	25
Assists	32	22
Clean Sheets (goalkeepers)	16	1
Yellow Cards	30	33
Red Cards	3	2
Full Internationals	4	3

Age/Height

Stoke City Age	Watford Age
27 yrs, 1 mo	**24 yrs, 4 mo**
Stoke City Height	Watford Height
6'	**5'11"**

Match Statistics

League Table after Fixture

			Played	Won	Drawn	Lost	For	Against	Pts
↑	3	Watford	7	4	2	1	15	8	14
↓	4	Luton	7	4	2	1	11	7	14
•	5	Southampton	7	3	3	1	8	5	12
•	6	Wolverhampton	7	3	3	1	9	7	12
•	7	Leeds	6	3	2	1	9	6	11
↑	8	Preston	7	3	2	2	10	8	11
↑	9	Crystal Palace	6	3	1	2	8	5	10
↓	10	Stoke	7	3	1	3	8	11	10
↓	11	Ipswich	7	3	1	3	6	10	10

Statistics

	Stoke	Watford
Goals	0	3
Shots on Target	7	8
Shots off Target	7	3
Hit Woodwork	1	0
Possession %	54	46
Corners	3	6
Offsides	2	3
Fouls	12	10
Disciplinary Points	24	4

0-1

Hull City ○
Stoke City ○

Championship

13.09.05

▶ Karl Henry gives Stuart Elliott little room in which to work

Event Line

37 ○ ▪	Elliott
43 ○ ▪	Henry
Half time 0-0	
46 ○ ⇄	Russell > Henry
46 ○ ⇄	Price > France
53 ○ ▪	Gallagher
65 ○ ⇄	Green > Brown
67 ○ ⇄	Burgess > Woodhouse
74 ○ ⊕	Gallagher / RF / OP / 6Y
	Assist: Harper
75 ○ ▪	Kolar
78 ○ ▪	Russell
83 ○ ▪	Sidibe
83 ○ ⇄	Dyer > Harper
90 ○ ⇄	Junior > Kolar
Full time 0-1	

Paul Gallagher was the man of the moment with the goal which clinched a hard-fought victory at the KC Stadium.

The Scottish Under-21 international striker, in the third appearance of his season-long loan from Blackburn Rovers, marked his first start by slotting home the winner fifteen minutes from time. Gallagher reacted smartly to Kevin Harper's low cross and his neat finish showed a glimpse of the quality he was to bring to the team over the next eight months.

It was a close call against the hungry Tigers, who nearly took the lead when Stuart Elliott rattled the crossbar with a close-range header on the stroke of half-time.

The introduction of Darel Russell at the interval pepped up City as an attacking force in the second-half and Mamady Sidibe headed against crossbar from Martin Kolar's cross.

That increasing threat was rewarded in the 75th minute with the move of the game and one which stretched the home defence and allowed Harper to pick out Gallagher for his decisive strike.

Quote

● **Johan Boskamp**

It was a very good result for us, because at 0-0 Hull were on top and we would have taken that score.

Championship Milestone

▶ **First Goal**

Paul Gallagher netted his first goal in the Championship.

Venue:	Kingston	Referee:	C.H.Webster - 05/06		**Hull City**
Attendance:	18,692	Matches:	7		**Stoke City**
Capacity:	25,504	Yellow Cards:	31		
Occupancy:	73%	Red Cards:	3		

Form Coming into Fixture

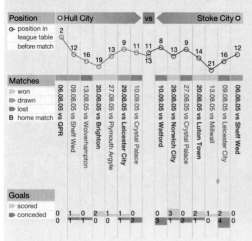

Position

- ◑ position in league table before match
- B home match

Matches
- won
- drawn
- lost

Goals
- scored
- conceded

Hull City: 06.08.05 vs QPR, 09.08.05 vs Sheff Wed, 13.08.05 vs Wolverhampton, 20.08.05 vs Brighton, 27.08.05 vs Plymouth Argyle, 29.08.05 vs Leicester City, 10.09.05 vs Crystal Palace

Stoke City: 10.09.05 vs Watford, 29.08.05 vs Norwich City, 27.08.05 vs Crystal Palace, 20.08.05 vs Luton Town, 13.08.05 vs Millwall, 09.08.05 vs Leicester City, 06.08.05 vs Sheff Wed

Goals scored: 0 1 0 2 1 1 0 | 0 3 0 2 1 2 0
Goals conceded: 0 1 1 0 0 1 2 | 3 1 2 1 0 4 0

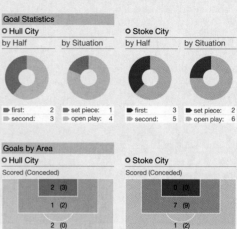

Goal Statistics

Hull City
by Half / by Situation
- first: 2
- second: 3
- set piece: 1
- open play: 4

Stoke City
by Half / by Situation
- first: 3
- second: 5
- set piece: 2
- open play: 6

Goals by Area

Hull City — Scored (Conceded)
- 2 (3)
- 1 (2)
- 2 (0)

Stoke City — Scored (Conceded)
- 0 (0)
- 7 (9)
- 1 (2)

Team Statistics

Starting Line-Ups

Hull City: Myhill; Edge, Elliott, Delaney, Woodhouse (Burgess), Brown (Green), Barmby, Cort, Welsh, Coles, France (Price) — 4/4/2

Stoke City: de Goey; Harper (Dyer), Buxton, Brammer, Hoefkens, Gallagher, Sidibe, Henry (Russell), Duberry, Kolar (Junior), Broomes — 4/4/2

Unused Sub: Duke, Ellison
Unused Sub: Duggan, Taggart

Championship Totals	◑ Hull	Stoke ◑
Championship Appearances	106	349
Team Appearances	69	261
Goals Scored	9	20
Assists	9	27
Clean Sheets (goalkeepers)	3	6
Yellow Cards	7	38
Red Cards	0	3
Full Internationals	2	4

Age/Height

	Hull City	Stoke City
Age	25 yrs, 1 mo	26 yrs, 10 mo
Height	6'	6'

Match Statistics

League Table after Fixture

		Played	Won	Drawn	Lost	For	Against	Pts
↑ 6	Stoke	8	4	1	3	9	11	13
↑ 7	Preston	8	3	3	2	10	8	12
↓ 8	Wolverhampton	8	3	3	2	10	9	12
↑ 9	QPR	8	3	3	2	7	9	12
↓ 10	Leeds	7	3	2	2	9	7	11
↑ 11	Ipswich	8	3	2	3	8	12	11
↓ 12	Crystal Palace	7	3	1	3	10	8	10
↓ 13	Derby	7	2	4	1	10	8	10
↓ 14	Hull	8	2	3	3	5	6	9

Statistics	◑ Hull	Stoke ◑
Goals	0	1
Shots on Target	9	2
Shots off Target	8	5
Hit Woodwork	1	1
Possession %	57	43
Corners	6	2
Offsides	4	3
Fouls	12	23
Disciplinary Points	4	20

0-1

Preston North End ○
Stoke City ○

➡ Paul Gallagher celebrates his 76th-minute winner

Event Line

31 ○ ⇄ Nowland > O'Neil	
Half time 0-0	
46 ○ ⇄ Harper > Chadwick	
51 ○ ⇄ Dyer > Sidibe	
62 ○ ▢ Lucketti	
66 ○ ▢ Nugent	
76 ○ ⊕ Gallagher / RF / OP / IA	
Assist: Kolar	
77 ○ ⇄ Anyinsah > Sedgwick	
86 ○ ⇄ Dichio > Agyemang	
Full time 0-1	

Paul Gallagher produced a clinical second-half strike to take his tally to two goals in two games and fire City up to fourth in the table.

The on-loan forward provided the decisive finish to stun Deepdale, just as he had done in the 1-0 win at Hull three nights earlier.

This time, last season's beaten play-off finalists Preston were the victims as the Scot provided the cutting edge to some fine work by Martin Kolar.

The Czech winger seized on casual play by the North End defence before cutting back a perfect ball into Gallagher's path, and he made no mistake with a low shot from 16 yards.

One goal always looked like it would be enough to settle a tight contest with defences dominating although Steve Simonsen had to make a brilliant double save from David Jones and Patrick Agyemang's follow-up in the 72nd minute.

Late home pressure produced a chance for David Nugent, but Simonsen's positioning was perfect, while in injury time Claude Davis was unable to keep his close-range header down.

Quote

● **Johan Boskamp**

When you win a game away from home you must always be happy, and it was a great result.

Venue:	Deepdale	Referee:	G.Laws - 05/06
Attendance:	12,453	Matches:	5
Capacity:	22,225	Yellow Cards:	25
Occupancy:	56%	Red Cards:	1

Preston North End
Stoke City

Form Coming into Fixture

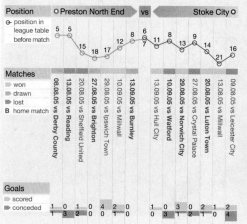

Position

o- position in league table before match

Matches
- won
- drawn
- lost
- B home match

5 5 15 18 17 12 8 6 11 7 8 13 9 14 21 16

08.08.05 vs Derby County
13.08.05 vs Reading
20.08.05 vs Sheffield United
27.08.05 vs Brighton
29.08.05 vs Ipswich Town
10.09.05 vs Millwall
13.09.05 vs Burnley
13.09.05 vs Hull City
10.09.05 vs Watford
29.08.05 vs Norwich City
27.08.05 vs Crystal Palace
20.08.05 vs Luton Town
13.08.05 vs Millwall
09.08.05 vs Leicester City

Goals
- scored
- conceded

| 1 | 0 | 1 | 0 | 4 | 2 | 0 | | 1 | 0 | 3 | 0 | 2 | 1 | 2 |
| 1 | 3 | 2 | 0 | 0 | 1 | 0 | | 0 | 3 | 1 | 2 | 1 | 0 | 4 |

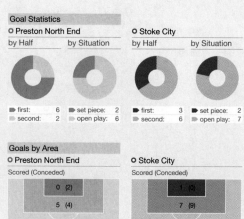

Goal Statistics

o Preston North End

by Half | by Situation

first: 6 | set piece: 2
second: 2 | open play: 6

o Stoke City

by Half | by Situation

first: 3 | set piece: 2
second: 6 | open play: 7

Goals by Area

o Preston North End
Scored (Conceded)

0 (2)
5 (4)
3 (1)

o Stoke City
Scored (Conceded)

1 (0)
7 (9)
1 (2)

Team Statistics

Starting Line-Ups

Davidson | Jones D | Chadwick / Harper | Buxton
Davis | O'Neil / Nowland | Russell | Hoefkens
Nash | Agyemang / Dichio | Gallagher | Simonsen
Lucketti | McKenna | Nugent | Sidibe / Dyer | Brammer | Duberry
Alexander | Sedgwick / Anyinsah | Kolar | Broomes

▶ 4 / 4 / 2   ▶ 4 / 4 / 1 / 1

Unused Sub: Mawene, Etuhu   Unused Sub: de Goey, Junior, Halls

Championship Totals

	o Preston	Stoke o
Championship Appearances	454	375
Team Appearances	378	255
Goals Scored	58	22
Assists	46	32
Clean Sheets (goalkeepers)	5	16
Yellow Cards	57	44
Red Cards	3	3
Full Internationals	5	3

Age/Height

Preston North End Age
▶ **27 yrs, 5 mo**

Stoke City Age
▶ **26 yrs, 4 mo**

Preston North End Height
▶ **6'**

Stoke City Height
▶ **6'**

Match Statistics

League Table after Fixture

		Played	Won	Drawn	Lost	For	Against	Pts
• 1	Sheff Utd	8	7	0	1	17	7	21
• 2	Reading	8	5	2	1	17	6	17
• 3	Watford	8	5	2	1	17	9	17
↑ 4	Stoke	9	5	1	3	10	11	16
↓ 5	Luton	8	4	2	2	11	8	14
↓ 6	Southampton	8	3	4	1	10	7	13
• 7	Preston	9	3	3	3	10	9	12
• 8	Wolverhampton	8	3	3	2	10	9	12
• 9	QPR	8	3	3	2	7	9	12

Statistics

	o Preston	Stoke o
Goals	0	1
Shots on Target	5	3
Shots off Target	6	4
Hit Woodwork	0	0
Possession %	50	50
Corners	12	4
Offsides	0	2
Fouls	18	12
Disciplinary Points	8	0

1-3

Stoke City ○
Wolves ○

► Martin Kolar takes on Ki-Hyeon Seol

Event Line

42 ○ ⊕ Cort / RF / OP / 6Y	
Assist: Seol	
Half time 0-1	
46 ○ ⇄ Harper > Chadwick	
48 ○ ⊕ Miller / H / OP / 6Y	
Assist: Seol	
58 ○ ■ Buxton	
66 ○ ⇄ Junior > Brammer	
71 ○ ⇄ Dyer > Kolar	
73 ○ ⊕ Naylor / LF / DFK / OA	
Assist: Cort	
85 ○ ⇄ Ndah > Miller	
90 ○ ⊕ Buxton / H / C / IA	
Assist: Gallagher	
Full time 1-3	

Topsy-turvy September continued as encouraging back-to-back away victories were followed by a deflating second successive home defeat.

Lewis Buxton's first goal for City was nothing more than a late consolation with the points already in the bag for the men from Molineux thanks to Carl Cort, Kenny Miller and Lee Naylor.

The deadlock was broken three minutes before the break when Cort tapped home Seol's low cross and Wolves doubled their advantage a minute into the second-half when Miller flicked Seol's cross beyond Simonsen.

Paul Gallagher missed a great chance to reduce the deficit, but blasted over, before the game was but beyond doubt 18 minutes from time when Lee Naylor rattled in a superb free-kick from 30 yards.

City kept going with Michael Duberry heading wide and volleying over before finally finding the net in injury time through Lewis Buxton's looping header.

Quote

● **Johan Boskamp**

Wolves were better than us. They were quicker on the ball and always found the free man and especially in the first-half we gave them lots of space and the chance to play.

Championship Milestone

► **First Goal**

Lewis Buxton netted his first goal in the Championship.

Venue:	Britannia Stadium	Referee:	M.Atkinson - 05/06		Stoke City
Attendance:	18,183	Matches:	6		Wolverhampton Wanderers
Capacity:	28,218	Yellow Cards:	14		
Occupancy:	64%	Red Cards:	0		

Form Coming into Fixture

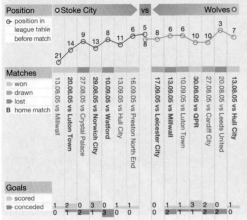

Position

- o– position in league table before match

Stoke City vs Wolves

21 14 9 13 8 11 6 5 8 8 6 6 10 10 3 7

Matches

- won
- drawn
- lost
- B home match

13.08.05 vs Millwall
20.08.05 vs Luton Town
27.08.05 vs Crystal Palace
29.08.05 vs Norwich City
10.09.05 vs Watford
13.09.05 vs Hull City
16.09.05 vs Preston North End
17.09.05 vs Leicester City
13.09.05 vs Millwall
10.09.05 vs Luton Town
30.08.05 vs QPR
27.08.05 vs Cardiff City
20.08.05 vs Leeds United
13.08.05 vs Hull City

Goals

- scored
- conceded

| scored | 1 | 2 | 0 | 3 | 0 | 1 | 1 | | 0 | 1 | 1 | 3 | 2 | 0 | 1 |
| conceded | 0 | 1 | 2 | 1 | 3 | 0 | 0 | | 0 | 2 | 1 | 1 | 2 | 2 | 0 |

Goal Statistics

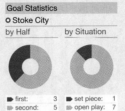

o Stoke City

by Half | by Situation

- first: 3
- second: 5
- set piece: 1
- open play: 7

o Wolverhampton Wanderers

by Half | by Situation

- first: 5
- second: 3
- set piece: 0
- open play: 7
- own goals: 1

Goals by Area

o Stoke City

Scored (Conceded)

1 (0)
6 (5)
1 (2)

o Wolverhampton Wanderers

Scored (Conceded)

5 (1)
3 (5)
0 (2)

Team Statistics

Starting Line-Ups

Broomes, Kolar, Dyer, Seol, Edwards, Cameron, Duberry, Brammer, Junior, Sidibe, Gyepes, Simonsen, Cort, Kennedy, Oakes, Hoefkens, Russell, Gallagher, Lescott, Ricketts, Buxton, Chadwick, Harper, Miller, Ndah, Naylor

4/4/1/1 | 4/3/3

Unused Sub: de Goey, Halls | Unused Sub: Postma, Craddock, Davies, Olofinjana

Championship Totals	o Stoke	Wolves o
Championship Appearances	394	417
Team Appearances	274	411
Goals Scored	23	55
Assists	34	51
Clean Sheets (goalkeepers)	17	8
Yellow Cards	44	37
Red Cards	4	1
Full Internationals	3	6

Age/Height

Stoke City Age	Wolverhampton Wanderers Age
26 yrs, 1 mo	27 yrs
Stoke City Height	Wolverhampton Wanderers Height
6'	6'

Match Statistics

League Table after Fixture

		Played	Won	Drawn	Lost	For	Against	Pts
↑ 5	Wolverhampton	10	4	4	2	13	10	16
↓ 6	Stoke	10	5	1	4	11	14	16
↓ 7	Southampton	10	3	6	1	12	9	15
↑ 8	QPR	10	4	3	3	9	11	15
↓ 9	Leeds	9	4	2	3	10	9	14
↑ 10	Ipswich	10	4	2	4	10	13	14
↓ 11	Preston	10	3	4	3	11	10	13
↓ 12	Derby	10	2	6	2	14	13	12
↑ 13	Hull	10	3	3	4	7	7	12

Statistics	o Stoke	Wolves o
Goals	1	3
Shots on Target	5	3
Shots off Target	6	5
Hit Woodwork	0	0
Possession %	52	48
Corners	5	2
Offsides	4	1
Fouls	14	15
Disciplinary Points	4	0

0-3

Stoke City ○
Cardiff City ○

▶ Michael Duberry brings the ball out of defence

Event Line

10 ○ ⊕	Jerome / RF / OP / OA	
	Assist: Ledley	
12 ○ ⊕	Purse / H / IFK / IA	
	Assist: Koumas	
14 ○ ▪	Russell	
20 ○ ▪	Ledley	
43 ○ ⊕	Jerome / LF / OP / OA	
	Assist: Ledley	
Half time 0-3		
71 ○ ▪	Jerome	
72 ○ ⇄	Lee > Ricketts	
79 ○ ⇄	Parry > Cooper	
84 ○ ⇄	Kolar > Chadwick	
Full time 0-3		

Three first-half defensive lapses proved costly as two goals from the highly-rated Cameron Jerome and another from Darren Purse sent Cardiff back to South Wales with three easy points.

Paul Gallagher was one of the brighter sparks on a bleak night and came closest to scoring when he struck the post in the second-half.

The game was well up by then, though, thanks to the Bluebirds' express start. Jerome raced onto a through ball from Jason Koumas after just ten minutes and fired clinically past Steve Simonsen. Cardiff doubled their advantage minutes later when Koumas' teasing free-kick was glanced beyond Simonsen by Purse.

It was three in the 42nd minute when Jerome latched onto another threaded pass, this time from Joe Ledley, and rounded Simonsen before planting into an empty net.

Gallagher rattled the woodwork with his free-kick and skipper Michael Duberry headed narrowly wide from a Gallagher corner in the closing minutes.

Quote

● **Johan Boskamp**

This was very poor, by far our worst performance of the season. We gave them a two-goal start and made it easy for them to win. It has been a very strange month for us.

Venue:	Britannia Stadium	Referee:	R.J.Beeby - 05/06		Stoke City
Attendance:	12,240	Matches:	10		Cardiff City
Capacity:	28,218	Yellow Cards:	21		
Occupancy:	43%	Red Cards:	1		

Form Coming into Fixture

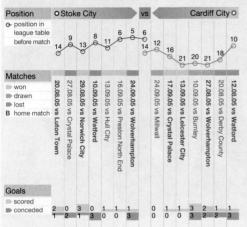

Position
Stoke City vs Cardiff City

- position in league table before match

Matches
- won
- drawn
- lost
- B home match

Matches:
20.08.05 vs Luton Town
27.08.05 vs Crystal Palace
29.08.05 vs Norwich City
10.09.05 vs Watford
13.09.05 vs Hull City
16.09.05 vs Preston North End
24.09.05 vs Wolverhampton
24.09.05 vs Millwall
17.09.05 vs Crystal Palace
13.09.05 vs Leicester City
10.09.05 vs Burnley
27.08.05 vs Wolverhampton
20.08.05 vs Derby County
12.08.05 vs Watford

Goals
- scored
- conceded

Stoke scored: 2 0 3 0 1 1 1
Stoke conceded: 1 2 1 3 0 0 3

Cardiff scored: 0 1 1 3 2 1 1
Cardiff conceded: 0 0 0 3 2 2 3

Goal Statistics

Stoke City
by Half | by Situation
- first: 2
- second: 6
- set piece: 2
- open play: 6

Cardiff City
by Half | by Situation
- first: 5
- second: 4
- set piece: 4
- open play: 5

Goals by Area

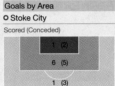

Stoke City — Scored (Conceded)
- 1 (2)
- 6 (5)
- 1 (3)

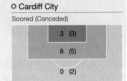

Cardiff City — Scored (Conceded)
- 3 (3)
- 6 (5)
- 0 (2)

Team Statistics

Starting Line-Ups

Broomes, Chadwick (Kolar), Koumas, Weston
Duberry, Junior, Sidibe, Ricketts (Lee), Whitley, Purse
Simonsen, Alexander
Hoefkens, Russell, Gallagher, Jerome, Ledley, Loovens
Buxton, Harper, Cooper (Parry), Barker

4/4/1/1 | 4/4/2

Unused Sub: de Goey, Halls, Henry, Dyer

Unused Sub: Margetson, Cox, Ardley

Championship Totals	Stoke	Cardiff
Championship Appearances	310	401
Team Appearances	226	296
Goals Scored	13	35
Assists	27	28
Clean Sheets (goalkeepers)	17	8
Yellow Cards	34	49
Red Cards	4	2
Full Internationals	3	7

Age/Height

	Stoke City Age	Cardiff City Age
	25 yrs, 5 mo	25 yrs, 3 mo
	Stoke City Height	Cardiff City Height
	6'	6'

Match Statistics

League Table after Fixture

		Played	Won	Drawn	Lost	For	Against	Pts
•	1 Sheff Utd	11	10	0	1	24	10	30
•	2 Reading	10	7	2	1	19	6	23
↑	3 Luton	11	6	3	2	17	10	21
↑	4 Wolverhampton	11	5	4	2	17	10	19
↓	5 Watford	10	5	3	2	19	12	18
↑	6 QPR	11	4	4	3	10	12	16
↓	7 Stoke	11	5	1	5	11	17	16
↓	8 Southampton	10	3	6	1	12	9	15
↑	9 Cardiff	10	4	3	3	14	12	15

Statistics	Stoke	Cardiff
Goals	0	3
Shots on Target	3	5
Shots off Target	7	7
Hit Woodwork	2	0
Possession %	50	50
Corners	6	1
Offsides	2	4
Fouls	13	17
Disciplinary Points	4	8

2-1

Plymouth Argyle ○
Stoke City ○

▶ Darel Russell is brought crashing to the ground

Event Line
Half time 0-0

46 ○ ⇄	Sigurdsson > Kolar	
47 ○ ⊕	Chadwick / RF / OP / 6Y	
	Assist: Gallagher	
50 ○ ⊕	Russell / LF / OG / 6Y	
	Assist: Capaldi	
53 ○ ⇄	Taylor > Chadwick	
53 ○ ⇄	Buzsaky > Gudjonsson	
70 ○ ▨	Gallagher	
71 ○ ⇄	Dyer > Sidibe	
76 ○ ▨	Buxton	
77 ○ ⊕	Buzsaky / LF / IFK / IA	
86 ○ ⇄	Henry > Chadwick	

Full time 2-1

This was a hard luck story in every sense – a fluke own goal from Darel Russell setting Plymouth on their way while the woodwork twice came to their rescue.

Good fortune certainly smiled on former City boss Tony Pulis on his home debut as Argyle manager after succeeding Bobby Williamson.

Luke Chadwick netted two minutes into the second-half after being set up by Paul Gallagher's clever pass and, after a dominating first-half performance, the points appeared to be on their way back to the Potteries. But the lead was short-lived when Tony Capaldi's shot was saved by Steve Simonsen, only for the ball to rebound off Russell and creep over the line.

Akos Buszaky then netted what proved to be the winning goal in the 77th minute after being left unmarked at a free-kick.

Paul Gallagher hit the post from 20 yards after 18 minutes and Hannes Sigurdsson did the same just after Plymouth's equaliser.

Quote
● **Johan Boskamp**

Fortune was not with us and we were denied a clear penalty. However, we cannot use that as a reason for losing.

Championship Milestone
▶ **First Goal**

Luke Chadwick netted his first goal in the Championship for Stoke.

Venue:	Home Park	Referee:	M.Russell - 05/06	Plymouth Argyle
Attendance:	12,604	Matches:	9	Stoke City
Capacity:	20,922	Yellow Cards:	16	
Occupancy:	60%	Red Cards:	1	

Form Coming into Fixture

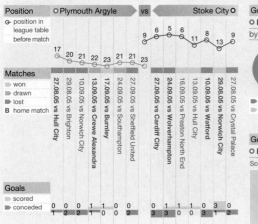

Position

○ Plymouth Argyle vs Stoke City ○

⊙ position in league table before match

Matches
- won
- drawn
- lost
- B home match

	27.08.05 vs Hull City	29.08.05 vs Brighton	10.09.05 vs Norwich City	13.09.05 vs Crewe Alexandra	17.09.05 vs Burnley	24.09.05 vs Southampton	27.09.05 vs Sheffield United	27.09.05 vs Cardiff City	24.09.05 vs Wolverhampton	16.09.05 vs Preston North End	13.09.05 vs Hull City	10.09.05 vs Watford

Goals
- scored
- conceded

| scored | 0 | 0 | 0 | 1 | 1 | 0 | 0 | | 0 | 1 | 1 | 1 | 0 | 3 | 0 |
| conceded | 1 | 2 | 2 | 1 | 0 | 0 | 2 | | 3 | 3 | 0 | 0 | 3 | 1 | 2 |

Goal Statistics

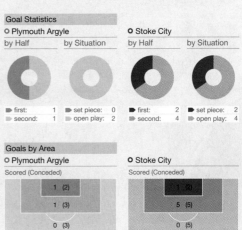

○ Plymouth Argyle

by Half | by Situation

■ first: 1 ▶ set piece: 0
■ second: 1 ▶ open play: 2

○ Stoke City

by Half | by Situation

■ first: 2 ▶ set piece: 2
■ second: 4 ▶ open play: 4

Goals by Area

○ Plymouth Argyle — Scored (Conceded)
- 1 (2)
- 1 (3)
- 0 (3)

○ Stoke City — Scored (Conceded)
- 1 (2)
- 5 (5)
- 0 (5)

Team Statistics

Starting Line-Ups

Brevett, Capaldi, Chadwick Henry, Buxton

Aljofree, Norris, Evans, Gallagher, Russell, Hoefkens

Larrieu, Simonsen

Doumbe, Wotton, Chadwick Taylor, Sidibe Dyer, Junior, Duberry

Barness, Gudjonsson Buzsaky, Kolar Sigurdsson, Broomes

▶ 4 / 4 / 2   ▶ 4 / 4 / 1 / 1

Unused Sub: McCormick, Connolly, Djordjic | Unused Sub: de Goey, Taggart

Championship Totals	○ Plymouth	Stoke ○
Championship Appearances	419	386
Team Appearances	399	268
Goals Scored	37	21
Assists	30	26
Clean Sheets (goalkeepers)	6	17
Yellow Cards	51	40
Red Cards	2	4
Full Internationals	4	4

Age/Height

Plymouth Argyle Age	Stoke City Age
▶ 27 yrs, 11 mo	▶ 25 yrs, 1 mo
Plymouth Argyle Height	Stoke City Height
▶ 5'11"	▶ 6'

Match Statistics

League Table after Fixture

		Played	Won	Drawn	Lost	For	Against	Pts
●	4 Wolverhampton	12	5	4	3	17	11	19
●	5 Watford	12	5	4	3	20	15	19
●	6 Leeds	11	5	3	3	13	10	18
●	7 Southampton	12	3	8	1	13	10	17
↑	8 Ipswich	12	5	2	5	12	17	17
↓	9 QPR	11	4	4	3	10	12	16
↓	10 Stoke	12	5	1	6	19	16	16
...	...	...	...	...	...	...	...	...
↑	20 Plymouth	12	3	3	6	9	16	12

Statistics	○ Plymouth	Stoke ○
Goals	2	1
Shots on Target	4	4
Shots off Target	4	8
Hit Woodwork	0	2
Possession %	59	41
Corners	1	3
Offsides	2	1
Fouls	8	17
Disciplinary Points	0	8

2-1

Derby County ○
Stoke City ○

▶ Hannes Sigurdsson fires the ball goalwards

Event Line

10 ○ ▪	Buxton	
28 ○ ▪	Russell	
37 ○ ▪	Johnson M	
45 ○ ⊕	Idiakez / RF / OP / OA	
	Assist: Peschisolido	

Half time 1-0

59 ○ ⊕	Hoefkens / RF / C / OA	
	Assist: Chadwick	
73 ○ ⇄	Bangoura > Sigurdsson	
74 ○ ⇄	Tudgay > El Hamdaoui	
82 ○ ⇄	Kolar > Chadwick	
84 ○ ⇄	Jackson > Smith	
86 ○ ⊕	Peschisolido / RF / OP / 6Y	
	Assist: Bisgaard	
90 ○ ⇄	Nyatanga > Peschisolido	

Full time 2-1

The Rams grabbed a late goal to snatch the points at Pride Park.

It was a former City favourite, Paul Peschisolido, who delivered the killer blow just four minutes from time.

Inigo Idiakez fired the home side ahead just before half-time but a draw looked on the cards after Carl Hoefkens equalised on the hour.

The game was always tight and while Derby had more possession in the opening half hour Hannes Sigurdsson went closest to scoring when his effort was hacked off the line by Peter Whittingham.

Paul Gallagher saw a header saved by Kevin Poole but it was the accuracy of Idiakez seconds before the half-time whistle which broke the deadlock as he found the bottom corner of Steve Simonsen's net from 18 yards.

Hoefkens' equaliser came via a deflection and Darel Russell and Mamady Sidibe both went close before Peschisolido turned home Morten Bisgaard's cross in the 86th minute to confirm a rather undeserved fourth successive league defeat for City.

Quote

● **Johan Boskamp**

In the second-half we were in control and after our equaliser I though we might win. But we didn't take our chances and gave the ball away too much.

Championship Milestone

▶ **First Goal**

Carl Hoefkens netted his first goal in the Championship.

Venue:	Pride Park	Referee:	K.Stroud - 05/06	Derby County
Attendance:	22,229	Matches:	12	Stoke City
Capacity:	33,597	Yellow Cards:	55	
Occupancy:	66%	Red Cards:	2	

Form Coming into Fixture

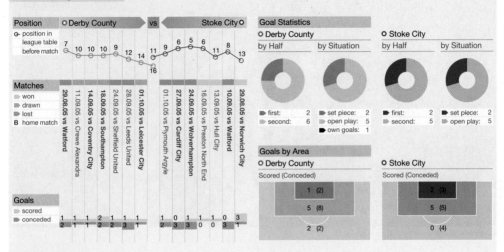

Position: Derby County vs Stoke City

- position in league table before match

Matches
- won
- drawn
- lost
- B home match

Goal Statistics

Derby County
by Half — first: 2, second: 6
by Situation — set piece: 2, open play: 5, own goals: 1

Stoke City
by Half — first: 2, second: 5
by Situation — set piece: 2, open play: 5

Goals by Area

Derby County — Scored (Conceded): 1 (2), 5 (8), 2 (2)

Stoke City — Scored (Conceded): 2 (3), 5 (5), 0 (4)

Goals
scored	1	1	1	2	1	1	1		1	0	1	1	1	0	3
conceded	2	1	1	2	2	3	1		2	3	3	0	0	3	1

Matches: 29.08.05 vs Watford, 11.09.05 vs Crewe Alexandra, 14.09.05 vs Coventry City, 18.09.05 vs Southampton, 24.09.05 vs Sheffield United, 28.09.05 vs Leeds United, 01.10.05 vs Leicester City, 01.10.05 vs Plymouth Argyle, 27.09.05 vs Cardiff City, 24.09.05 vs Wolverhampton, 16.09.05 vs Preston North End, 13.09.05 vs Hull City, 10.09.05 vs Watford, 29.08.05 vs Norwich City

Team Statistics

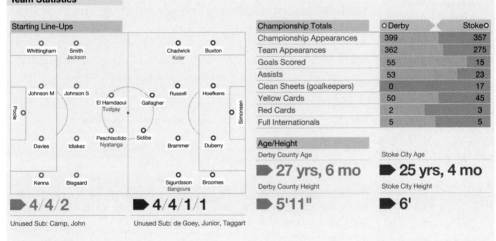

Starting Line-Ups

Derby County (4/4/2)
Whittingham, Smith, Jackson, Chadwick, Kolar, Buxton, Johnson M, Johnson S, El Hamdaoui / Tudgay, Gallagher, Russell, Hoefkens, Poole, Davies, Idiakez, Peschisolido / Nyatanga, Sidibe, Brammer, Duberry, Kenna, Bisgaard, Sigurdsson / Bangoura, Broomes, Simonsen

Stoke City (4/4/1/1)

Unused Sub: Camp, John
Unused Sub: de Goey, Junior, Taggart

Championship Totals	Derby	Stoke
Championship Appearances	399	357
Team Appearances	362	275
Goals Scored	55	15
Assists	53	23
Clean Sheets (goalkeepers)	0	17
Yellow Cards	50	45
Red Cards	2	3
Full Internationals	5	5

Age/Height

	Derby County	Stoke City
Age	27 yrs, 6 mo	25 yrs, 4 mo
Height	5'11"	6'

Match Statistics

League Table after Fixture

		Played	Won	Drawn	Lost	For	Against	Pts
↑	12 Derby	13	3	7	3	18	18	16
●	13 Norwich	13	4	4	5	14	14	16
↓	14 Stoke	13	5	1	7	13	21	16
↑	15 Leicester	13	3	6	4	14	16	15
↓	16 Preston	13	3	6	4	13	15	15
●	17 Hull	13	3	5	5	10	11	14
↓	18 Burnley	13	3	4	6	19	18	13
↑	19 Plymouth	13	3	4	6	10	17	13
↓	20 Coventry	13	2	6	5	16	22	12

Statistics	Derby	Stoke
Goals	2	1
Shots on Target	11	7
Shots off Target	11	6
Hit Woodwork	0	0
Possession %	55	45
Corners	3	7
Offsides	3	4
Fouls	15	12
Disciplinary Points	4	8

2-0

Stoke City ○
Crewe Alexandra ○

▶ Michael Duberry makes sure of the points

Event Line

41 ○ ⊕	Bangoura / RF / OP / OA	
	Assist: Sigurdsson	
Half time 1-0		
63 ○ ⇄	Roberts G > Cochrane	
64 ○ ⊕	Duberry / H / OP / IA	
	Assist: Russell	
70 ○ ▢	Jones B	
75 ○ ⇄	Jones S > Vaughan	
78 ○ ⇄	Sidibe > Chadwick	
81 ○ ⇄	Suhaj > Rodgers	
85 ○ ⇄	Henry > Gallagher	
90 ○ ▢	Duberry	
	Violent Conduct	
90 ○ ⇄	Sweeney > Sigurdsson	
Full time 2-0		

A goal in each half from debutant Sam Bangoura and Michael Duberry clinched the first of the local derby honours.

After a typically tense derby start, Bangoura fired past Ben Williams from the edge of the area to tip the balance of play four minutes before the break.

Duberry then headed home his first goal for City after rising to meet Darel Russell's teasing cross and thus put the outcome beyond any doubt.

There might have been more goals after that, but Williams twice foiled Paul Gallagher while Hannes Sigurdsson shot over.

Crewe fought hard in search of a way back into the game, but it was simply not their night as substitute Pavol Suhaj saw an effort disallowed in the closing minutes and Duberry cleared off the line from Luke Varney after Simonsen saved from Kenny Lunt.

Duberry's night turned from triumph to despair in stoppage time when he was controversially dismissed by referee Nigel Miller for allegedly using an elbow in an aerial challenge with Suhaj.

Quote

● **Jan De Koning**

I'm very pleased for the boys, for ourselves and for the fans and it was a great game for Sam Bangoura with a well-taken goal.

Championship Milestone

▶ **50**

Sambegou Bangoura's goal was the 50th scored in the Championship by Stoke.

Venue:	Britannia Stadium	Referee:	N.Miller - 05/06		Stoke City
Attendance:	14,080	Matches:	12		Crewe Alexandra
Capacity:	28,218	Yellow Cards:	33		
Occupancy:	50%	Red Cards:	7		

Form Coming into Fixture

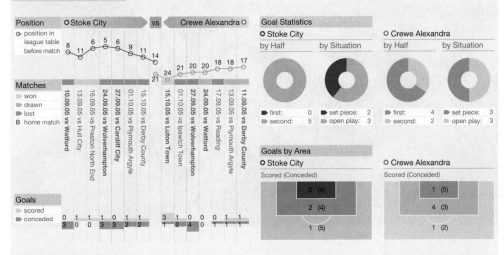

Goal Statistics

Stoke City

by Half | by Situation

- first: 0
- second: 5
- set piece: 2
- open play: 3

Crewe Alexandra

by Half | by Situation

- first: 4
- second: 2
- set piece: 3
- open play: 3

Goals by Area

Stoke City — Scored (Conceded)

2 (4)
2 (4)
1 (5)

Crewe Alexandra — Scored (Conceded)

1 (5)
4 (3)
1 (2)

Team Statistics

Starting Line-Ups

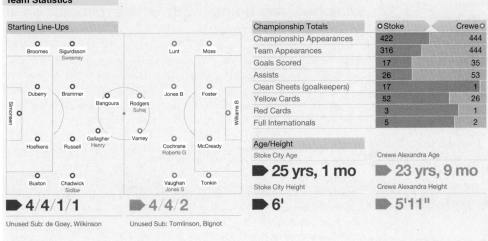

Broomes, Sigurdsson (Sweeney), Lunt, Moss, Duberry, Brammer, Bangoura, Rodgers (Suhaj), Jones B, Foster, Simonsen, Williams B, Hoefkens, Russell, Gallagher (Henry), Varney, Cochrane (Roberts G), McCready, Buxton, Chadwick (Sidibe), Vaughan (Jones S), Tonkin

4/4/1/1   **4/4/2**

Unused Sub: de Goey, Wilkinson   Unused Sub: Tomlinson, Bignot

Championship Totals	Stoke	Crewe
Championship Appearances	422	444
Team Appearances	316	444
Goals Scored	17	35
Assists	26	53
Clean Sheets (goalkeepers)	17	1
Yellow Cards	52	26
Red Cards	3	1
Full Internationals	5	2

Age/Height

Stoke City Age — **25 yrs, 1 mo**   Crewe Alexandra Age — **23 yrs, 9 mo**

Stoke City Height — **6'**   Crewe Alexandra Height — **5'11"**

Match Statistics

League Table after Fixture

		Played	Won	Drawn	Lost	For	Against	Pts
●	3 Luton	14	8	3	3	24	16	27
●	4 Leeds	13	7	3	3	17	12	24
●	5 Crystal Palace	13	6	2	5	20	13	20
●	6 Wolverhampton	14	5	5	4	18	13	20
●	7 Watford	14	5	5	4	22	18	20
↑	8 Cardiff	13	5	4	4	19	17	19
↑	9 Stoke	14	6	1	7	15	21	19
...	...	...	...	...	...	...	...	...
↓	23 Crewe	14	2	6	6	14	23	12

Statistics	Stoke	Crewe
Goals	2	0
Shots on Target	15	7
Shots off Target	8	4
Hit Woodwork	0	0
Possession %	54	46
Corners	9	6
Offsides	7	1
Fouls	13	10
Disciplinary Points	12	4

0-1

Stoke City ○
Reading ○

► Carl Hoefkens gets to grips with Kevin Doyle

Event Line

17 ○ ▨	Makin	
35 ○	Little	
Half time 0-0		
46 ○ ⇄	Sidibe > Chadwick	
46 ○ ⇄	Sweeney > Kolar	
53 ○ ⇄	Sidwell > Makin	
69 ○ ▨	Hoefkens	
73 ○ ⇄	Oster > Little	
76 ○ ▨	Buxton	
77 ○ ⊕	Kitson / LF / P / IA	
	Assist: Kitson	
87 ○ ⇄	Wilkinson > Taggart	
90 ○ ▨	Bangoura	
90 ○ ⇄	Hunt > Convey	
Full time 0-1		

Early pacesetters Reading kept it tight and then snatched the points with a late penalty on a frustrating afternoon.

Royals' striker Dave Kitson slotted home the decisive spot-kick fourteen minutes from time after being felled by Lewis Buxton.

The emergence of Mamady Sidibe and Peter Sweeney for Martin Kolar and Luke Chadwick after the break sparked life into the game.

Buxton saw a header saved by Marcus Hahnemann, before the Royals 'keeper was caught wrong-footed minutes later as Paul Gallagher's deflected drive flew agonisingly wide.

It spurred Reading into action and after former Potter Brynjar Gunnarsson tested Simonsen and Bobby Convey curled over a free-kick, the deadlock was broken after Kitson was bundled over going for another Convey cross.

The striker picked himself up and made no mistake from twelve yards to extend Reading's unbeaten run to an impressive sixteen games.

Quote

● **Johan Boskamp**

Defensively we were ok but attacking-wise we struggled. We didn't penetrate their box enough and we played a little bit differently today, so maybe that's why we lost.

Championship Milestone

► **50**

Mamady Sidibe made his 50th appearance in the Championship.

Venue:	Britannia Stadium	Referee:	G.Salisbury - 05/06		Stoke City
Attendance:	13,484	Matches:	11		Reading
Capacity:	28,218	Yellow Cards:	26		
Occupancy:	48%	Red Cards:	2		

Form Coming into Fixture

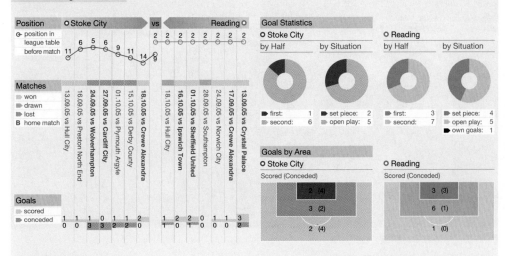

Position

O Stoke City vs Reading O

- position in league table before match

Stoke City: 11, 6, 5, 6, 9, 11, 14
Reading: 2, 2, 2, 2, 2, 2, 2, 2, 9

Matches
- won
- drawn
- lost
- B home match

Stoke City:
- 13.09.05 vs Hull City
- 16.09.05 vs Preston North End
- 24.09.05 vs Wolverhampton
- 27.09.05 vs Cardiff City
- 01.10.05 vs Plymouth Argyle
- 15.10.05 vs Derby County
- 18.10.05 vs Crewe Alexandra

Reading:
- 18.10.05 vs Hull City
- 16.10.05 vs Ipswich Town
- 01.10.05 vs Sheffield United
- 28.09.05 vs Southampton
- 24.09.05 vs Norwich City
- 17.09.05 vs Crewe Alexandra
- 13.09.05 vs Crystal Palace

Goals
- scored: 1 1 1 0 1 1 2 | 1 2 2 0 1 1 3
- conceded: 0 0 3 3 2 2 0 | 1 0 1 0 0 0 2

Goal Statistics

O Stoke City

by Half		by Situation	
first:	1	set piece:	2
second:	6	open play:	5

O Reading

by Half		by Situation	
first:	3	set piece:	4
second:	7	open play:	5
		own goals:	1

Goals by Area

O Stoke City — Scored (Conceded)

2 (4)
3 (2)
2 (4)

O Reading — Scored (Conceded)

3 (3)
6 (1)
1 (0)

Team Statistics

Starting Line-Ups

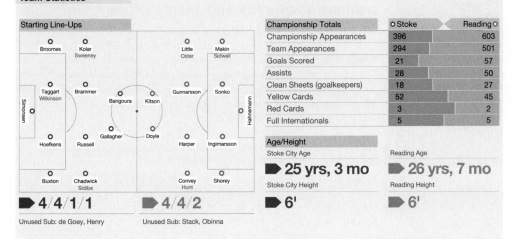

Stoke City:
- Broomes, Kolar (Sweeney)
- Little (Oster), Makin (Sidwell)
- Simonsen
- Taggart (Wilkinson), Brammer, Bangoura, Kitson
- Gunnarsson, Sonko, Hahnemann
- Hoefkens, Russell, Gallagher, Doyle
- Harper, Ingimarsson
- Buxton, Chadwick (Sidibe)
- Convey, Shorey (Hunt)

Stoke City: 4/4/1/1
Reading: 4/4/2

Unused Sub: de Goey, Henry
Unused Sub: Stack, Obinna

Championship Totals	O Stoke	Reading O
Championship Appearances	396	603
Team Appearances	294	501
Goals Scored	21	57
Assists	28	50
Clean Sheets (goalkeepers)	18	27
Yellow Cards	52	45
Red Cards	3	2
Full Internationals	5	5

Age/Height

Stoke City Age	Reading Age
25 yrs, 3 mo	26 yrs, 7 mo
Stoke City Height	Reading Height
6'	6'

Match Statistics

League Table after Fixture

		Played	Won	Drawn	Lost	For	Against	Pts
● 2	Reading	15	10	4	1	25	8	34
...		...	...	...	...	...	...	...
↓ 11	Stoke	15	6	1	8	15	22	19
↑ 12	Hull	15	4	6	5	13	13	18
↓ 13	Ipswich	15	5	3	7	14	22	18
↓ 14	Derby	15	3	8	4	20	21	17
↑ 15	Preston	15	3	8	4	16	18	17
↓ 16	Burnley	15	4	4	7	20	20	16
↓ 17	Norwich	15	4	4	7	16	21	16

Statistics	O Stoke	Reading O
Goals	0	1
Shots on Target	5	8
Shots off Target	2	9
Hit Woodwork	0	0
Possession %	49	51
Corners	5	6
Offsides	5	2
Fouls	14	9
Disciplinary Points	12	8

2-0

Southampton ○
Stoke City ○

▶ Mamady Sidibe surges forward

Event Line

2	○ ■	Brammer
16	○ ⊕	Walcott / RF / OP / IA
		Assist: Quashie
40	○ ■	Broomes
		Violent Conduct

Half time 1-0

77	○ ⇄	Jones > Fuller
83	○ ⇄	Paterson > Gallagher
86	○ ⇄	Sweeney > Sigurdsson
90	○ ⊕	Belmadi / RF / OP / IA
		Assist: Jones

Full time 2-0

Southampton took the points after an incident-packed encounter and plenty of controversy at St. Mary's.

Goals at either end of the game were enough to decide the outcome, but referee Ray Olivier took centre stage after sending off both Potters defender Marlon Broomes and manager Johan Boskamp minutes before half-time. Broomes saw red for an alleged elbow off-the-ball on Theo Walcott, while Boskamp was sent to the stand for contesting the official's decision.

Hannes Sigurdsson had two early chances but the deadlock was broken in the 16th minute when Ricardo Fuller released Walcott, who raced clear to slot confidently past Steve Simonsen.

Dave Brammer came within inches of an instant response when his fierce volley flew narrowly wide, before Niemi was on hand to block Sigurdsson's low drive.

City kept battling on but it was the home side who dominated and Simonsen kept them at bay with a string of fine saves to deny Fuller, Djamel Belmadi and Kenwyne Jones until Djamel Belmadi wrapped up the victory in the dying seconds with a smart finish at the back post.

Quote

● Johan Boskamp

I don't think 2-0 was a fair reflection of the game. The linesman gave the decision that Marlon elbowed Walcott, but everybody could see that didn't happen.

Form Coming into Fixture

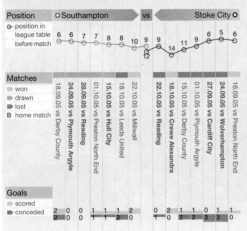

Position

position in league table before match

Southampton vs Stoke City

6 6 7 7 8 8 10 9 9 11 9 6 5 6
12 14

Matches
- won
- drawn
- lost
- B home match

18.09.05 vs Derby County
24.09.05 vs Plymouth Argyle
28.09.05 vs Reading
01.10.05 vs Preston North End
15.10.05 vs Hull City
18.10.05 vs Leeds United
22.10.05 vs Millwall

22.10.05 vs Reading
18.10.05 vs Crewe Alexandra
15.10.05 vs Plymouth Argyle
01.10.05 vs Derby County
27.09.05 vs Cardiff City
24.09.05 vs Wolverhampton
16.09.05 vs Preston North End

Goals
- scored
- conceded

| 2 | 0 | 0 | 1 | 1 | 1 | 2 | | 0 | 2 | 1 | 1 | 0 | 1 | 1 |
| 2 | 0 | 0 | 1 | 1 | 2 | 0 | | 1 | 0 | 2 | 2 | 3 | 3 | 0 |

Goal Statistics

Southampton

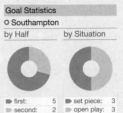

by Half | by Situation

- first: 5
- second: 2

- set piece: 3
- open play: 3
- own goals: 1

Stoke City

by Half | by Situation

- first: 1
- second: 5

- set piece: 2
- open play: 4

Goals by Area

Southampton

Scored (Conceded)

0 (1)

5 (4)

2 (1)

Stoke City

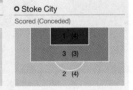

Scored (Conceded)

1 (4)

3 (3)

2 (4)

Team Statistics

Starting Line-Ups

Higginbotham, McCann, Russell, Halls

Svensson, Quashie, Walcott, Junior, Wilkinson

Niemi, Gallagher, Paterson, Simonsen

Lundekvam, Wise, Fuller/Jones, Sidibe, Brammer, Hoefkens

Delap, Belmadi, Sigurdsson/Sweeney, Broomes

4/4/2 **4/4/1/1**

Unused Sub: Smith, Powell, Folly, Kosowski

Unused Sub: de Goey, Henry, Kolar

Championship Totals

	Southampton	Stoke
Championship Appearances	162	327
Team Appearances	122	257
Goals Scored	19	16
Assists	13	20
Clean Sheets (goalkeepers)	7	18
Yellow Cards	27	37
Red Cards	1	3
Full Internationals	10	4

Age/Height

Southampton Age **28 yrs, 7 mo** | Stoke City Age **24 yrs, 3 mo**

Southampton Height **5'11"** | Stoke City Height **6'**

Match Statistics

League Table after Fixture

		Played	Won	Drawn	Lost	For	Against	Pts
↑ 7	Southampton	16	5	9	2	19	13	24
↑ 8	QPR	16	6	6	4	18	18	24
↓ 9	Cardiff	15	6	5	4	25	18	23
↓ 10	Wolverhampton	16	5	6	5	20	17	21
● 11	Burnley	16	5	4	7	21	20	19
↑ 12	Leicester	16	4	7	5	16	18	19
↑ 13	Ipswich	16	5	4	7	15	23	19
↓ 14	Stoke	16	6	1	9	15	24	19
↓ 15	Hull	16	4	6	6	13	14	18

Statistics

	Southampton	Stoke
Goals	2	0
Shots on Target	13	5
Shots off Target	8	5
Hit Woodwork	0	0
Possession %	53	47
Corners	7	3
Offsides	5	0
Fouls	13	10
Disciplinary Points	0	16

1-2

Coventry City ○
Stoke City ○

 Dave Brammer celebrates a memorable away win

Event Line

12 ○ ⊕ Nalis / LF / OP / 6Y		
	Assist: Adebola	
37 ○ ⊕ Taggart / LF / OP / OA		
	Assist: Bangoura	
Half time 1-1		
55 ○ ⊕ Gallagher / RF / OP / OA		
	Assist: Bangoura	
59 ○ ⇄ Davis > Nalis		
60 ○ ⇄ Thornton > Impey		
66 ○ ▨ Thornton		
71 ○ ▨ Gallagher		
79 ○ ▨ Heath		
81 ○ ⇄ Henry > Gallagher		
Full time 1-2		

Paul Gallagher kept up his knack of grabbing vital goals away from home with the decisive strike to kill off Coventry at the new Ricoh Arena.

The Scot struck eleven minutes after the break to turn the tables after Lilian Nalis' first-half opener. Nalis steered home Dele Adebola's centre following a defensive mix-up in the 12th minute.

Steve Simonsen then had to be on his toes to foil Adebola, while a towering header from Matt Heath crashed against the post as Coventry threatened to pull away.

However, six minutes before the interval, the scores were levelled. Gerry Taggart, starting only third game of the season (and what ultimately proved to be his last in a Potters shirt) unleashed a powerful drive which flew through a crowd of bodies on its way past Marton Fulop.

Gallagher had the final say, giving Fulop no chance from 20 yards with a superbly executed right-foot shot.

Quote

● **Jan De Koning**

It was a fantastic response. We started very poorly but worked very hard after that, scored two fantastic goals and I think we deserved the win in the end.

Venue:	Ricoh Arena	Referee:	L.Probert - 05/06		Coventry City
Attendance:	16,617	Matches:	15		Stoke City
Capacity:	32,000	Yellow Cards:	71		
Occupancy:	52%	Red Cards:	1		

Form Coming into Fixture

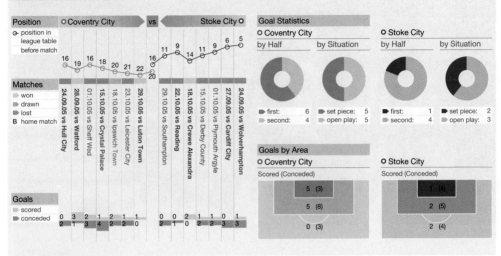

Position
- position in league table before match

Coventry City vs **Stoke City**

Coventry City: 16, 19, 16, 18, 20, 21, 22
Stoke City: 16, 20, 11, 9, 11, 9, 14, 6, 5

Matches
- won
- drawn
- lost
- B home match

Coventry matches:
24.09.05 vs Hull City (B)
28.08.05 vs Watford
01.10.05 vs Sheff Wed
15.10.05 vs Crystal Palace
18.10.05 vs Ipswich Town
23.10.05 vs Leicester City
29.10.05 vs Luton Town (B)

Stoke matches:
29.10.05 vs Southampton
22.10.05 vs Reading
18.10.05 vs Crewe Alexandra (B)
15.10.05 vs Derby County
01.10.05 vs Plymouth Argyle
27.09.05 vs Cardiff City (B)
24.09.05 vs Wolverhampton

Goals
- scored
- conceded

Coventry scored: 0 3 2 1 2 1 1
Coventry conceded: 2 1 3 4 2 2 0

Stoke scored: 0 0 2 1 1 0 1
Stoke conceded: 2 1 0 2 2 3 3

Goal Statistics

Coventry City

by Half — first: 6, second: 4
by Situation — set piece: 5, open play: 5

Stoke City

by Half — first: 1, second: 4
by Situation — set piece: 2, open play: 3

Goals by Area

Coventry City — Scored (Conceded)
5 (3)
5 (8)
0 (3)

Stoke City — Scored (Conceded)
1 (4)
2 (5)
2 (4)

Team Statistics

Starting Line-Ups

Coventry City 4/4/2

Fulop
Duffy, Page, Nalis, Davis
Impey, Thornton
Heath, Hughes, Adebola, Bangoura
Scowcroft, Sidibe
Hall, Doyle

Unused Sub: Ince, Shaw, Wood

Stoke City 4/4/2

Simonsen
Sigurdsson, Brammer, Russell, Gallagher
Henry
Buxton, Taggart, Hoefkens, Halls

Unused Sub: de Goey, Junior, Wilkinson, Kolar

Championship Totals	Coventry	Stoke
Championship Appearances	427	374
Team Appearances	261	339
Goals Scored	36	16
Assists	35	19
Clean Sheets (goalkeepers)	1	18
Yellow Cards	59	55
Red Cards	3	4
Full Internationals	4	6

Age/Height

	Coventry City	Stoke City
Age	26 yrs, 10 mo	25 yrs, 6 mo
Height	6'	6'1"

Match Statistics

League Table after Fixture

		Played	Won	Drawn	Lost	For	Against	Pts
● 6	Crystal Palace	15	7	3	5	24	15	24
● 7	Southampton	16	5	9	2	19	13	24
● 8	QPR	17	6	6	5	19	21	24
● 9	Cardiff	16	6	5	5	25	19	23
● 10	Wolverhampton	17	5	7	5	21	18	22
● 11	Burnley	17	6	4	7	23	21	22
↑ 12	Stoke	17	7	1	9	17	25	22
...	...	...	...	...	...	...	...	...
↓ 21	Coventry	17	3	7	7	21	28	16

Statistics	Coventry	Stoke
Goals	1	2
Shots on Target	5	5
Shots off Target	8	3
Hit Woodwork	0	0
Possession %	38	62
Corners	3	2
Offsides	1	4
Fouls	15	21
Disciplinary Points	8	4

3-0

Stoke City ○
Brighton & Hove Albion ○

Championship
05.11.05

▶ Sambegou Bangoura is the hero for Stoke

Event Line

31 ○ ■	Russell	
35 ○ ⊕	Bangoura / RF / OP / IA	
	Assist: Gallagher	
39 ○ ■	McShane	
40 ○ ■	Bangoura	
Half time 1-0		
46 ○ ⇄	Chadwick > Sigurdsson	
64 ○ ⇄	McPhee > Robinson	
68 ○ ⊕	Russell / RF / OP / 6Y	
	Assist: Sidibe	
72 ○ ⇄	Turienzo > Kazim-Richards	
75 ○ ⊕	Bangoura / H / OP / IA	
	Assist: Halls	
82 ○ ■	Brammer	
86 ○ ⇄	Henry > Gallagher	
87 ○ ■	Duberry	
88 ○ ⇄	Junior > Bangoura	
Full time 3-0		

Sam Bangoura provided the fireworks as Brighton fizzled out in the build-up to Bonfire Night.

The striker helped himself to a brace either side of setting-up Darel Russell for his first goal of the season to complete a second City victory in four days.

Bangoura set the ball rolling in the 35th minute after some early Brighton pressure nearly saw the visitors nose ahead. Steve Simonsen blocked bravely at the feet of Dean Hammond before turning away two dangerous free-kicks from Alex Frutos.

City took time to get going, but when Paul Gallagher's pass set Bangoura clear he calmly slotted past Alan Blayney.

Luke Chadwick's introduction as a half-time substitute livened things up further and Gallagher nearly made it 2-0 when he fired against the crossbar. It was 2-0, though, when Russell steamed in to slide home from close range after good work from Gallagher and Bangoura.

There was still time for Bangoura to complete the rout by sending a firm header from a John Halls' cross past Blayney.

Quote

● Johan Boskamp

Sammy Bangoura did his job out there again – we brought him to the club to score goals and he's doing that regularly.

Venue:	Britannia Stadium	Referee:	K.Wright - 05/06		**Stoke City**
Attendance:	15,274	Matches:	11		**Brighton & Hove Albion**
Capacity:	28,218	Yellow Cards:	41		
Occupancy:	54%	Red Cards:	2		

Form Coming into Fixture

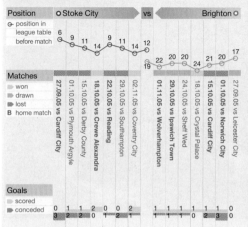

Position — Stoke City vs Brighton

position in league table before match

Stoke City: 6, 9, 11, 14, 9, 11, 14, 12
Brighton: 19, 22, 20, 20, 24, 21, 20, 17

Matches
- won
- drawn
- lost
- B home match

Stoke City matches: 27.09.05 vs Cardiff City, 01.10.05 vs Plymouth Argyle, 15.10.05 vs Derby County, 18.10.05 vs Crewe Alexandra, 22.10.05 vs Reading, 29.10.05 vs Southampton, 02.11.05 vs Coventry City

Brighton matches: 01.11.05 vs Wolverhampton, 29.10.05 vs Ipswich Town, 24.10.05 vs Sheff Wed, 18.10.05 vs Crystal Palace, 15.10.05 vs Cardiff City, 01.10.05 vs Norwich City, 27.09.05 vs Leicester City

Goals
- scored
- conceded

Stoke City: scored 0 1 1 2 0 0 2 / conceded 3 2 2 0 1 2 1
Brighton: scored 1 1 1 1 1 1 0 / conceded 1 1 1 0 2 3 0

Goal Statistics

○ Stoke City — by Half / by Situation

| first: | 2 | set piece: | 1 |
| second: | 4 | open play: | 5 |

○ Brighton & Hove Albion — by Half / by Situation

| first: | 2 | set piece: | 2 |
| second: | 4 | open play: | 4 |

Goals by Area

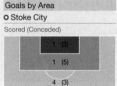

○ Stoke City — Scored (Conceded)

1 (3)
1 (5)
4 (3)

○ Brighton & Hove Albion — Scored (Conceded)

1 (3)
4 (5)
1 (0)

Team Statistics

Starting Line-Ups

Stoke City:
Simonsen
Buxton, Sigurdsson (Chadwick), Duberry, Brammer, Sidibe, Kazim-Richards (Turienzo), Bangoura (Junior), Russell, Robinson (McPhee), Hoefkens, Halls, Gallagher (Henry)

Brighton:
Blayney
Carole, Hart, Nicolas, McShane, Hammond, Butters, Frutos, Reid

▶ 4/4/2   **▶ 4/4/2**

Unused Sub: de Goey, Wilkinson

Unused Sub: Chaigneau, Dodd, Mayo

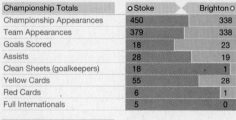

Championship Totals	○ Stoke	Brighton ○
Championship Appearances	450	338
Team Appearances	379	338
Goals Scored	18	23
Assists	28	19
Clean Sheets (goalkeepers)	18	1
Yellow Cards	55	28
Red Cards	6	1
Full Internationals	5	0

Age/Height

Stoke City Age	Brighton & Hove Albion Age
▶ 25 yrs	**▶ 23 yrs, 11 mo**
Stoke City Height	Brighton & Hove Albion Height
▶ 6'	**▶ 5'11"**

Match Statistics

League Table after Fixture

		Played	Won	Drawn	Lost	For	Against	Pts
●	3 Watford	18	9	5	4	31	21	32
●	4 Luton	18	8	4	6	27	25	28
●	5 Leeds	17	7	6	4	19	15	27
↑	6 Southampton	17	5	10	2	19	13	25
↑	7 Wolverhampton	18	6	7	5	23	18	25
↑	8 Burnley	18	7	4	7	26	23	25
↑	9 Stoke	18	8	1	9	20	25	25
...	...	...	...	...	...	...	...	...
↓	22 Brighton	18	2	10	6	17	25	16

Statistics	○ Stoke	Brighton ○
Goals	3	0
Shots on Target	7	1
Shots off Target	3	7
Hit Woodwork	1	0
Possession %	57	43
Corners	3	8
Offsides	1	1
Fouls	21	17
Disciplinary Points	16	4

49

1-2

Crewe Alexandra ○
Stoke City ○

► Hannes Sigurdsson looks to make progress down the wing

Event Line

16 ○ ⊕ Bangoura / RF / IFK / IA	
Assist: Brammer	
34 ○ ▨ Bangoura	
37 ○ ▨ Gallagher	
Half time 0-1	
51 ○ ▨ Tonkin	
56 ○ ⇄ Rivers > Vaughan	
72 ○ ⇄ Johnson > Roberts G	
79 ○ ⇄ Sigurdsson > Chadwick	
88 ○ ▨ Halls	
89 ○ ⊕ Gallagher / RF / IFK / IA	
90 ○ ⇄ Henry > Gallagher	
90 ○ ⊕ Johnson / RF / OP / 6Y	
Assist: Jones S	
Full time 1-2	

Goals from Sam Bangoura and Paul Gallagher ensured the derby honours remained firmly in the Potteries for a second successive season.

Crewe grabbed a late reply through Eddie Johnson, but it was too little too late as City edged an action packed encounter at the Alexandra Stadium and completed a league double.

Alex 'keeper Ben William was powerless in the 16th minute when Bangoura's clever flick from a Dave Brammer free-kick crept into the bottom corner.

The home side rallies and Michael Higdon heading against the crossbar before Mamady Sidibe fired narrowly over and Darel Russell was again thwarted by the in-form Williams.

Williams' best save came shortly after the break when he kept out a Bangoura header before Billy Jones spurned a great opportunity to equalise from close-range.

Gallagher put the game beyond doubt in the 88th minute, bending a superb effort from the edge of the area beyond Williams and Johnson's scrambled effort reduced the arrears deep into stoppage time.

Quote

● **Jan De Koning**

The game was played at a high tempo and it felt like a derby game from start to finish. We deserved to win because we worked hard and didn't give Crewe the chance to play.

Venue:	Gresty Road	Referee:	A.Woolmer - 05/06	Crewe Alexandra
Attendance:	8,942	Matches:	12	Stoke City
Capacity:	10,066	Yellow Cards:	35	
Occupancy:	89%	Red Cards:	2	

Form Coming into Fixture

Position

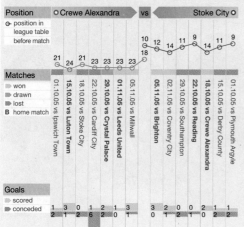

- ⊙ position in league table before match

Crewe Alexandra vs **Stoke City**

	21	24	21	23	23	23	23	18								
									10	12	14	11	9	14	11	9

Matches
- ▶ won
- ▶ drawn
- ▶ lost
- B home match

01.10.05 vs Ipswich Town
15.10.05 vs Luton Town
18.10.05 vs Stoke City
22.10.05 vs Cardiff City
29.10.05 vs Crystal Palace
01.11.05 vs Leeds United
05.11.05 vs Millwall
05.11.05 vs Brighton
02.11.05 vs Coventry City
29.10.05 vs Southampton
22.10.05 vs Reading
18.10.05 vs Crewe Alexandra
15.10.05 vs Derby County
01.10.05 vs Plymouth Argyle

Goals
- ▶ scored
- ▶ conceded

scored	1	3	0	1	2	1	3		3	2	0	0	2	1	1
conceded	2	1	2	6	2	0	1		0	1	2	1	0	2	2

Goal Statistics

○ Crewe Alexandra

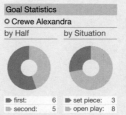

by Half — by Situation

- ▶ first: 6
- ▶ second: 5
- ▶ set piece: 3
- ▶ open play: 8

○ Stoke City

by Half — by Situation

- ▶ first: 3
- ▶ second: 6
- ▶ set piece: 1
- ▶ open play: 8

Goals by Area

○ Crewe Alexandra

Scored (Conceded)

- 1 (1)
- 9 (10)
- 1 (3)

○ Stoke City

Scored (Conceded)

- 2 (3)
- 3 (4)
- 4 (1)

Team Statistics

Starting Line-Ups

Crewe: Williams B; Tonkin, Foster, Jones B, Walker, Moss, Roberts G (Johnson), Lunt, Higdon, Bangoura, Jones S (Rivers), Vaughan

Stoke: Simonsen; Chadwick (Sigurdsson), Halls, Russell, Hoefkens, Brammer, Duberry, Sidibe, Gallagher (Henry), Buxton

▶ 4/4/2 ▶ 4/4/2

Unused Sub: Tomlinson, Moses, Rodgers

Unused Sub: de Goey, Junior, Kolar

Championship Totals	○ Crewe	Stoke ○
Championship Appearances	536	453
Team Appearances	510	382
Goals Scored	57	21
Assists	57	30
Clean Sheets (goalkeepers)	2	19
Yellow Cards	30	59
Red Cards	1	5
Full Internationals	2	5

Age/Height

Crewe Alexandra Age	Stoke City Age
▶ **24 yrs**	▶ **25 yrs, 2 mo**
Crewe Alexandra Height	Stoke City Height
▶ **5'11"**	▶ **6'1"**

Match Statistics

League Table after Fixture

			Played	Won	Drawn	Lost	For	Against	Pts
●	2	Reading	19	13	5	1	33	11	44
●	3	Watford	19	10	5	4	33	22	35
↑	4	Leeds	18	8	6	4	23	18	30
↓	5	Wolverhampton	19	7	7	5	26	18	28
↑	6	Burnley	19	8	4	7	27	23	28
↓	7	Luton	19	8	4	7	27	27	28
↑	8	Stoke	19	9	1	9	22	26	28
...			...	...	...	...	...	...	...
↓	19	Crewe	19	4	7	8	22	34	19

Statistics	○ Crewe	Stoke ○
Goals	1	2
Shots on Target	5	9
Shots off Target	8	6
Hit Woodwork	1	0
Possession %	51	49
Corners	6	5
Offsides	1	6
Fouls	9	15
Disciplinary Points	4	12

1-2

Stoke City ○
Derby County ◎

▶ Sambegou Bangoura threatens the Derby defence

Event Line

33 ○ ⊕ Bangoura / RF / OP / 6Y	
Assist: Sidibe	
Half time 1-0	
53 ○ ▬ Edworthy	
64 ○ ⊕ Smith / RF / OP / IA	
Assist: Blackstock	
66 ○ ▬ Johnson S	
69 ○ ⊕ Nyatanga / H / IFK / IA	
Assist: Idiakez	
76 ○ ⇄ Sigurdsson > Gallagher	
86 ○ ▬ Russell	
88 ○ ▬ Nyatanga	
90 ○ ⇄ Bolder > Idiakez	
90 ○ ⇄ Doyle > Tudgay	
Full time 1-2	

This was a Ram-raid in every sense of the word as Derby came from behind to snatch the points.

A fourth consecutive league win looked very much on the cards for City after Sam Bangoura volleyed home in style on the half-hour. Another goal would have ended the one-sided contest, but although the County defence wobbled, it stood firm. And that laid the platform for a dramatic second-half fight-back.

Tommy Smith gave them hope when he nipped in with a 65th minute equaliser and then 17-year-old defender Lewin Nyatanga popped in a close-range header less than five minutes later.

Bangoura's goal was typically clinical as he thumped the ball into the net from eight yards after Mamady Sidibe flicked on John Halls' long throw.

Luke Chadwick twice went close to extending the lead and Paul Gallagher three times as Derby withstood heavy pressure.

Smith levelled with a looping effort from a Dexter Blackstock through-ball and Nyatanga nodded home his first senior goal from an excellent Inigo Idiakez cross.

Quote	Championship Milestone
● **Jan De Koning**	▶ **50**
It was another good goal by Sammy and he probably could have had another in the second-half, but everything seemed to be against us today.	Steve Simonsen made his 50th appearance in the Championship.

Venue:	Britannia Stadium	Referee:	M.J.Jones - 05/06
Attendance:	13,205	Matches:	12
Capacity:	28,218	Yellow Cards:	38
Occupancy:	47%	Red Cards:	2

**Stoke City
Derby County**

Form Coming into Fixture

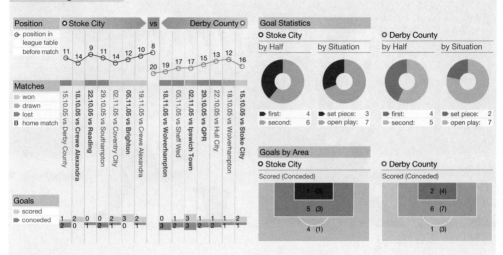

Team Statistics

Starting Line-Ups

▶ 4/4/2   ▶ 4/5/1

Unused Sub: de Goey, Junior, Kolar, Sweeney

Unused Sub: Poole, Bisgaard, Holmes

Championship Totals	O Stoke	Derby O
Championship Appearances	406	418
Team Appearances	335	353
Goals Scored	21	50
Assists	27	45
Clean Sheets (goalkeepers)	19	14
Yellow Cards	51	47
Red Cards	5	5
Full Internationals	5	1

Age/Height

Stoke City Age	Derby County Age
▶ **24 yrs, 8 mo**	▶ **24 yrs, 3 mo**
Stoke City Height	Derby County Height
▶ **6'1"**	▶ **5'11"**

Match Statistics

League Table after Fixture

		Played	Won	Drawn	Lost	For	Against	Pts
↑ 9	Preston	20	6	10	4	23	19	28
↓ 10	Burnley	20	8	4	8	27	25	28
↓ 11	Stoke	20	9	1	10	23	28	28
↓ 12	Southampton	19	5	11	3	23	18	26
● 13	QPR	20	6	6	8	21	28	24
● 14	Ipswich	20	6	6	8	22	31	24
● 15	Norwich	20	6	4	10	19	25	22
● 16	Leicester	19	4	9	6	18	21	21
↑ 17	Derby	20	4	9	7	27	32	21

Statistics	O Stoke	Derby O
Goals	1	2
Shots on Target	6	4
Shots off Target	2	2
Hit Woodwork	0	0
Possession %	47	53
Corners	1	0
Offsides	0	1
Fouls	11	11
Disciplinary Points	4	12

0-2

Sheffield Wednesday ○
Stoke City ○

▶ Dave Brammer demonstrates his ball skills

Event Line

5 ○ ■	Diallo	
13 ○ ■	Duberry	
17 ○ ⊕	Bangoura / RF / OP / IA	
	Assist: Hoefkens	
36 ○ ■	Broomes	
Half time 0-1		
46 ○ ⇄	Sidibe > Sigurdsson	
58 ○ ■	Gallagher	
67 ○ ■	Bangoura	
71 ○ ⇄	McGovern > Graham	
71 ○ ⇄	O'Brien > Heckingbottom	
76 ○ ⇄	Agbonlahor > Partridge	
79 ○ ⇄	Henry > Chadwick	
83 ○ ■	Halls	
86 ○ ⊕	Sidibe / LF / OP / 6Y	
	Assist: Gallagher	
90 ○ ⇄	Buxton > Bangoura	
Full time 0-2		

Sam Bangoura was on the mark again with his fifth goal in four games as the Owls fell prey to City's continuing fine away record.

A sixth league win on the road was set up by Bangoura's 16th minute strike and sealed with substitute Mamady Sidibe effort five minutes from time.

Bangoura's goal was well-timed and took the early sting out the game as he seized on Carl Hoefkens' ball to prod a shot past Nicky Weaver.

Wednesday might have gone ahead moments earlier, but Steve Simonsen saved well from Daryl Murphy and then Chris Brunt.

Bangoura nearly followed up his strike with a second, but Weaver pulled off a fine save and the game remained in the balance with Simonsen producing another excellent stop to deny Brunt again.

Sidibe, though, sealed victory when he rounded off the best move a bitterly cold afternoon by converting Paul Gallagher's near-post cross after Karl Henry's pass sliced open the home defence.

Quote

● **Johan Boskamp**

Mama needed that goal and it was a perfect way for us to finish off the match. It was nice Sammy scored also, he's doing what we bought him for.

Championship Milestone

▶ **50**

Luke Chadwick made his 50th appearance in the Championship.

Venue:	Hillsborough	Referee:	A.R.Hall - 05/06	**Sheffield Wednesday**
Attendance:	21,970	Matches:	14	**Stoke City**
Capacity:	39,859	Yellow Cards:	54	
Occupancy:	55%	Red Cards:	6	

Form Coming into Fixture

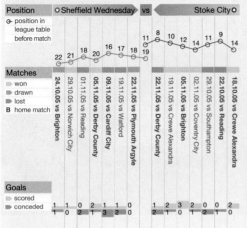

Goal Statistics

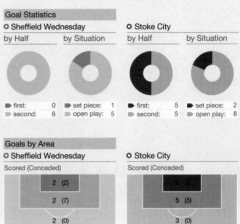

Sheffield Wednesday — by Half / by Situation

first:	0	set piece:	1
second:	6	open play:	5

Stoke City — by Half / by Situation

first:	5	set piece:	2
second:	5	open play:	8

Goals by Area

Sheffield Wednesday — Scored (Conceded)

- 2 (2)
- 2 (7)
- 2 (0)

Stoke City — Scored (Conceded)

- 2 (0)
- 5 (5)
- 3 (0)

Team Statistics

Starting Line-Ups

Sheffield Wednesday: Weaver; Heckingbottom, O'Brien, Brunt; Coughlan, Rocastle, Murphy D, Bangoura (Buxton); Diallo, Whelan, Graham McGovern — Sigurdsson Sidibe; Simek, Partridge (Agbonlahor)

4/4/2

Unused Sub: Wood, Corr

Stoke City: Simonsen; Chadwick, Halls; Russell, Hoefkens; Brammer, Duberry; Gallagher, Broomes

4/4/2

Unused Sub: de Goey, Kolar

Championship Totals

	○ Sheff Wed	Stoke ○
Championship Appearances	253	505
Team Appearances	147	423
Goals Scored	13	26
Assists	15	33
Clean Sheets (goalkeepers)	1	19
Yellow Cards	23	66
Red Cards	1	6
Full Internationals	2	5

Age/Height

	Sheffield Wednesday	Stoke City
Age	**25 yrs, 1 mo**	**25 yrs, 4 mo**
Height	**6'**	**6'**

Match Statistics

League Table after Fixture

		Played	Won	Drawn	Lost	For	Against	Pts
●	1 Reading	21	15	5	1	38	11	50
●	2 Sheff Utd	21	14	4	3	42	21	46
●	3 Watford	21	10	7	4	36	25	37
●	4 Leeds	20	10	6	4	26	18	36
●	5 Luton	21	10	4	7	33	28	34
↑	6 Burnley	21	9	4	8	30	25	31
↑	7 Stoke	21	10	1	10	25	28	31
...	...	...	...	...	...	...	...	...
↓	20 Sheff Wed	21	4	8	9	17	27	20

Statistics

	○ Sheff Wed	Stoke ○
Goals	0	2
Shots on Target	7	4
Shots off Target	9	3
Hit Woodwork	0	0
Possession %	47	53
Corners	3	3
Offsides	0	2
Fouls	5	10
Disciplinary Points	4	20

1-2

Stoke City ○
Queens Park Rangers ○

▶ Sambegou Bangoura is first to the ball

Event Line

2 ○ ⊕ Furlong / RF / IFK / IA	
	Assist: Ainsworth
12 ○ ▪ Brammer	
23 ○ ▪ Milanese	
26 ○ ⊕ Bangoura / H / IFK / IA	
	Assist: Sweeney
43 ○ ▪ Ainsworth	
Half time 1-1	
51 ○ ▪ Halls	
	Disent
52 ○ ⊕ Langley / RF / P / IA	
	Assist: Furlong
57 ○ ▪ Bean	
59 ○ ⇄ Evatt > Dyer	
76 ○ ⇄ Sigurdsson > Sweeney	
79 ○ ▪ Rowlands	
83 ○ ▪ Sigurdsson	
88 ○ ⇄ Cook > Ainsworth	
90 ○ ⇄ Baidoo > Moore	
Full time 1-2	

A dramatic start, another Sam Bangoura goal, a controversial sending-off and a debatable penalty – QPR's visit to the Potteries just about had it all.

From the moment Paul Furlong fired Rangers ahead after just 80 seconds, it was never going to be a dull afternoon. In a match packed full of incidents and talking points, Powerade Player of the Month Bangoura responded with his sixth goal in five games to level the scores after 25 minutes, rising highest to sneak a header inside the post from Peter Sweeney's teasing free-kick. Sweeney then saw an effort bound for the bottom corner blocked, while Marcus Bignot's timely intervention stopped Bangoura grabbing his second from a Mamady Sidibe cross.

The smart money at half-time was on a home win, but referee Andre Marriner changed all that when he controversially red-carded John Halls – and pointed to the spot – after a 51st minute clash with Furlong. Richard Langley stepped up and sent Steve Simonsen the wrong way, but even against ten men Rangers were forced back.

Bangoura forced Simon Royce into action with an overhead kick and Sidibe headed a great chance wide, but the equaliser proved elusive.

Quote

● **Johan Boskamp**

This defeat was very disappointing for us because our ball circulation was very good and it was one of the best games we have played at home so far.

Venue:	Britannia Stadium	Referee:	A.Marriner - 05/06		Stoke City
Attendance:	15,367	Matches:	5		Queens Park Rangers
Capacity:	28,218	Yellow Cards:	12		
Occupancy:	54%	Red Cards:	3		

Form Coming into Fixture

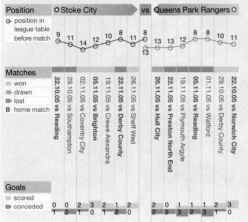

Position ○ Stoke City vs Queens Park Rangers ○

- ⊙ position in league table before match

Stoke City: 9, 11, 14, 12, 10, 8, 11, 8, 13, 13, 13, 12, 8, 8, 10, 11

Matches
- won
- drawn
- lost
- B home match

Stoke City matches: 22.10.05 vs Reading, 29.10.05 vs Southampton, 02.11.05 vs Coventry City, 05.11.05 vs Brighton, 19.11.05 vs Crewe Alexandra, 22.11.05 vs Derby County, 26.11.05 vs Sheff Wed

QPR matches: 26.11.05 vs Hull City, 22.11.05 vs Preston North End, 19.11.05 vs Plymouth Argyle, 05.11.05 vs Reading, 01.11.05 vs Watford, 29.10.05 vs Derby County, 22.10.05 vs Norwich City

Goals
- scored
- conceded

Stoke scored: 0 0 2 3 2 1 2 | conceded: 1 2 1 0 1 2 0
QPR scored: 2 0 1 1 1 2 3 | conceded: 2 2 3 2 3 1 0

Goal Statistics

○ Stoke City

by Half	by Situation

- first: 5
- second: 5
- set piece: 2
- open play: 8

○ Queens Park Rangers

by Half	by Situation

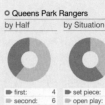

- first: 4
- second: 6
- set piece: 6
- open play: 4

Goals by Area

○ Stoke City — Scored (Conceded)

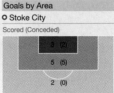

3 (2)
5 (5)
2 (0)

○ Queens Park Rangers — Scored (Conceded)

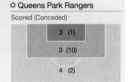

3 (1)
3 (10)
4 (2)

Team Statistics

Starting Line-Ups

Stoke City: Simonsen; Broomes, Sweeney, Sigurdsson, Duberry, Brammer, Sidibe, Moore/Baidoo, Bangoura, Hoefkens, Henry, Halls, Chadwick

Queens Park Rangers: Royce; Ainsworth, Bignot, Cook, Langley, Shittu, Furlong, Bean, Milanese, Rowlands, Dyer/Evatt

Stoke City: ▶ 4/4/2
Queens Park Rangers: ▶ 4/4/2

Unused Sub: de Goey, Buxton, Kolar, Junior

Unused Sub: Cole, Donnelly

Championship Totals	○ Stoke	QPR ○
Championship Appearances	436	483
Team Appearances	330	439
Goals Scored	22	46
Assists	32	48
Clean Sheets (goalkeepers)	20	10
Yellow Cards	48	61
Red Cards	6	4
Full Internationals	4	3

Age/Height

Stoke City Age	Queens Park Rangers Age
▶ 25 yrs, 8 mo	▶ 27 yrs, 1 mo
Stoke City Height	Queens Park Rangers Height
▶ 6'1"	▶ 5'11"

Match Statistics

League Table after Fixture

		Played	Won	Drawn	Lost	For	Against	Pts
● 5	Luton	22	10	4	8	33	31	34
↑ 6	Preston	22	7	11	4	26	20	32
● 7	Burnley	22	9	5	8	31	26	32
↑ 8	Crystal Palace	20	9	4	7	32	23	31
↑ 9	Wolverhampton	22	7	10	5	27	19	31
↓ 10	Cardiff	22	8	7	7	32	26	31
↓ 11	Stoke	22	10	1	11	26	30	31
● 12	Southampton	21	5	13	3	24	19	28
● 13	QPR	22	7	7	8	25	31	28

Statistics	○ Stoke	QPR ○
Goals	1	2
Shots on Target	3	4
Shots off Target	3	2
Hit Woodwork	0	0
Possession %	53	47
Corners	5	5
Offsides	3	1
Fouls	17	19
Disciplinary Points	20	16

3-2

Stoke City ○
Leicester City ○

➡ Sambegou Bangoura unleashes a venomous drive

Event Line

21 ○ ⊕ Gudjonsson / RF / IFK / OA		
	Assist: Hume	
34 ○ ▢ Douglas		
36 ○ ⊕ Gallagher / RF / P / IA		
	Assist: Bangoura	
Half time 1-1		
48 ○ ⊕ Hammond / RF / OP / IA		
	Assist: Hume	
49 ○ ▢ Gudjonsson		
64 ○ ⇄ Sigurdsson > Sweeney		
75 ○ ⊕ Sidibe / H / OP / IA		
	Assist: Brammer	
78 ○ ▢ Bangoura		
78 ○ ⊕ Bangoura / H / OP / IA		
	Assist: Brammer	
80 ○ ▢ Stearman		
84 ○ ⇄ Williams > Stearman		
85 ○ ⇄ de Vries > Hammond		
89 ○ ⇄ Henry > Gallagher		
90 ○ ▢ Russell		
Full time 3-2		

A stunning late comeback sealed a swift return to winning ways in front of the Sky TV cameras.

In-form Sammy Bangoura was the matchwinner, providing a sting in the tail to a thrilling game which was going the visitors' way until the final 15 minutes.

The Foxes got their noses in front on 20 minutes thanks to Joey Gudjonsson's cleverly-worked and superbly-executed free-kick. But their lead lasted just 16 minutes when Paul Gallagher's defence-splitting pass set Bangoura clear and he was brought down by goalkeeper Rab Douglas. Gallagher confidently stepped up score from the penalty spot – twice, as it happened, after the kick was retaken after his initial effort was ruled out due to encroachment.

Elvis Hammond's fine finish saw Leicester regain the initiative two minutes after the break and Gudjonsson almost put the game beyond reach when his thunderous 25-yard effort struck the crossbar. That was the break City needed and on 75 minutes Dave Brammer crossed for Sidibe to loop a header over Douglas from the edge of the area.

Just two minutes later, Brammer was again the supplier and Bangoura stole in to nod home the winner.

Quote

● **Jan De Koning**

We ended up with everything out of nothing whereas against QPR we had nothing out of everything. We didn't play great football but showed fantastic character to come from behind.

Form Coming into Fixture

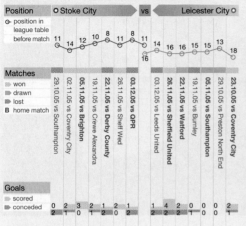

Position | O Stoke City vs Leicester City O
- position in league table before match

Matches
- won
- drawn
- lost
- B home match

Goals
- scored
- conceded

	29.10.05 vs Southampton	02.11.05 vs Coventry City	05.11.05 vs Brighton	19.11.05 vs Crewe Alexandra	22.11.05 vs Derby County	26.11.05 vs Sheff Wed	03.12.05 vs QPR		03.12.05 vs Leeds United	26.11.05 vs Sheffield United	22.11.05 vs Watford	19.11.05 vs Burnley	05.11.05 vs Southampton	29.10.05 vs Preston North End	23.10.05 vs Coventry City
scored	0	2	3	2	1	2	1		1	4	2	0	0	0	2
conceded	2	1	0	1	2	0	2		2	2	2	1	0	0	1

Goal Statistics

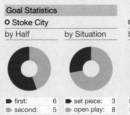

O Stoke City — by Half / by Situation

first:	6	set piece:	3
second:	5	open play:	8

O Leicester City — by Half / by Situation

first:	5	set piece:	4
second:	4	open play:	5

Goals by Area

O Stoke City — Scored (Conceded)

| 3 (2) |
| 6 (6) |
| 2 (0) |

O Leicester City — Scored (Conceded)

| 2 (4) |
| 7 (2) |
| 0 (2) |

Team Statistics

Starting Line-Ups

Broomes, Sweeney, Sigurdsson, Duberry, Brammer, Sidibe, Hammond de Vries, Bangoura, Hume, Simonsen, Hoefkens, Russell, Buxton, Gallagher, Henry

Sylla, Stearman, Williams, Gudjonsson, Dublin, Kisnorbo, Gerrbrand, Douglas, Smith, Maybury

▶ 4/4/2 ▶ 4/4/2

Unused Sub: de Goey, Harper, Junior

Unused Sub: Johansson, Hamill, Tiatto

Championship Totals

	O Stoke	Leicester O
Championship Appearances	474	344
Team Appearances	400	344
Goals Scored	27	29
Assists	30	24
Clean Sheets (goalkeepers)	20	5
Yellow Cards	68	55
Red Cards	5	2
Full Internationals	5	8

Age/Height

Stoke City Age	Leicester City Age
▶ 25 yrs, 3 mo	▶ 26 yrs, 2 mo
Stoke City Height	Leicester City Height
▶ 6'1"	▶ 6'

Match Statistics

League Table after Fixture

			Played	Won	Drawn	Lost	For	Against	Pts
●	1	Reading	22	16	5	1	41	11	53
●	2	Sheff Utd	22	15	4	3	43	21	49
●	3	Leeds	21	11	6	4	28	19	39
●	4	Watford	22	10	8	4	37	26	38
●	5	Luton	22	10	4	8	33	31	34
↑	6	Stoke	23	11	1	11	29	32	34
↓	7	Preston	22	7	11	4	26	20	32
...			...	...	...	...	...	...	...
●	16	Leicester	22	5	9	8	25	28	24

Statistics

	O Stoke	Leicester O
Goals	3	2
Shots on Target	5	6
Shots off Target	4	4
Hit Woodwork	0	1
Possession %	48	52
Corners	4	1
Offsides	2	1
Fouls	10	7
Disciplinary Points	8	12

2-3

Luton Town ○
Stoke City ○

▶ Paul Gallagher just beats Carlos Edwards to the ball

Event Line

21 ○ ⊕ Brkovic / LF / OP / IA	
Assist: Vine	
43 ○ ▇ Robinson	
45 ○ ⊕ Gallagher / RF / OP / 6Y	
Assist: Sidibe	
Half time 1-1	
46 ○ ⇄ Harper > Chadwick	
75 ○ ⇄ Feeney > Vine	
76 ○ ⇄ Sweeney > Sigurdsson	
78 ○ ▇ Coyne	
81 ○ ▇ Brammer	
83 ○ ⊕ Gallagher / RF / OP / IA	
Assist: Sidibe	
88 ○ ⊕ Nicholls / RF / P / IA	
Assist: Howard	
88 ○ ⇄ Shownumi > Robinson	
89 ○ ▇ Gallagher	
90 ○ ▇ Sweeney	
90 ○ ⊕ Coyne / RF / OG / IA	
Assist: Duberry	
Full time 2-3	

Sam Bangoura missed the game through suspension, but Paul Gallagher seized the goalscoring mantle in an epic encounter at Kenilworth Road.

The Scot bagged a brace during a see-saw contest, which was settled deep into stoppage time when Hatters defender Chris Coyne lobbed into his own net.

Just moments earlier, it seemed as though Kevin Nicholls' 87th minute penalty, controversially awarded by referee Trevor Kettle, would earn the home side a draw. Kettle whistled immediately after the faintest of touches from Karl Henry forced Steve Howard to hit the deck.

Ahmet Brkovic had put the home side ahead with an angled drive after 21 minutes, but Gallagher restored parity on the stroke of half-time, tapping in from close-range after Mamady Sidibe rounded goalkeeper Dean Brill. Sidibe was again the provider seven minutes from time, driving in a low cross which Gallagher finished neatly on the near post.

Kettle brought things to the boil with his penalty award, but City steamed in for three points in the dying seconds when Coyne diverted past Brill.

Quote	Championship Milestone
● **Michael Duberry**	➡ **50**
Paul has the world at his feet and he showed today he's the kind of player who can turn a game in our favour.	Karl Henry made his 50th appearance in the Championship.

Venue:	Kenilworth Road	Referee:	T.Kettle - 05/06	**Luton Town**
Attendance:	8,296	Matches:	18	**Stoke City**
Capacity:	10,300	Yellow Cards:	80	
Occupancy:	81%	Red Cards:	6	

Form Coming into Fixture

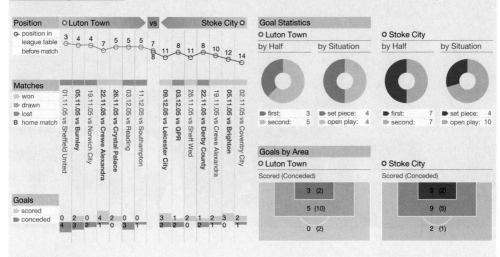

Team Statistics

Championship Totals	○ Luton	Stoke ○
Championship Appearances	219	519
Team Appearances	219	422
Goals Scored	25	23
Assists	24	43
Clean Sheets (goalkeepers)	1	20
Yellow Cards	19	64
Red Cards	2	4
Full Internationals	5	4

Age/Height

	Luton Town Age	Stoke City Age
	▶ 26 yrs, 7 mo	▶ 25 yrs, 6 mo
	Luton Town Height	Stoke City Height
	▶ 6'	▶ 6'

Unused Sub: Beckwith, Barnett, Holmes

Unused Sub: de Goey, Dickinson, Junior

Match Statistics

League Table after Fixture

		Played	Won	Drawn	Lost	For	Against	Pts
●	2 Sheff Utd	24	16	5	3	46	21	53
●	3 Watford	24	10	9	5	39	31	39
●	4 Leeds	23	11	6	6	28	21	39
↑	5 Stoke	24	12	1	11	32	34	37
↑	6 Wolverhampton	24	8	11	5	29	20	35
↓	7 Cardiff	24	9	8	7	33	26	35
↑	8 Burnley	24	10	5	9	35	30	35
↓	9 Preston	24	7	13	4	27	21	34
↓	10 Luton	24	10	4	10	35	35	34

Statistics	○ Luton	Stoke ○
Goals	2	3
Shots on Target	8	5
Shots off Target	7	1
Hit Woodwork	0	0
Possession %	45	55
Corners	4	4
Offsides	1	6
Fouls	14	18
Disciplinary Points	8	12

1-0

Burnley ○
Stoke City ○

Championship
26.12.05

▶ Dave Brammer in midfield action

Event Line

35 ○ ▨ Duff	
Half time 0-0	
54 ○ ▨ Hyde	
56 ○ ⊕ Akinbiyi / LF / OP / 6Y	
Assist: Duff	
86 ○ ⇄ Thomas > Branch	
90 ○ ▨ Sinclair	
Full time 1-0	

Former Potter Ade Akinbiyi landed the Boxing Day knockout blow as Burnley edged a feisty encounter at Turf Moor.

Akinbiyi bundled home Michael Duff's low cross in the 56th minute to inflict a first away defeat in more than two months and move the Clarets above City in the play-off zone.

Ex-City star Gifton Noel-Williams spurned the opening period's best opportunity when he rattled a header against the crossbar from Wade Elliott's cross.

Sam Bangoura, kept in close check all match by Frank Sinclair, headed over following some industrious wing play from Luke Chadwick shortly after the restart before Micah Hyde fired over from 20 yards at the other end.

The deadlock was broken when Akinbiyi scrambled a shot past Steve Simonsen from five yards to spark a frantic last half-hour.

Noel-Williams and Graham Branch wasted chances to double Burnley's advantage, while Darel Russell dragged an effort wide before Mamady Sidibe was foiled by Brian Jensen.

Quote

● **Johan Boskamp**

We played well in the first-half and Burnley played well in the second-half. Sometimes you win, sometimes you lose. We did it well and lost today, but that's football.

Championship Milestone

▶ **50**

Michael Duberry made his 50th appearance in the Championship.

Venue:	Turf Moor	Referee:	N.Miller - 05/06		Burnley
Attendance:	17,912	Matches:	19		Stoke City
Capacity:	22,546	Yellow Cards:	47		
Occupancy:	79%	Red Cards:	8		

Form Coming into Fixture

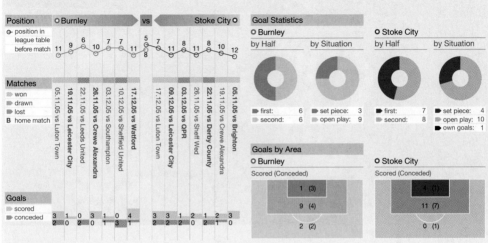

Position

Burnley vs Stoke City

- position in league table before match

Burnley: 11, 9, 6, 10, 7, 7, 5, 8
Stoke City: 7, 11, 8, 11, 8, 10, 12

Matches
- won
- drawn
- lost
- B home match

Burnley matches: 05.11.05 vs Luton Town, 19.11.05 vs Leicester City, 22.11.05 vs Leeds United, 26.11.05 vs Crewe Alexandra, 03.12.05 vs Southampton, 10.12.05 vs Sheffield United, 17.12.05 vs Watford

Stoke matches: 17.12.05 vs Luton Town, 09.12.05 vs Leicester City, 03.12.05 vs QPR, 26.11.05 vs Sheff Wed, 22.11.05 vs Derby County, 19.11.05 vs Crewe Alexandra, 05.11.05 vs Brighton

Goals
- scored
- conceded

Burnley scored: 3, 1, 0, 3, 1, 0, 4
Burnley conceded: 2, 0, 2, 0, 1, 3, 1

Stoke scored: 3, 3, 1, 2, 1, 2, 3
Stoke conceded: 2, 2, 2, 0, 2, 1, 0

Goal Statistics

Burnley

by Half — first: 6, second: 6
by Situation — set piece: 3, open play: 9

Stoke City

by Half — first: 7, second: 8
by Situation — set piece: 4, open play: 10, own goals: 1

Goals by Area

Burnley — Scored (Conceded)

1 (3)
9 (4)
2 (2)

Stoke City — Scored (Conceded)

4 (1)
11 (7)
0 (1)

Team Statistics

Starting Line-Ups

Burnley: Jensen; Harley, Branch/Thomas, McGreal, O'Connor J; Noel-Williams, Bangoura; Sinclair, Hyde, Akinbiyi, Sidibe; Duff, Elliott

Stoke City: Simonsen; Chadwick, Halls, Russell, Hoefkens; Brammer, Duberry; Gallagher, Broomes

Burnley: ▶ 4/4/2
Stoke City: ▶ 4/4/2

Unused Sub: Grant L, Karbassiyoon, O'Connor G, Spicer

Unused Sub: de Goey, Buxton, Henry, Sweeney, Junior

Championship Totals	Burnley	Stoke
Championship Appearances	638	456
Team Appearances	480	374
Goals Scored	59	33
Assists	49	39
Clean Sheets (goalkeepers)	17	20
Yellow Cards	91	64
Red Cards	9	7
Full Internationals	4	4

Age/Height

Burnley Age	Stoke City Age
▶ 29 yrs, 5 mo	▶ 26 yrs, 3 mo
Burnley Height	Stoke City Height
▶ 5'11"	▶ 6'

Match Statistics

League Table after Fixture

			Played	Won	Drawn	Lost	For	Against	Pts
↑	5	Burnley	25	11	5	9	36	30	38
↓	6	Stoke	25	12	1	12	32	35	37
↑	7	Crystal Palace	23	10	5	8	35	26	35
↓	8	Wolverhampton	25	8	11	6	29	22	35
●	9	Preston	25	7	14	4	27	21	35
↓	10	Cardiff	25	9	8	8	33	28	35
↓	11	Luton	25	10	5	10	36	36	35
↑	12	Norwich	25	9	5	11	29	32	32
↓	13	Southampton	24	6	13	5	26	25	31

Statistics	Burnley	Stoke
Goals	1	0
Shots on Target	2	4
Shots off Target	5	7
Hit Woodwork	1	0
Possession %	54	46
Corners	9	1
Offsides	2	3
Fouls	15	3
Disciplinary Points	12	0

0-1

Stoke City °
Leeds United °°

▶ Michael Duberry holds off Rob Hulse

Event Line

26 ○ ▪ Chadwick	
Half time 0-0	
66 ○ ⇄ Miller > Healy	
69 ○ ⊕ Lewis / RF / OP / IA	
Assist: Cresswell	
75 ○ ⇄ Buxton > Halls	
81 ○ ▪ Gallagher	
82 ○ ⇄ Hulse > Blake	
82 ○ ⇄ Sigurdsson > Broomes	
Full time 0-1	

The largest crowd of the season crammed into the Britannia Stadium for the visit of play-off chasing Leeds United.

But a solitary strike from Eddie Lewis twenty minutes from time saw the visitors earn a result which barely reflected the game.

Kevin Blackwell's side were second-best throughout and certainly enjoyed their share of luck on their way to victory - never more so than in injury time when Michael Duberry was denied an equaliser against his former club when his shot crashed off the crossbar.

Earlier, Neil Sullivan saved Paul Gallagher's 18th minute penalty after Mamady Sidibe was impeded in the area.

Gallagher and Luke Chadwick went close to scoring, as did the visitors when substitute Richard Cresswell was foiled by a last-ditch Duberry tackle.

American international Lewis had no trouble making the breakthrough though, arriving late on the scene to drill home Jonathan Douglas' cross from eight yards.

Quote

● **Johan Boskamp**

We had a lot of possibilities to score but didn't do it. We made pressure for eight minutes but every time we create chances we don't put them away.

Venue:	Britannia Stadium	Referee:	M.R.Halsey - 05/06
Attendance:	20,408	Matches:	19
Capacity:	28,218	Yellow Cards:	30
Occupancy:	72%	Red Cards:	5

Form Coming into Fixture

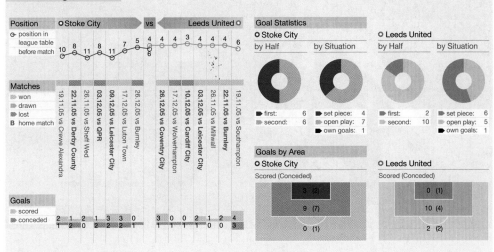

Team Statistics

Championship Totals

	Stoke	Leeds
Championship Appearances	514	630
Team Appearances	432	446
Goals Scored	34	80
Assists	40	72
Clean Sheets (goalkeepers)	20	16
Yellow Cards	73	93
Red Cards	7	7
Full Internationals	5	7

Age/Height

	Stoke City	Leeds United
Age	25 yrs, 8 mo	28 yrs
Height	6'1"	5'11"

Starting Line-Ups
Stoke City: 4/4/2 — Unused Sub: de Goey, Henry, Sweeney
Leeds United: 4/3/3 — Unused Sub: Bennett, Pugh, Richardson

Match Statistics

League Table after Fixture

		Played	Won	Drawn	Lost	For	Against	Pts
↑ 3	Leeds	25	13	6	6	32	22	45
↓ 4	Watford	26	11	10	5	42	31	43
↑ 5	Crystal Palace	24	11	5	8	37	26	38
↑ 6	Wolverhampton	26	9	11	6	31	22	38
↓ 7	Burnley	26	11	5	10	37	32	38
↑ 8	Luton	26	11	5	10	39	36	38
↓ 9	Stoke	26	12	1	13	32	36	37
↓ 10	Preston	25	7	14	4	27	21	35
↓ 11	Cardiff	26	9	8	9	33	29	35

Statistics

	Stoke	Leeds
Goals	0	1
Shots on Target	2	2
Shots off Target	4	3
Hit Woodwork	2	0
Possession %	48	52
Corners	8	3
Offsides	0	1
Fouls	9	10
Disciplinary Points	8	0

2-1

Sheffield United ○
Stoke City ○

▶ Darel Russell flicks the ball away from Alan Quinn

Event Line

18 ○ ⊕	Montgomery / RF / IFK / OA	
	Assist: Jagielka	
Half time 1-0		
46 ○ ⇄	Sigurdsson > Gallagher	
52 ○ ▥	Unsworth	
56 ○ ⇄	Kozluk > Unsworth	
57 ○ ⊕	Sidibe / RF / OP / IA	
	Assist: Broomes	
59 ○ ⇄	Ifill > Kabba	
74 ○ ⇄	Tonge > Montgomery	
87 ○ ⇄	Henry > Chadwick	
90 ○ ▥	Bromby	
90 ○ ▥	Tonge	
90 ○ ⊕	Morgan / H / OP / IA	
	Assist: Jagielka	
90 ○ ▥	Duberry	
Full time 2-1		

Chris Morgan's late, late header handed Sheffield United the points in a dramatic end to 2005 at Bramall Lane.

The Blades' skipper headed home deep into stoppage time to inflict the cruellest of defeats on City, who were more than a match for Neil Warnock's high-flyers over 90 minutes.

Mamady Sidibe's 57th minute strike seemed certain to have earned a deserved draw after levelling out Nick Montgomery's 18th minute opener, which came against the run of play.

Paddy Kenny was the busier of the two goalkeepers at the start as he turned away Sam Bangoura's volley before denying Luke Chadwick.

Bangoura saw two more efforts charged down before Sidibe poked home from close range after Leigh Bromby blocked Chadwick's low drive.

Darel Russell almost grabbed a late winner but was denied by Kenny's outstretched foot before United substitute Michael Tonge crossed for Morgan to direct his looping header over Steve Simonsen.

Quote

● **Johan Boskamp**

With one or two minutes left to play, we have to kick the ball into the stands and not try to play football – because of this we ended up with nothing.

Venue:	Bramall Lane	Referee:	L.Mason - 05/06		**Sheffield United**
Attendance:	21,279	Matches:	14		**Stoke City**
Capacity:	30,558	Yellow Cards:	39		
Occupancy:	70%	Red Cards:	2		

Form Coming into Fixture

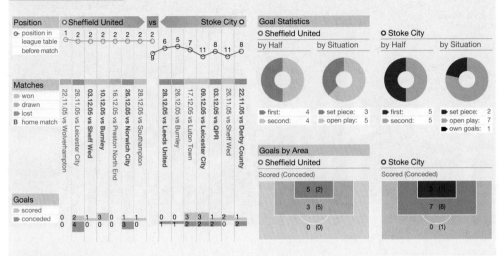

Position — Sheffield United vs Stoke City

- position in league table before match

Sheffield United: 1 2 2 2 2 2 2 2 9
Stoke City: 6 5 7 11 8 11 8

Matches
- won
- drawn
- lost
- B home match

Sheffield United matches:
- 22.11.05 vs Wolverhampton
- 26.11.05 vs Leicester City
- 03.12.05 vs Sheff Wed
- 10.12.05 vs Burnley
- 16.12.05 vs Preston North End
- 26.12.05 vs Norwich City
- 28.12.05 vs Southampton

Stoke City matches:
- 28.12.05 vs Leeds United
- 26.12.05 vs Burnley
- 17.12.05 vs Luton Town
- 09.12.05 vs Leicester City
- 03.12.05 vs QPR
- 26.11.05 vs Sheff Wed
- 22.11.05 vs Derby County

Goals
- scored
- conceded

Sheffield United scored: 0 2 1 3 0 1 1
Sheffield United conceded: 0 4 0 0 0 3 0

Stoke City scored: 0 0 3 3 1 2 1
Stoke City conceded: 1 1 2 2 2 0 2

Goal Statistics

Sheffield United

by Half / by Situation
- first: 4
- second: 4
- set piece: 3
- open play: 5

Stoke City

by Half / by Situation
- first: 5
- second: 5
- set piece: 2
- open play: 7
- own goals: 1

Goals by Area

Sheffield United — Scored (Conceded)
- 5 (2)
- 3 (5)
- 0 (0)

Stoke City — Scored (Conceded)
- 3 (1)
- 7 (8)
- 0 (1)

Team Statistics

Starting Line-Ups

Sheffield United (4/3/3): Kenny; Unsworth, Kozluk, Morgan, Bromby, Geary; Quinn A, Jagielka, Shipperley, Montgomery Tonge, Webber; Kabba Ifill, Bangoura, Sidibe

Stoke City (4/4/2): Simonsen; Chadwick Henry, Broomes, Russell, Hoefkens, Duberry; Brammer, Gallagher Sigurdsson, Buxton

▶ 4/3/3   ▶ 4/4/2

Unused Sub: Gillespie, Shaw
Unused Sub: de Goey, Sweeney, Junior

Championship Totals	Sheff Utd	Stoke
Championship Appearances	679	542
Team Appearances	616	460
Goals Scored	83	32
Assists	65	40
Clean Sheets (goalkeepers)	24	20
Yellow Cards	76	74
Red Cards	5	5
Full Internationals	4	5

Age/Height

	Sheffield United	Stoke City
Age	▶ 26 yrs, 6 mo	▶ 25 yrs, 7 mo
Height	▶ 5'11"	▶ 6'1"

Match Statistics

League Table after Fixture

	Played	Won	Drawn	Lost	For	Against	Pts
● 2 Sheff Utd	27	18	5	4	50	25	59
...	...	...	...	...	...	...	...
↓ 12 Stoke	27	12	1	14	33	38	37
● 13 QPR	27	9	8	10	32	38	35
↑ 14 Ipswich	27	8	8	11	28	40	32
↓ 15 Southampton	26	6	13	7	27	28	31
↓ 16 Hull	27	7	9	11	26	31	30
↑ 17 Derby	27	5	14	8	33	38	29
↓ 18 Coventry	27	6	11	10	32	41	29

Statistics	Sheff Utd	Stoke
Goals	2	1
Shots on Target	5	5
Shots off Target	4	5
Hit Woodwork	0	0
Possession %	55	45
Corners	2	8
Offsides	0	0
Fouls	8	6
Disciplinary Points	12	4

2-2

Stoke City ○
Ipswich Town ○

► Mamady Sidibe celebrates earning a point

Event Line

7 ○ ⊕ De Vos / H / C / IA	
	Assist: Currie
18 ○ ⊕ Wilnis / RF / OP / IA	
27 ○ ⊕ Russell / RF / OP / IA	
	Assist: Bangoura
41 ○ ▢ Chadwick	
45 ○ ▢ Broomes	
Half time 1-2	
46 ○ ⇄ Henry > Broomes	
60 ○ ⇄ Harper > Chadwick	
70 ○ ⇄ Kopteff > Gallagher	
71 ○ ⇄ Juan > Magilton	
73 ○ ⊕ Sidibe / H / C / 6Y	
	Assist: Brammer
88 ○ ⇄ Proudlock > McDonald	
Full time 2-2	

The New Year began in exciting style with a thrilling comeback to snatch a draw from the jaws of defeat.

Ipswich might have thought the points were in the bag when they roared into a two-goal lead inside the opening 20 minutes. Skipper Jason De Vos began the early flurry when he outjumped both Michael Duberry and Marlon Broomes to plant a firm header beyond Steve Simonsen. Fabian Wilnis doubled the advantage, hammering home at the second attempt after his initial effort was blocked by Simonsen.

But Darel Russell led the fight-back on the half-hour when he slammed home after being set up by Sam Bangoura. Bangoura then saw a powerful header saved by Shane Supple before Darren Currie forced Simonsen to turn aside a free-kick.

Supple was again alert to deny the lively Bangoura on the hour, but the breakthrough finally arrived when the goalkeeper failed to gather Dave Brammer's corner and Mamady Sidibe rose highest to head home from close range.

New signing Peter Kopteff almost made a flying start to his career, but Supple reacted well to save from the Finland international.

Quote

● **Johan Boskamp**

If you see the first-half I think we won one point, but if you see the second-half then I think we lost two points.

Championship Milestone

► **Debut**

Peter Kopteff made his Championship debut.

Venue:	Britannia Stadium	Referee:	L.Probert - 05/06		**Stoke City**
Attendance:	14,493	Matches:	21		**Ipswich Town**
Capacity:	28,218	Yellow Cards:	88		
Occupancy:	51%	Red Cards:	3		

Form Coming into Fixture

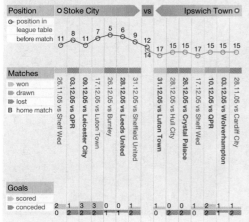

Goal Statistics

Stoke City

by Half / by Situation

■ first:	4	▶ set piece:	2
■ second:	6	▶ open play:	7
		▶ own goals:	1

Ipswich Town

by Half / by Situation

■ first:	1	▶ set piece:	5
■ second:	5	▶ open play:	1

Goals by Area

Stoke City — Scored (Conceded)

2 (1)
8 (7)
0 (2)

Ipswich Town — Scored (Conceded)

1 (2)
4 (5)
1 (2)

Team Statistics

Starting Line-Ups

Simonsen
Buxton / Gallagher (Koptteff)
Duberry / Brammer
Sidibe / Currie
Bangoura / McDonald (Proudlock)
Hoefkens / Russell
Broomes (Henry) / Chadwick (Harper)

Williams / Wilnis
Magilton (Juan) / Collins
Supple
Westlake / De Vos
Richards / Barron

▶ 4/4/2

▶ 4/4/1/1

Unused Sub: de Goey, Sweeney

Unused Sub: Price, Garvan, Horlock

Championship Totals

	○ Stoke	Ipswich ○
Championship Appearances	563	432
Team Appearances	479	394
Goals Scored	34	34
Assists	47	55
Clean Sheets (goalkeepers)	20	1
Yellow Cards	75	34
Red Cards	5	2
Full Internationals	5	3

Age/Height

Stoke City Age	Ipswich Town Age
▶ **26 yrs, 2 mo**	▶ **25 yrs, 4 mo**
Stoke City Height	Ipswich Town Height
▶ **6'**	▶ **5'11"**

Match Statistics

League Table after Fixture

		Played	Won	Drawn	Lost	For	Against	Pts
↓ 7	Wolverhampton	28	9	12	7	32	25	39
↑ 8	Burnley	28	11	6	11	39	35	39
↑ 9	Luton	28	11	5	12	40	39	38
↓ 10	Cardiff	28	10	8	10	36	35	38
● 11	Norwich	28	11	5	12	32	36	38
● 12	Stoke	28	12	2	14	35	40	38
● 13	QPR	28	9	9	10	33	39	36
↑ 14	Southampton	27	7	13	7	29	29	34
↓ 15	Ipswich	28	8	9	11	30	42	33

Statistics

	○ Stoke	Ipswich ○
Goals	2	2
Shots on Target	9	8
Shots off Target	8	5
Hit Woodwork	0	0
Possession %	46	54
Corners	11	5
Offsides	2	2
Fouls	16	13
Disciplinary Points	8	0

0-0

Stoke City ○
Tamworth ○

FA Cup

07.01.06

▶ Darel Russell tries to get his head to the ball

Event Line
Half time 0-0
53 ○ ▨ Bampton
54 ○ ⇄ Sweeney > Kopteff
64 ○ ⇄ Storer > Wright
75 ○ ▨ Henry
76 ○ ⇄ Sigurdsson > Gallagher
79 ○ ⇄ Harper > Chadwick
83 ○ ⇄ Cooper > Bampton
90 ○ ▨ Simonsen
Full time 0-0

Tamworth played their part on a memorable weekend for non-league sides as they held out for a replay.

The Lambs joined Conference neighbours Burton Albion – who held Manchester United – and Conference North outfit Nuneaton – who drew at home to Middlesbrough – to earn a second bite at a Third Round upset.

A gallant defensive display continually frustrated City and plenty of chances to put the tie to bed went begging.

The best of all fell to Mamady Sidibe midway through the second-half, but Lambs 'keeper Scott Bevan pulled of one of a string of fine saves to ensure the draw.

Bevan, a former City loanee during his days as a Southampton trainee, had to be alert right from the word go as recent signing Peter Kopteff, making his first start, put in a low effort before Paul Gallagher saw a similar shot comfortably dealt with.

Gallagher tried his luck again moments later only to find Bevan a formidable presence before the visitors created their best opening of the half on 34 minutes.

Eddie Anaclet latched onto a lose ball on the edge of the area, but with the goal gaping, fired straight into the arms of Steve Simonsen.

Simonsen was called into action again just after the break to stop a header from giant defender Matthew Redmile.

But Sidibe should have finally broken the stubborn resistance when he raced through on goal following a mix-up in the Tamworth defence only for Bevan to

▶ Carl Hoefkens prepares to send over a cross

Match Statistics

Starting Line-Ups

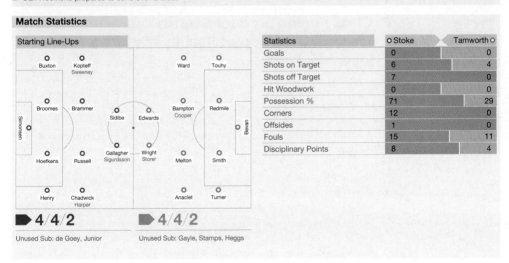

Statistics	○ Stoke	Tamworth ○
Goals	0	0
Shots on Target	6	4
Shots off Target	7	0
Hit Woodwork	0	0
Possession %	71	29
Corners	12	0
Offsides	1	0
Fouls	15	11
Disciplinary Points	8	4

▶ 4/4/2   ▶ 4/4/2

Unused Sub: de Goey, Junior   Unused Sub: Gayle, Stamps, Heggs

spread himself well and charge down the effort.

Bevan kept arguably his most important save for last when Darel Russell came out second-best as the in-form 'keeper pushed away a shot bound for the bottom corner in the closing stages.

There was still time for Tamworth to nearly steal victory though when Jake Edwards squandered two excellent late chances.

The striker fired narrowly wide of the target following a mazy run on goal and then, after another run, rounded Simonsen but delayed his shot and Marlon Broomes put in a vital block.

Quote

● **Johan Boskamp**

If you think you are better than the other team, then it's your own fault you don't win.

1-0

Watford ○
Stoke City ○

▶ Luke Chadwick fires the ball across goal

Event Line
Half time 0-0

54 ○ ⊕	Eagles / RF / OP / IA
70 ○ ⇄	Bangura > McNamee
78 ○ ⇄	Dyer > Harper
81 ○ ⇄	Bouazza > Henderson

Full time 1-0

Chris Eagles produced a rare moment of quality to edge a scrappy affair in Watford's favour at Vicarage Road.

The Hornets winger, on loan from Manchester United, struck the decisive blow shortly after the break.

A bobbly playing surface made for a poor-quality contest, but City were always in the hunt for at least a point.

Marlon King went closest to a goal early on with a fierce drive pushed away by Steve Simonsen. Luke Chadwick saw two efforts blocked and Junior fired over, before the game's key moment arrived nine minutes after half-time when Carl Hoefkens' clearance fell into the path of Eagles, who fired crisply home.

Paul Gallagher shot wide and Luke Chadwick was denied by Watford's former Stoke 'keeper Ben Foster in response.

Chadwick missed the best, and final, chance to level the scores with 15 minutes left to play when he scooped over from close range.

Quote

● **Johan Boskamp**

If one of the chances had fallen to Sammy Bangoura then it's normally Bingo, but we cannot have him for five weeks – so we need other people to score.

Championship Milestone

▶ **50**

Michael Duberry made his 50th appearance in the Championship for Stoke.

Venue:	Vicarage Road	Referee:	P.Crossley - 05/06		**Watford**
Attendance:	12,247	Matches:	9		**Stoke City**
Capacity:	22,100	Yellow Cards:	27		
Occupancy:	55%	Red Cards:	2		

Form Coming into Fixture

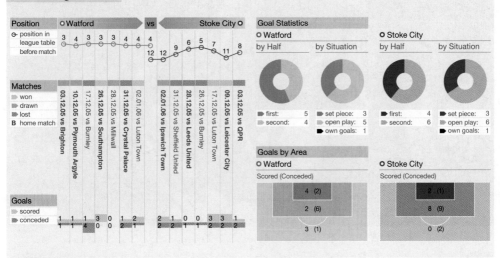

Goal Statistics

○ Watford

by Half | by Situation

▶ first: 5 ▶ set piece: 3
▶ second: 4 ▶ open play: 5
 ▶ own goals: 1

○ Stoke City

by Half | by Situation

▶ first: 4 ▶ set piece: 3
▶ second: 6 ▶ open play: 6
 ▶ own goals: 1

Goals by Area

○ Watford — Scored (Conceded)

4 (2)
2 (6)
3 (1)

○ Stoke City — Scored (Conceded)

2 (1)
8 (9)
0 (2)

Team Statistics

Starting Line-Ups

Watford (4/4/2): Foster; Stewart, McNamee (Bangura), Mackay, Mahon; Henderson/Bouazza, King, Harper/Dyer, Sidibe; DeMerit, Spring; Doyley, Eagles

Stoke City (4/4/1/1): Simonsen; Chadwick, Henry, Junior, Hoefkens; Brammer, Duberry; Gallagher, Broomes

4 / 4 / 2

4 / 4 / 1 / 1

Unused Sub: Chamberlain, Chambers, Mariappa

Unused Sub: Duggan, Dickinson, Kopteff, Sweeney

Championship Totals

	○ Watford	Stoke ○
Championship Appearances	554	524
Team Appearances	396	394
Goals Scored	56	34
Assists	39	51
Clean Sheets (goalkeepers)	7	20
Yellow Cards	49	53
Red Cards	4	6
Full Internationals	2	3

Age/Height

Watford Age	Stoke City Age
24 yrs, 4 mo	**26 yrs, 11 mo**
Watford Height	Stoke City Height
5'11"	**6'**

Match Statistics

League Table after Fixture

		Played	Won	Drawn	Lost	For	Against	Pts
● 4	Watford	29	13	10	6	46	34	49
...		...	...	...	...	...	...	...
↓ 13	Stoke	29	12	2	15	35	41	38
● 14	Southampton	28	7	13	8	29	30	34
● 15	Ipswich	29	8	10	11	31	43	34
↑ 16	Derby	29	6	14	9	39	41	32
↓ 17	Coventry	29	7	11	11	34	43	32
↓ 18	Hull	29	7	9	13	28	36	30
↑ 19	Sheff Wed	29	7	9	13	24	34	30

Statistics

	○ Watford	Stoke ○
Goals	1	0
Shots on Target	7	2
Shots off Target	8	7
Hit Woodwork	0	0
Possession %	49	51
Corners	9	5
Offsides	2	6
Fouls	15	11
Disciplinary Points	0	0

1-1 a.e.t Tamworth ○
Stoke City ○

▶ Paul Gallagher finds himself under intense pressure

Event Line

33 ○ ▪	Smith
42 ○ ⊕	Jackson / RF / OP / IA
	Assist: Heggs
43 ○ ▪	Heggs
Half time 1-0	
46 ○ ⇄	Junior > Brammer
46 ○ ⇄	Kopteff > Chadwick
66 ○ ⇄	Turner > Wright
80 ○ ⊕	Gallagher / RF / C / 6Y
	Assist: Rooney
80 ○ ⇄	Rooney > Broomes
83 ○ ⇄	Storer > Melton
97 ○ ▪	Harper
101 ○ ▪	Junior
116 ○ ⇄	Stamps > Ward
Full time 1-1	

Penalties were needed before Tamworth were eventually put to the sword in a dramatic FA Cup third round replay at The Lamb.

Goalkeeper Steve Simonsen emerged as the hero, saving two spot-kicks in the shootout before Carl Hoefkens lashed home the decisive strike in sudden-death.

It was all square after 120 minutes of edge-of-the-seat action as Paul Gallagher's 80th minute strike cancelled out Nathan Jackson's first-half opener.

A hatful of chances went begging to put the contest beyond the Conference outfit and Gallagher was the early culprit when he twice fired over from close range. Dave Brammer tried his luck from further out, but fired over, and then found the hands of Scott Bevan with another effort. Another chance came and went as Gallagher sent Kevin Harper clear, but Mamady Sidibe couldn't make contact as the ball bobbled across goal.

Simonsen was a virtual spectator as Luke Chadwick sent a stinging volley against the crossbar, but he could do nothing in the 42nd minute when the non-leaguers grabbed the lead. Michael Duberry's clearance was charged down by Carl Heggs and, with Simonsen stranded, he squared for strike partner Jackson to tuck home into an empty net.

Tamworth piled men behind the ball after that, but Marlon Broomes led the pursuit of an equaliser and struck the post.

Gallagher saw an effort blocked on the line by Matthew Redmile, but he wasn't to be denied ten minutes from time when he reacted quickest to hook acrobatically past Scott Bevan after the 'keeper had saved from debutant Adam Rooney.

➡ Steve Simonsen helps City to a place in Round Four

Match Statistics

Starting Line-Ups

Statistics	○ Tamworth	Stoke ○
Goals	1	1
Shots on Target	2	7
Shots off Target	3	12
Hit Woodwork	0	1
Possession %	40	60
Corners	4	11
Offsides	1	5
Fouls	19	22
Disciplinary Points	8	8

➡ 4/4/2   ➡ 4/4/1/1

Unused Sub: Gayle, Cooper   Unused Sub: Duggan, Sweeney

Chances were few and far between during extra-time as nerves and fatigue took hold and, in the end, 310 minutes of cup action were settled by 12 penalty kicks.

After Gallagher and Peter Kopteff both converted, Simonsen's save from Eddie Anaclet at 2-2 handed City the advantage, but Harper missed and Heggs scored to put the tie back in the balance. Karl Henry then sent Bevan the wrong way before Lewis Buxton stepped up and kept his cool to force the game into sudden death.

After Michael Touhy's tame effort was blocked by Simonsen's legs, Hoefkens' revelled under the pressure and confidently slotted home to book a place in the fourth round.

Quote

● **Jan De Koning**

It's a lottery, but lucky for us, Steve Simonsen did his job and we took our kicks well.

0-3

Stoke City ○
Hull City ○

▶ Luke Chadwick tries to get away from Stuart Elliott

Event Line

7 ○ ⊕	Russell / LF / OG / 6Y
20 ○ ▪	France
35 ○ ▪	Elliott
38 ○ ▪	Broomes
Half time 0-1	
50 ○ ▪	Collins
55 ○ ⊕	Parkin / LF / OP / IA
	Assist: Delaney
63 ○ ⇄	Duffy > Price
70 ○ ⇄	Harper > Chadwick
78 ○ ⇄	Rooney > Harper
80 ○ ▪	Fagan
81 ○ ⊕	Duffy / RF / OP / OA
	Assist: Fagan
83 ○ ⇄	Wiseman > Fagan
86 ○ ⇄	Ellison > Elliott
89 ○ ▪	Duberry
90 ○ ▪	Rooney
Full time 0-3	

Penalties played a big part as two missed spot-kicks allowed Hull to claim all three points.

Paul Gallagher and Luke Chadwick both failed to convert from the spot and the visitors also had the luck when they needed it because a fluke own-goal from Darel Russell set them on their way before second-half strikes from Jon Parkin and Darryl Duffy put the contest beyond doubt.

The Tigers were ahead after just six minutes when Marlon Broomes' goal-line clearance cannoned back off the unfortunate Russell and into the net.

Gallagher's penalty miss came just after the break when he was pulled back by Sam Collins in the area – the striker seeing his effort saved by Boaz Myhill. Parkin made the most of the reprieve shortly after as he swivelled past Carl Hoefkens before tucking beyond Steve Simonsen.

Collins was again the culprit when he pulled down Peter Sweeney to hand City a second chance from the spot, but Myhill was on hand to deny Chadwick.

Substitute Duffy added insult to injury in the 80th minute when he broke clear to fire home.

Quote

⬤ **Johan Boskamp**

This is the first time I'm a little bit down after a game. Today we were not supposed to lose and yet we lost 3-0 at home to Hull.

Championship Milestone

▶ **Debut**

Adam Rooney made his Championship debut.

Form Coming into Fixture

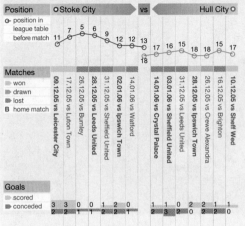

Goal Statistics

○ Stoke City

by Half	by Situation
first: 3	set piece: 2
second: 6	open play: 6
	own goals: 1

○ Hull City

by Half	by Situation
first: 4	set piece: 2
second: 4	open play: 6

Goals by Area

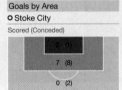

○ Stoke City — Scored (Conceded)

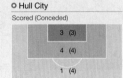

○ Hull City — Scored (Conceded)

Team Statistics

Starting Line-Ups

Unused Sub: de Goey, Kopteff, Junior

▶ 4/4/2

Unused Sub: Leite, Paynter

▶ 4/4/2

Championship Totals	○Stoke	Hull○
Championship Appearances	533	251
Team Appearances	425	231
Goals Scored	28	16
Assists	41	16
Clean Sheets (goalkeepers)	20	6
Yellow Cards	62	14
Red Cards	5	1
Full Internationals	3	1

Age/Height

Stoke City Age	Hull City Age
▶ **25 yrs**	▶ **24 yrs, 10 mo**
Stoke City Height	Hull City Height
▶ **6'**	▶ **6'**

Match Statistics

League Table after Fixture

		Played	Won	Drawn	Lost	For	Against	Pts
↑	9 Luton	30	12	5	13	43	41	41
↓	10 Burnley	30	11	6	13	39	40	39
↓	11 Norwich	30	11	6	13	35	40	39
↓	12 QPR	30	10	9	11	34	41	39
●	13 Stoke	30	12	2	16	35	44	38
↑	14 Ipswich	30	9	10	11	33	43	37
↑	15 Coventry	30	8	11	11	40	44	35
↓	16 Southampton	29	7	13	9	29	32	34
↑	17 Hull	30	8	9	13	31	36	33

Statistics	○Stoke	Hull○
Goals	0	3
Shots on Target	11	8
Shots off Target	8	3
Hit Woodwork	0	0
Possession %	47	53
Corners	6	8
Offsides	1	1
Fouls	14	21
Disciplinary Points	12	16

2-1

Stoke City ○
Walsall ○

▶ Marlon Broomes looks to get forward

Event Line

21	○ ■	Hoefkens
42	○ ■	Leary
45	○ ⊕	Sidibe / LF / OP / IA
		Assist: Henry
Half time 1-0		
49	○ ⊕	Chadwick / LF / OP / OA
		Assist: Gallagher
51	○ ⊕	James / RF / OP / 6Y
		Assist: Wright
52	○ ⇄	Nicholls > McDermott
60	○ ⇄	de Goey > Simonsen
69	○ ⇄	Standing > Wright
77	○ ⇄	Kopteff > Chadwick
90	○ ⇄	Sigurdsson > Gallagher
Full time 2-1		

Luke Chadwick's brilliant goal helped shrug off the challenge of Walsall and earned an interesting FA Cup fifth round tie at home to Birmingham.

The lively winger fired home his second goal for City from long-range shortly after the break to add to Mamady Sidibe's first-half opener.

Kevin James' quick reply set up a nervy finish, but substitute goalkeeper Ed De Goey shared the plaudits with match-winner Chadwick when he pulled off two fine saves after replacing the injured Steve Simonsen on the hour.

A bright opening saw plenty of goalmouth action at both ends of the field, with Daniel Fox and Mads Timm going close for the Saddlers from long-range after Mamady Sidibe blasted high and wide from a promising position.

But, shortly after a Paul Gallagher strike whistled past the post, Sidibe made amends.

Anthony Gerrard charged down Karl Henry's goalbound effort and the ball fell invitingly at Sidibe's feet and he made no mistake with a powerful drive from eight yards.

Chadwick's moment of skill doubled the advantage in the 49th minute, exchanging passes with Gallagher and embarking on a mazy run before curling a left-footed strike past Andy Oakes from the edge of the area.

James immediately reduced arrears, nipping in front of his marker to turn Mark

► Carl Hoefkens evades a sliding tackle

Match Statistics

Starting Line-Ups

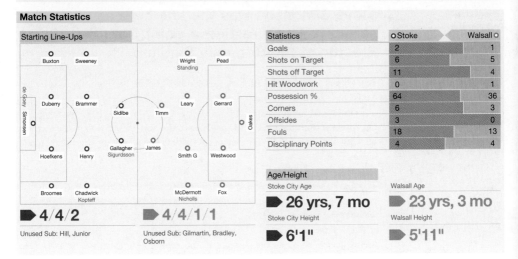

Statistics	o Stoke	Walsall o
Goals	2	1
Shots on Target	6	5
Shots off Target	11	4
Hit Woodwork	0	1
Possession %	64	36
Corners	6	3
Offsides	3	0
Fouls	18	13
Disciplinary Points	4	4

Age/Height

Stoke City Age	Walsall Age
► **26 yrs, 7 mo**	► **23 yrs, 3 mo**
Stoke City Height	Walsall Height
► **6'1"**	► **5'11"**

► 4/4/2 ► 4/4/1/1

Unused Sub: Hill, Junior

Unused Sub: Gilmartin, Bradley, Osborn

Wright's cross past Simonsen, who limped off with a hand injury shortly afterwards.

De Goey stepped into the breach and was immediately put to the test as Grant Smith's drive cracked against the post.

Dave Brammer tried his luck from 25 yards only to see Oakes tip over, but it was the visitors who applied the late pressure.

Despite making only his third appearance of the season, De Goey was on his toes to thwart a dangerous effort from Michael Standing before a magnificent one-handed save to deny Alex Nicholls in the dying seconds.

Quote

● **Luke Chadwick**

Ed's saves stopped the game from going to a replay. He does that kind of thing day in, day out, in training.

0-0

Stoke City ○
Preston North End ○

▶ Karl Henry closes down Tyrone Mears

Event Line

28 ○ ⇄ Neal L > Alexander	
30 ○ ▨ Mawene	
43 ○ ▨ O'Neil	
Half time 0-0	
46 ○ ⇄ Sigurdsson > Gallagher	
55 ○ ▨ Russell	
	Violent Conduct
56 ○ ⇄ Lucketti > O'Neil	
58 ○ ▨ Chadwick	
63 ○ ⇄ Junior > Sweeney	
82 ○ ⇄ Agyemang > Sedgwick	
90 ○ ▨ Nugent	
Full time 0-0	

Steve Simonsen was the late hero as an under-strength side wrestled a point from high-flying Preston at the Britannia Stadium.

The Potters 'keeper saved Paul McKenna's 88th minute penalty to stave off what would have been an undeserved defeat.

Up against it from the moment Darel Russell was sent-off early on in the second-off, City battled bravely in the face of adversity to claim only the third draw of the season.

The first-half was a tight affair with chances few and far between at both ends, but Paul Gallagher did go close with angled drive and David Nugent dragged an effort wide for the visitors.

Preston began to apply the pressure in the second period with their extra man advantage after Russell saw red for an off the ball clash with McKenna. They looked like cashing in right at the death, when former Lilywhite Marlon Broomes upended Tyrone Mears' probing run into the area. McKenna stepped up to take the spot-kick, but Simonsen read his mind.

Quote

● **Johan Boskamp**

Preston haven't lost for twenty-odd games so we're glad to get a point.

Championship Milestone

▶ **25**

Paul Gallagher made his 25th appearance in the Championship.

Venue:	Britannia Stadium	Referee:	B.Curson - 05/06		**Stoke City**
Attendance:	13,218	Matches:	25		**Preston North End**
Capacity:	28,218	Yellow Cards:	58		
Occupancy:	47%	Red Cards:	3		

Form Coming into Fixture

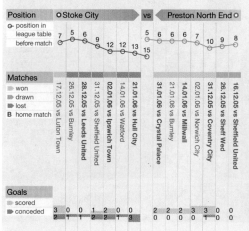

Position
- position in league table before match

Stoke City: 7 5 6 9 12 12 13 15
vs Preston North End: 5 6 6 6 7 10 9 8

Matches
- won
- drawn
- lost
- B home match

Stoke: 17.12.05 vs Luton Town · 26.12.05 vs Burnley · 28.12.05 vs Leeds United · 31.12.05 vs Sheffield United · 02.01.06 vs Ipswich Town · 14.01.06 vs Watford · 21.01.06 vs Hull City

Preston: 31.01.06 vs Crystal Palace · 21.01.06 vs Burnley · 14.01.06 vs Millwall · 02.01.06 vs Norwich City · 31.12.05 vs Coventry City · 26.12.05 vs Sheffield Wed · 16.12.05 vs Sheffield United

Goals
- scored
- conceded

Stoke: scored 3 0 0 1 2 0 0 / conceded 2 1 1 2 2 1 3
Preston: scored 2 2 2 3 3 0 0 / conceded 0 0 0 0 1 0 0

Goal Statistics

Stoke City

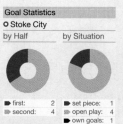

by Half / by Situation
- first: 2
- second: 4
- set piece: 1
- open play: 4
- own goals: 1

Preston North End

by Half / by Situation
- first: 7
- second: 5
- set piece: 6
- open play: 6

Goals by Area

Stoke City — Scored (Conceded)

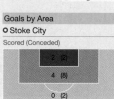

2 (2)
4 (8)
0 (2)

Preston North End — Scored (Conceded)

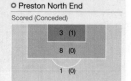

3 (1)
8 (0)
1 (0)

Team Statistics

Starting Line-Ups

Stoke City:
Simonsen · Buxton · Sweeney (Junior) · Duberry · Henry · Sidibe · Ormerod · Hoefkens · Russell · Gallagher (Sigurdsson) · Nugent · Broomes · Chadwick

Preston North End:
Nash · Sedgwick (Agyemang) · Mears · O'Neil (Lucketti) · Mawene · McKenna · Davis · Davidson · Alexander (Neal L)

▶ 4/4/2   **▶ 4/4/2**

Unused Sub: de Goey, Hill, Kopteff   Unused Sub: Whaley, Dichio

Championship Totals	Stoke	Preston
Championship Appearances	546	734
Team Appearances	440	647
Goals Scored	27	73
Assists	36	62
Clean Sheets (goalkeepers)	20	16
Yellow Cards	64	90
Red Cards	6	2
Full Internationals	4	5

Age/Height

	Stoke City Age	Preston North End Age
	▶ 24 yrs, 11 mo	**▶ 28 yrs, 2 mo**
	Stoke City Height	Preston North End Height
	▶ 6'1"	**▶ 6'**

Match Statistics

League Table after Fixture

		Played	Won	Drawn	Lost	For	Against	Pts
↓ 6	Preston	31	12	15	4	39	22	51
• 7	Cardiff	32	12	9	11	42	38	45
• 8	Luton	32	13	5	14	47	44	44
• 9	Wolverhampton	31	10	13	8	34	27	43
• 10	Burnley	32	12	7	13	40	40	43
↑ 11	Coventry	32	10	11	11	44	45	41
• 12	Norwich	31	11	6	14	35	44	39
↑ 13	Stoke	31	12	3	16	35	44	39
↓ 14	QPR	32	10	9	13	36	46	39

Statistics	Stoke	Preston
Goals	0	0
Shots on Target	3	3
Shots off Target	1	5
Hit Woodwork	0	1
Possession %	48	52
Corners	0	6
Offsides	2	3
Fouls	16	17
Disciplinary Points	16	12

3-0

Cardiff City ○
Stoke City ○

➡ Peter Sweeney bursts forward down the left

Event Line

9	○ ▨	Ndumbu-Nsungu
18	○ ⊕	Cooper / LF / OP / OA
25	○ ▨	Purse
30	○ ⊕	Cox / RF / C / 6Y
		Assist: Scimeca
37	○ ▨	Sidibe
Half time 2-0		
46	○ ⇄	Kopteff > Sweeney
68	○ ⇄	Hill > Broomes
68	○ ⊕	Cox / H / IFK / IA
		Assist: Ardley
77	○ ⇄	Junior > Brammer
Full time 3-0		

There was little joy down in South Wales as play-off chasing Cardiff powered to victory at Ninian Park.

The home side took the lead against the run of play in the 18th minute through Kevin Cooper, but took control after that and a brace from Neil Cox settled the outcome.

Cooper opened the scoring with a 20-yard drive from a tight angle and 12 minutes later supplied the cross for Cox to stroke home from close range.

It was an uphill battle after that, although the Bluebirds were made to work hard for their third goal as Mamady Sidibe and Hannes Sigurdsson went close.

But it came in the 68th minute and it was Cox again, ghosting in at the back post to glance home a header.

It nearly got worse when Darren Purse rattled the crossbar, but one bonus was the return of defender Clint Hill after a long injury lay-off for the final 20 minutes and he almost notched a late consolation when he saw a powerful header saved.

Quote

● **Johan Boskamp**

We were in control for the first 20 minutes but after that the team fell down. I think we have conceded 20 goals now through set-pieces.

Championship Milestone

➡ **Debut**

Josip Skoko made his Championship debut.

Form Coming into Fixture

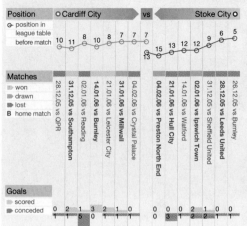

Goal Statistics

Cardiff City

by Half | by Situation

first: 4 | set piece: 1
second: 5 | open play: 8

Stoke City

by Half | by Situation

first: 1 | set piece: 1
second: 2 | open play: 2

Goals by Area

Cardiff City
Scored (Conceded)

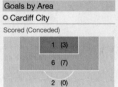

1 (3)
6 (7)
2 (0)

Stoke City
Scored (Conceded)

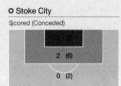

2 (6)
0 (2)

Team Statistics

Starting Line-Ups

4/4/2   **4/4/2**

Unused Sub: Margetson, Weston, Mulryne, Whitley, Ferretti

Unused Sub: de Goey, Rooney

Championship Totals

	Cardiff	Stoke
Championship Appearances	481	508
Team Appearances	372	434
Goals Scored	42	17
Assists	42	33
Clean Sheets (goalkeepers)	14	21
Yellow Cards	37	59
Red Cards	3	7
Full Internationals	1	5

Age/Height

Cardiff City Age	Stoke City Age
27 yrs, 8 mo	**26 yrs, 3 mo**

Cardiff City Height	Stoke City Height
6'	**6'**

Match Statistics

League Table after Fixture

		Played	Won	Drawn	Lost	For	Against	Pts
● 7	Cardiff	33	13	9	11	45	38	48
...		...	...	...	...	...	...	...
↓ 16	Stoke	32	12	3	17	35	47	39
● 17	Hull	33	9	10	14	36	41	37
● 18	Southampton	33	7	15	11	30	36	36
↑ 19	Leicester	33	8	11	14	35	43	35
↓ 20	Derby	33	6	16	11	40	48	34
↓ 21	Sheff Wed	33	8	10	15	25	39	34
● 22	Brighton	33	5	14	14	31	51	29

Statistics

	Cardiff	Stoke
Goals	3	0
Shots on Target	5	4
Shots off Target	0	8
Hit Woodwork	1	0
Possession %	53	47
Corners	4	4
Offsides	1	2
Fouls	17	16
Disciplinary Points	8	4

0-0

Stoke City o
Plymouth Argyle o

▶ Josip Skoko tries to stay on his feet

Event Line

15 O ■	Doumbe
18 O ⇄	Sigurdsson > Sidibe
Half time 0-0	
60 O ⇄	Evans > Chadwick
67 O ⇄	Sweeney > Kopteff
81 O ■	Barness
83 O ■	Chadwick
Full time 0-0	

Tony Pulis brought his Plymouth side to the Britannia Stadium and battled it out for a point.

A game of few chances might have been settled by Sam Bangoura on his return from the African Cup of Nations, but Argyle 'keeper Roman Larrieu made a superb fingertip save from his stooping header. Nick Chadwick also missed two great chances to score for Plymouth in the second-half, but overall the draw was a fair reflection of a frustrating game.

Peter Kopteff called Larrieu into action early on, while at the other end Paul Wotton and David Norris both fired wide before Lilian Nalis tested Steve Simonsen from long range.

The visitors should have taken the lead just after half-time through Chadwick, who twice failed to finish off promising attacks in the space of three minutes.

Carl Hoefkens, switched to right-back to accommodate the full return of Clint Hill from injury in the centre of defence, drilled a thunderous effort narrowly wide.

Bangoura nearly broke through on the hour when he connected with a Dave Brammer cross, but Larrieu sprawled across his goal to make a brilliant save.

Quote

● **Johan Boskamp**

Plymouth put ten men behind the ball and made it very difficult for us to score. But I'm happy we didn't concede.

Venue:	Britannia Stadium	Referee:	M.A.Riley - 05/06		**Stoke City**
Attendance:	10,242	Matches:	28		**Plymouth Argyle**
Capacity:	28,218	Yellow Cards:	94		
Occupancy:	36%	Red Cards:	7		

Form Coming into Fixture

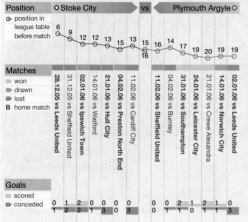

Position — ⊙ Stoke City vs Plymouth Argyle ⊙
- ⊙ position in league table before match

Matches
- won
- drawn
- lost
- B home match

Goals
- scored
- conceded

Goal Statistics

⊙ Stoke City

by Half	by Situation
first: 1	set piece: 1
second: 2	open play: 2

⊙ Plymouth Argyle

by Half	by Situation
first: 4	set piece: 4
second: 2	open play: 1
	own goals: 1

Goals by Area

⊙ Stoke City

Scored (Conceded)

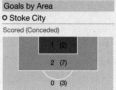

1 (2)	
2 (7)	
0 (3)	

⊙ Plymouth Argyle

Scored (Conceded)

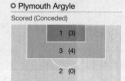

| 1 (3) |
| 3 (4) |
| 2 (0) |

Team Statistics

Starting Line-Ups

Simonsen — Broomes, Kopteff, Sweeney, Hill, Skoko, Sidibe, Sigurdsson, Pericard, Duberry, Brammer, Bangoura, Chadwick, Evans, Hoefkens, Chadwick

Norris, Connolly, Wotton, Doumbe, Larrieu, Nalis, Ward, Capaldi, Barness

▶ 4/4/2   ▶ 4/4/2

Unused Sub: de Goey, Dickinson, Junior

Unused Sub: McCormick, Aljofree, Buzsaky, Hodges

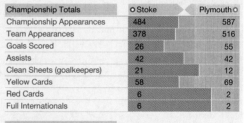

Championship Totals	⊙ Stoke	Plymouth ⊙
Championship Appearances	484	587
Team Appearances	378	516
Goals Scored	26	55
Assists	42	42
Clean Sheets (goalkeepers)	21	12
Yellow Cards	58	69
Red Cards	6	2
Full Internationals	6	2

Age/Height

Stoke City Age	Plymouth Argyle Age
▶ **26 yrs, 9 mo**	▶ **27 yrs**
Stoke City Height	Plymouth Argyle Height
▶ **6'**	▶ **6'**

Match Statistics

League Table after Fixture

		Played	Won	Drawn	Lost	For	Against	Pts
●	15 Plymouth	33	9	13	11	29	37	40
●	16 Stoke	33	12	4	17	35	47	40
●	17 Hull	34	9	11	14	37	42	38
●	18 Southampton	33	7	15	11	30	36	36
●	19 Leicester	34	8	12	14	37	45	36
●	20 Derby	34	6	17	11	42	50	35
●	21 Sheff Wed	33	8	10	15	25	39	34
●	22 Brighton	34	5	14	15	31	54	29
●	23 Millwall	34	5	13	16	24	46	28

Statistics	⊙ Stoke	Plymouth ⊙
Goals	0	0
Shots on Target	2	1
Shots off Target	1	3
Hit Woodwork	0	0
Possession %	56	44
Corners	4	3
Offsides	3	
Fouls	10	11
Disciplinary Points	4	8

0-1

Stoke City ○
Birmingham City ○

➡ Dave Brammer sends the ball upfield

Event Line

23 ○ ■	Junior	
Half time 0-0		
47 ○ ⊕	Forssell / RF / C / 6Y	
	Assist: Latka	
50 ○ ■	Latka	
70 ○ ⇄	Sigurdsson > Sweeney	
76 ○ ⇄	Jarosik > Forssell	
86 ○ ⇄	Rooney > Broomes	
87 ○ ■	Clemence	
88 ○ ■	Hoefkens	
88 ○ ⇄	Clapham > Pennant	
90 ○ ■	Brammer	
Full time 0-1		

Mikael Forssell's second-half goal settled a tense and closely-fought FA Cup fifth round tie.

The Finnish international striker steered Birmingham into the last eight of the competition, but their real hero was goalkeeper Maik Taylor. Taylor made two stunning saves and a series of timely interventions to keep the Potters at bay and frustrate a large home crowd.

Forssell and former England international Emile Heskey both fired in early warning shots before the visitors were forced onto the back foot.

Luke Chadwick saw a vicious effort cannon off a defender before Sam Bangoura, sporting a lightweight cast on his hand to protect a broken bone, was first to test Taylor.

There were muted shouts for a penalty when Peter Sweeney's cross appeared to strike the hand of Nicky Butt, but referee Mike Dean wasn't impressed.

Dave Brammer tried his luck from long range and then Bangoura cracked a shot just wide of the mark, while Jermaine Pennant's hopeful long-ranger offered a rare reply.

The best chance of the half fell at the feet of Carl Hoefkens. The Belgian full-back unleashed a stinging effort from 25-yards which forced a full-stretch Taylor into a magnificent one-handed save.

Birmingham went in at half-time lucky to be on level terms, but found themselves ahead on 47 minutes when Martin Latka flicked Pennant's corner into the path of Forssell and he hooked the ball beyond Simonsen from close range.

Venue:	Britannia Stadium	Referee:	M.L.Dean - 05/06
Attendance:	18,768	Matches:	25
Capacity:	28,218	Yellow Cards:	67
Occupancy:	67%	Red Cards:	6

Stoke City
Birmingham City

► Sambegou Bangoura demonstrates his aerial prowess

Match Statistics

Starting Line-Ups

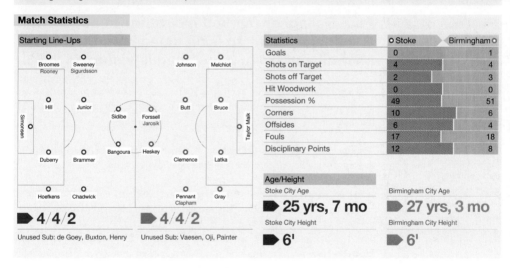

Statistics	O Stoke	Birmingham O
Goals	0	1
Shots on Target	4	4
Shots off Target	2	3
Hit Woodwork	0	0
Possession %	49	51
Corners	10	6
Offsides	6	4
Fouls	17	18
Disciplinary Points	12	8

Starting Line-Ups (Stoke):
Broomes, Sweeney, Rooney, Sigurdsson, Hill, Junior, Sidibe, Forssell/Jarosik, Bangoura, Heskey, Simonsen, Duberry, Brammer, Hoefkens, Chadwick

4/4/2

Unused Sub: de Goey, Buxton, Henry

Starting Line-Ups (Birmingham):
Johnson, Melchiot, Butt, Bruce, Taylor Maik, Clemence, Latka, Pennant, Clapham, Gray

4/4/2

Unused Sub: Vaesen, Oji, Painter

Age/Height

	Stoke	Birmingham
Age	► **25 yrs, 7 mo**	► **27 yrs, 3 mo**
Height	► **6'**	► **6'**

Skipper Michael Duberry led the response, but found Taylor in top form again when the Northern Ireland stopper somehow pawed away a powerful header bound for the top corner.

And the drama didn't end there. The Premiership side enjoyed a huge let-off when Bangoura's header from a superb Mamady Sidibe cross flew straight into Taylor's arms.

City continued to press in search of a deserved equaliser, but it wasn't to be and the Birmingham defence held firm under a barrage of pressure to earn a quarter-final tie at home to Liverpool.

Quote

● **Johan Boskamp**

We played our football against a Premiership team and that is a great compliment to us.

2-1

Stoke City ○
Millwall ○

▶ Josip Skoko runs at the Millwall defence

Event Line

8 ○ ⊕	May / H / C / IA	
	Assist: Craig	
14 ○ ▪	Lawrence	
15 ○ ⊕	Hoefkens / RF / P / IA	
	Assist: Hoefkens	
37 ○ ⇄	Gallagher > Sweeney	
Half time 1-1		
57 ○ ⊕	Gallagher / RF / OP / OA	
	Assist: Chadwick	
61 ○ ⇄	Powel > May	
66 ○	Skoko	
80 ○ ⇄	Russell > Skoko	
80 ○ ⇄	Williams > Asaba	
85 ○	Whitbread	
Full time 2-1		

Paul Gallagher marked his return to action with a stunning goal to sink relegation-threatened Millwall and claim a first league victory in 2006.

The Scottish under-21 international, back after a three-match absence with a knee injury, wasted no time in making an impact with the winning strike after 57 minutes.

Gallagher had been on the field for just 20 minutes after replacing the injured Peter Sweeney when he curled home a sweet strike from 18 yards.

It helped settle nerves on a tense afternoon which began with the lowly Lions taking an early lead when Ben May headed in Marvin Elliott's 8th minute cross.

The lead lasted for just seven minutes though, as Tony Craig impeded Carl Hoefkens' run into the area and the Belgian picked himself up to confidently stroke home the equaliser from the spot.

From that moment on, the Potters were firmly in control and Hannes Sigurdsson twice went close before Gallagher's winner, and after that Clint Hill and Gallagher, again, were both thwarted by Andy Marshall.

Quote

● **Carl Hoefkens**

We deserved victory. At the beginning we had difficulties after conceding another goal from a set-piece but, after that, I felt we were the best team and could have won by more.

Form Coming into Fixture

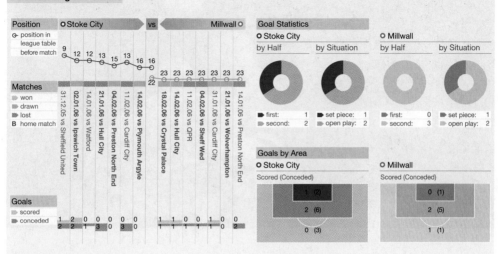

Position — ○ Stoke City vs Millwall ○

o position in league table before match

9, 12, 12, 13, 15, 13, 16, 16 — 23, 23, 23, 23, 23, 23, 23
22

Matches
- won
- drawn
- lost
- B home match

31.12.05 vs Sheffield United
02.01.06 vs Ipswich Town
14.01.06 vs Watford
21.01.06 vs Hull City
04.02.06 vs Preston North End
11.02.06 vs Cardiff City
14.02.06 vs Plymouth Argyle
18.02.06 vs Crystal Palace
14.02.06 vs Hull City
11.02.06 vs QPR
04.02.06 vs Sheff Wed
31.01.06 vs Cardiff City
21.01.06 vs Wolverhampton
14.01.06 vs Preston North End

Goals
- scored: 1 2 0 0 0 0 0 | 1 1 0 0 1 0 0
- conceded: 2 2 1 3 0 3 0 | 1 1 1 1 0 0 2

Goal Statistics

○ Stoke City — by Half | by Situation

| | first: | 1 | | set piece: | 1 |
| | second: | 2 | | open play: | 2 |

○ Millwall — by Half | by Situation

| | first: | 0 | | set piece: | 1 |
| | second: | 3 | | open play: | 2 |

Goals by Area

○ Stoke City — Scored (Conceded)

1 (2)
2 (6)
0 (3)

○ Millwall — Scored (Conceded)

0 (1)
2 (5)
1 (1)

Team Statistics

Starting Line-Ups

Simonsen
Broomes, Sweeney Gallagher
Hill, Skoko Russell, Sigurdsson, Asaba Williams
Duberry, Brammer, Sidibe, May Powel
Hoefkens, Chadwick

Dunne, Lawrence
Elliott, Robinson P
Marshall
Livermore, Whitbread
Dyer, Craig

▶ 4/4/2 ▶ 4/4/2

Unused Sub: de Goey, Buxton, Junior — Unused Sub: Doyle, Ifil, Braniff

Championship Totals	○ Stoke	Millwall ○
Championship Appearances	573	502
Team Appearances	467	448
Goals Scored	29	21
Assists	43	31
Clean Sheets (goalkeepers)	22	10
Yellow Cards	74	73
Red Cards	7	11
Full Internationals	5	0

Age/Height

Stoke City Age	Millwall Age
▶ **26 yrs, 6 mo**	▶ **24 yrs, 10 mo**
Stoke City Height	Millwall Height
▶ **6'**	▶ **6'**

Match Statistics

League Table after Fixture

		Played	Won	Drawn	Lost	For	Against	Pts
↓	14 Burnley	35	12	7	16	41	44	43
↓	15 Plymouth	35	10	13	12	32	39	43
●	16 Stoke	34	13	4	17	37	48	43
↑	17 Southampton	35	8	16	11	33	36	40
↓	18 Hull	36	9	11	16	39	46	38
↑	19 Derby	36	7	17	12	43	52	38
↓	20 Leicester	36	8	13	15	38	48	37
●	21 Sheff Wed	36	8	10	18	27	46	34
●	22 Millwall	36	5	14	17	26	49	29

Statistics	○ Stoke	Millwall ○
Goals	2	1
Shots on Target	8	0
Shots off Target	8	1
Hit Woodwork	0	0
Possession %	48	52
Corners	10	4
Offsides	1	0
Fouls	13	13
Disciplinary Points	4	8

2-1

Norwich City ○
Stoke City ○

► Michael Duberry towers above Leon McKenzie

Event Line
Half time 0-0

52 ○ ⊕	McKenzie / LF / OP / IA
	Assist: McVeigh
58 ○ ⊕	Gallagher / RF / DFK / OA
	Assist: Bangoura
78 ○ ▢	Broomes
80 ○ ⇄	Sweeney > Gallagher
85 ○ ⇄	Etuhu > Hughes
85 ○ ▢	Buxton
86 ○ ⇄	Johansson > McKenzie
89 ○ ⊕	Johansson / RF / OP / IA
	Assist: McVeigh

Full time 2-1

The agony of conceding a last-minute goal at Carrow Road all but ended hopes of resurrecting a late-season play-off bid.

Paul Gallagher cancelled out Leon McKenzie's opener and Sam Bangoura almost claimed the points late on, but Norwich substitute Jonatan Johansson delivered the knockout blow deep into injury time.

McKenzie brought the game to life shortly after the restart with a crisp finish past Steve Simonsen after a darting run into the area. City's response was instant, Gallagher levelling matters with a speculative free-kick which squirmed away from England 'keeper Robert Green and found the bottom corner.

Darren Huckerby tested Simonsen as the home side pressed for a winner, but Bangoura almost grabbed the points in the final minute when Green brilliantly saved his fierce header from a Skoko corner.

Near triumph then turned to despair in the dying seconds when Paul McVeigh sent Johansson through and the Finnish international steadied himself and made no mistake from six yards.

Quote

● **Johan Boskamp**

We deserved a lot more than we got today. Sammy could have given us the win and then with the next attack it was bingo for Norwich because everyone was out of position.

Venue:	Carrow Road	Referee:	P.Crossley - 05/06		**Norwich City**
Attendance:	24,223	Matches:	15		**Stoke City**
Capacity:	27,470	Yellow Cards:	44		
Occupancy:	88%	Red Cards:	2		

Form Coming into Fixture

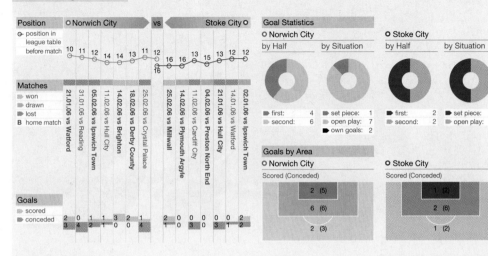

Position

○ Norwich City vs Stoke City ○

G- position in league table before match

10 11 12 14 14 13 11 12 16 16 13 15 13 12 12
16

21.01.06 vs Watford	31.01.06 vs Reading	05.02.06 vs Ipswich Town	11.02.06 vs Hull City	14.02.06 vs Brighton	18.02.06 vs Derby County	25.02.06 vs Crystal Palace	25.02.06 vs Millwall	14.02.06 vs Plymouth Argyle	11.02.06 vs Cardiff City	04.02.06 vs Preston North End	21.01.06 vs Hull City	14.01.06 vs Watford	02.01.06 vs Ipswich Town

Matches
- won
- drawn
- lost
- B home match

Goals
- scored
- conceded

scored	2	0	1	1	3	2	1		2	0	0	0	0	2
conceded	3	4	2	1	0	0	4		1	0	3	0	3	1	2

Goal Statistics

○ Norwich City

by Half / by Situation

first:	4	set piece:	1
second:	6	open play:	7
		own goals:	2

○ Stoke City

by Half / by Situation

| first: | 2 | set piece: | 2 |
| second: | 2 | open play: | 2 |

Goals by Area

○ Norwich City

Scored (Conceded)

2 (5)
6 (6)
2 (3)

○ Stoke City

Scored (Conceded)

1 (2)
2 (6)
1 (2)

Team Statistics

Starting Line-Ups

Charlton, Huckerby, Shackell, Robinson, McKenzie, Johansson, Bangoura, Doherty, Hughes, Etuhu, Earnshaw, Fleming, McVeigh, Green

Chadwick, Buxton, Junior, Duberry, Skoko, Hill, Russell, Gallagher, Sweeney, Broomes, Simonsen

▶ 4/4/2

▶ 4/5/1

Unused Sub: Gallacher, Colin, Henderson

Unused Sub: de Goey, Wilkinson, Kopteff, Rooney

Championship Totals	○ Norwich	Stoke ○
Championship Appearances	391	463
Team Appearances	258	392
Goals Scored	32	29
Assists	22	27
Clean Sheets (goalkeepers)	7	22
Yellow Cards	45	68
Red Cards	2	8
Full Internationals	6	3

Age/Height

Norwich City Age	Stoke City Age
▶ **28 yrs, 2 mo**	▶ **25 yrs, 7 mo**
Norwich City Height	Stoke City Height
▶ **6'**	▶ **6'**

Match Statistics

League Table after Fixture

		Played	Won	Drawn	Lost	For	Against	Pts
↑	10 Norwich	37	14	7	16	45	52	49
↓	11 Luton	37	14	6	17	56	58	48
↓	12 Coventry	37	12	12	13	49	54	48
↑	13 Plymouth	36	11	13	12	33	39	46
↓	14 QPR	36	12	10	14	41	50	46
↓	15 Burnley	36	12	7	17	41	47	43
●	16 Stoke	35	13	4	18	38	50	43
●	17 Southampton	36	8	17	11	34	37	41
↑	18 Leicester	37	9	13	15	41	50	40

Statistics	○ Norwich	Stoke ○
Goals	2	1
Shots on Target	5	5
Shots off Target	7	3
Hit Woodwork	0	0
Possession %	56	44
Corners	7	5
Offsides	2	0
Fouls	14	16
Disciplinary Points	0	8

0-0

Wolves ○
Stoke City ○

➡ Sambegou Bangoura shields the ball from Joleon Lescott

Event Line

5 ○ ■	Chadwick
12 ○ ⇄	Ince > Anderton
Half time 0-0	
46 ○ ⇄	Sidibe > Chadwick
64 ○ ⇄	Ricketts > Rosa
73 ○ ⇄	Frankowski > Cort
82 ○ ⇄	Junior > Skoko
Full time 0-0	

A gutsy performance against play-off chasing Wolves did enough to erase memories of the last-minute defeat at Norwich three days earlier.

It was nearly even better, because Clint Hill rattled the crossbar while Paul Gallagher almost grabbed a late winner.

In torrential conditions, a boggy surface restricted the quality of the early play as Josip Skoko flashed a header over and a long range shot wide before Wolves' reply saw Jeremie Aliadiere's acrobatic overhead-kick fail to test Steve Simonsen.

The best chance of the half fell to Carl Cort, but after bursting clear his attempt to lob Simonsen was inches off-target. Gallagher then drew a smart save from Stefan Postma and Sam Bangoura went close, before Postma clawed Hill's looping header from a Gallagher set-play onto the woodwork.

The home side hit back with Lee Naylor's hopeful cross also bouncing back off the crossbar and Aliadiere skewing wide of a gaping goal.

Bangoura's tame header failed to trouble Postma before Gallagher's last–gasp effort flew past the outstretched 'keeper but drifted narrowly over.

Quote

● **Jan De Koning**

The defenders were masters of this game. We sat deeper than we usually do and that made it difficult for them to score.

Venue:	Molineux	Referee:	B.Curson - 05/06	**Wolverhampton Wanderers**
Attendance:	22,439	Matches:	31	**Stoke City**
Capacity:	29,400	Yellow Cards:	74	
Occupancy:	76%	Red Cards:	5	

Form Coming into Fixture

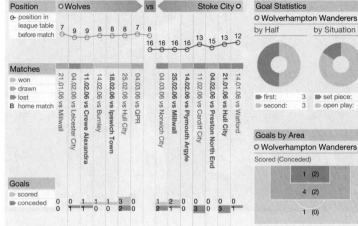

Position

Wolves — vs — Stoke City

- position in league table before match

Wolves: 7, 9, 9, 8, 8, 8, 7, 8
Stoke City: 16, 16, 16, 8, 13, 15, 13, 12

Matches
- won
- drawn
- lost
- B home match

Wolves matches:
21.01.06 vs Millwall
04.02.06 vs Leicester City
11.02.06 vs Crewe Alexandra
14.02.06 vs Burnley
18.02.06 vs Ipswich Town
25.02.06 vs Hull City
04.03.06 vs QPR

Stoke matches:
04.03.06 vs Norwich City
25.02.06 vs Millwall
14.02.06 vs Plymouth Argyle
11.02.06 vs Cardiff City
04.02.06 vs Preston North End
21.01.06 vs Hull City
14.01.06 vs Watford

Goals
- scored
- conceded

Wolves scored: 0 0 1 1 1 3 0
Wolves conceded: 0 1 1 0 0 2 0

Stoke scored: 1 2 0 0 0 0 0
Stoke conceded: 2 1 0 3 0 3 1

Goal Statistics

Wolverhampton Wanderers

by Half		by Situation	
first:	3	set piece:	1
second:	3	open play:	5

Stoke City

by Half		by Situation	
first:	1	set piece:	2
second:	2	open play:	1

Goals by Area

Wolverhampton Wanderers
Scored (Conceded)

1 (2)
4 (2)
1 (0)

Stoke City
Scored (Conceded)

0 (2)
1 (6)
2 (2)

Team Statistics

Starting Line-Ups

Wolves: Postma; Naylor, Lescott, Edwards, Ross; Kennedy, Anderton (Ince), Cort (Frankowski), Rosa (Ricketts); Miller, Aliadiere

4/3/3

Stoke: Simonsen; Hoefkens, Russell, Duberry, Hill, Broomes; Chadwick (Sidibe), Bangoura, Skoko (Junior), Brammer, Gallagher

4/5/1

Unused Sub: Oakes, Gyepes

Unused Sub: de Goey, Buxton, Sweeney

Championship Totals	Wolves	Stoke
Championship Appearances	528	572
Team Appearances	521	490
Goals Scored	67	38
Assists	53	47
Clean Sheets (goalkeepers)	10	22
Yellow Cards	56	77
Red Cards	1	8
Full Internationals	8	5

Age/Height

	Wolverhampton Wanderers	Stoke City
Age	**27 yrs, 11 mo**	**26 yrs, 9 mo**
Height	**6'**	**6'**

Match Statistics

League Table after Fixture

		Played	Won	Drawn	Lost	For	Against	Pts
↑ 7	Wolverhampton	37	13	16	8	40	30	55
↓ 8	Cardiff	37	15	10	12	51	43	55
● 9	Ipswich	36	13	11	12	42	48	50
● 10	Norwich	37	14	7	16	45	52	49
● 11	Luton	37	14	6	17	56	58	48
● 12	Coventry	37	12	12	13	49	54	48
● 13	Plymouth	37	11	14	12	33	39	47
● 14	QPR	36	12	10	14	41	50	46
↑ 15	Stoke	36	13	5	18	38	50	44

Statistics	Wolves	Stoke
Goals	0	0
Shots on Target	0	3
Shots off Target	4	8
Hit Woodwork	0	1
Possession %	37	63
Corners	3	9
Offsides	0	5
Fouls	13	13
Disciplinary Points	0	4

1-3

Stoke City ○
Crystal Palace ○

➡ Hannes Sigurdsson tries to find a way past Ben Watson

Event Line

25 ○ ⇄	Buxton > Hoefkens
30 ○ ⊕	Sidibe / LF / OG / 6Y
	Assist: Boyce
31 ○ ▣	Broomes
Half time 0-1	
47 ○ ⊕	Skoko / LF / OP / 6Y
48 ○ ⊕	McAnuff / RF / OP / IA
	Assist: Hughes
58 ○ ⊕	Johnson / RF / OP / IA
	Assist: McAnuff
72 ○ ⇄	Sigurdsson > Gallagher
84 ○ ⇄	Leigertwood > Watson
87 ○ ⇄	Soares > McAnuff
Full time 1-3	

The Sky TV cameras arrived at the Britannia Stadium, but Crystal Palace took the plaudits from an end-to-end clash.

Josip Skoko's first goal for City wasn't enough as an own goal from Mamady Sidibe, a deflected drive from Jobi McAnuff and a clinical finish from Andy Johnson gave the Eagles the points.

It was the visitors who drew first blood in rather fortunate fashion when Sidibe turned Emerson Boyce's teasing cross into his own net.

Skoko brought the scores level two minutes after the break, latching onto Sidibe's flick-on to scoop the ball over Gabor Kiraly from an acute angle. The joy lasted less than a minute though, as McAnuff's hopeful drive ricocheted off Clint Hill and wrong-footed Steve Simonsen.

Sam Bangoura led the fightback, twice going close before Darel Russell scuffed an excellent opportunity straight at Kiraly.

But the result was put beyond reach on the hour when Johnson raced through on goal and confidently slotted home.

Quote

● **Johan Boskamp**

It was a game that could have gone either way. We scored to make it 1-1 very quickly and then they made it 2-1 in the same minute.

Championship Milestone

➡ **75**

Josip Skoko's goal was the 75th scored in the Championship by Stoke and his first in the competition.

Venue:	Britannia Stadium	Referee:	A.R.Leake - 05/06		**Stoke City**
Attendance:	10,121	Matches:	30		**Crystal Palace**
Capacity:	28,218	Yellow Cards:	66		
Occupancy:	36%	Red Cards:	3		

Form Coming into Fixture

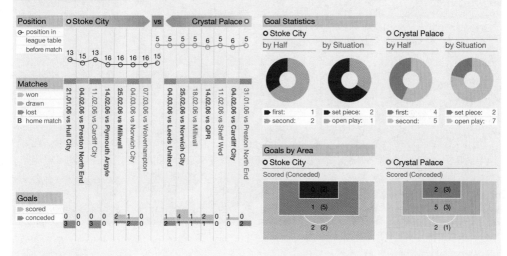

Goal Statistics

Stoke City

by Half — first: 1, second: 2
by Situation — set piece: 2, open play: 1

Crystal Palace

by Half — first: 4, second: 5
by Situation — set piece: 2, open play: 7

Goals by Area

Stoke City — Scored (Conceded)

0 (2), 1 (5), 2 (2)

Crystal Palace — Scored (Conceded)

2 (3), 5 (3), 2 (1)

Team Statistics

Starting Line-Ups

Stoke City: 4/5/1

Crystal Palace: 4/4/2 (Diamond)

Unused Sub: de Goey, Junior, Kopteff

Unused Sub: Speroni, Reich, Freedman

Championship Totals	Stoke	C. Palace
Championship Appearances	566	457
Team Appearances	516	370
Goals Scored	37	44
Assists	39	40
Clean Sheets (goalkeepers)	23	12
Yellow Cards	81	63
Red Cards	7	2
Full Internationals	6	6

Age/Height

Stoke City Age: **26 yrs, 6 mo**

Crystal Palace Age: **25 yrs, 8 mo**

Stoke City Height: **6'**

Crystal Palace Height: **5'11"**

Match Statistics

League Table after Fixture

		Played	Won	Drawn	Lost	For	Against	Pts
● 5	Crystal Palace	37	18	9	10	56	37	63
...		...	...	...	...	...	...	...
● 15	Stoke	37	13	5	19	39	53	44
● 16	Leicester	38	10	13	15	43	51	43
● 17	Burnley	37	12	7	18	41	50	43
● 18	Southampton	37	8	18	11	35	38	42
● 19	Derby	38	8	18	12	48	54	42
● 20	Hull	38	10	11	17	42	49	41
● 21	Sheff Wed	38	8	11	19	28	48	35

Statistics	Stoke	C. Palace
Goals	1	3
Shots on Target	8	5
Shots off Target	13	3
Hit Woodwork	0	1
Possession %	46	54
Corners	8	3
Offsides	0	3
Fouls	13	11
Disciplinary Points	4	0

1-0

Stoke City ○
Burnley ○

▶ Paul Gallagher tucks away the only goal of the game

Event Line

29 ○ ▪	Ricketts
Half time 0-0	
46 ○ ⇄	Buxton > Broomes
52 ○ ⊕	Gallagher / RF / OP / IA
	Assist: Brammer
56 ○ ▪	Russell
56 ○ ▪	Harley
62 ○ ⇄	Chadwick > Russell
64 ○ ⇄	Elliott > O'Connor G
67 ○ ▪	Bardsley
69 ○ ▪	Gallagher
79 ○ ⇄	Noel-Williams > McCann
80 ○ ⇄	Sigurdsson > Bangoura
85 ○ ⇄	Spicer > Branch
Full time 1-0	

Paul Gallagher's solitary strike ensured a less-than-satisfactory return to the Britannia Stadium for former City boss Steve Cotterill.

The Scottish under-21 star struck home a sweet volley after 52 minutes to claim his 11th goal of the campaign and all but mathematically guarantee Coca-Cola Championship football at the Brit for another season.

Gallagher's strike earned much from a superb cross from Dave Brammer and opened up the game after an uneventful opening.

There were half-hearted appeals for a penalty when Gallagher's shot appeared to hit the arm of Potters old boy Wayne Thomas before Sam Bangoura sent a header narrowly wide of goal.

Substitute Hannes Sigurdsson should have settled nerves with ten minutes remaining when he powered a header over the crossbar.

But, despite Burnley debutant Andy Gray going close to an equaliser in stoppage time with a glancing header, any lingering fears of a late-season relegation battle were banished by a timely and most welcome victory.

Quote	Championship Milestone
● **Johan Boskamp**	▶ **75**
This wasn't a victory for me – it was for everyone at the club. The nerves are gone now because we are fourteen points away from danger.	Dave Brammer made his 75th appearance in the Championship.

Venue:	Britannia Stadium	Referee:	M.Fletcher - 05/06		**Stoke City**
Attendance:	12,082	Matches:	23		**Burnley**
Capacity:	28,218	Yellow Cards:	95		
Occupancy:	43%	Red Cards:	4		

Form Coming into Fixture

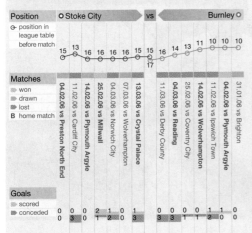

Goal Statistics

Stoke City

by Half	by Situation
first: 1	set piece: 2
second: 3	open play: 2

Burnley

by Half	by Situation
first: 2	set piece: 0
second: 0	open play: 2

Goals by Area

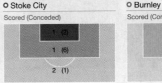

Stoke City — Scored (Conceded)

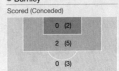

Burnley — Scored (Conceded)

Team Statistics

Starting Line-Ups

Stoke City: Broomes, Gallagher, Buxton, Hill, Skoko, Bangoura, Sigurdsson, Ricketts, Duberry, Brammer, Sidibe, Gray, Simonsen, Hoefkens, Russell, Chadwick

Burnley: O'Connor G, Bardsley, Elliott, O'Connor J, Thomas, McCann, Noel-Williams, Duff, Branch, Spicer, Harley, Jensen

4/4/2   **4/4/2**

Unused Sub: de Goey, Junior   Unused Sub: Karbassiyoon, Lafferty

Championship Totals	○ Stoke	Burnley ○
Championship Appearances	642	668
Team Appearances	560	442
Goals Scored	40	69
Assists	47	50
Clean Sheets (goalkeepers)	23	20
Yellow Cards	89	75
Red Cards	7	8
Full Internationals	6	3

Age/Height

Stoke City Age	Burnley Age
26 yrs, 5 mo	**26 yrs, 5 mo**
Stoke City Height	Burnley Height
6'	**6'**

Match Statistics

League Table after Fixture

		Played	Won	Drawn	Lost	For	Against	Pts
↓	10 Coventry	39	13	13	13	52	55	52
↓	11 Ipswich	39	13	13	13	46	54	52
●	12 Luton	39	15	6	18	58	60	51
↑	13 QPR	38	12	12	14	43	52	48
↓	14 Plymouth	39	11	14	14	33	41	47
●	15 Stoke	38	14	5	19	40	53	47
●	16 Leicester	39	11	13	15	44	51	46
↑	17 Hull	39	11	11	17	43	49	44
↓	18 Burnley	38	12	7	19	41	51	43

Statistics	○ Stoke	Burnley ○
Goals	1	0
Shots on Target	4	1
Shots off Target	7	3
Hit Woodwork	0	0
Possession %	55	45
Corners	5	3
Offsides	5	2
Fouls	16	23
Disciplinary Points	8	12

0-0

Leeds United ○
Stoke City ○

► Steve Simonsen comes to the rescue

Event Line
Half time 0-0

46 ○ ⇄	Sigurdsson >	Bangoura
47 ○ ▨	Gregan	
57 ○ ▨	Russell	
61 ○ ⇄	Brammer >	Junior
63 ○ ⇄	Beckford >	Healy
68 ○ ⇄	Blake >	Douglas
74 ○ ⇄	Griffiths >	Lewis
74 ○ ⇄	Sweeney >	Gallagher
90 ○ ▨	Butler	

Full time 0-0

No goals, but a deserved point at Elland Road severely dented Leeds' hopes of gaining automatic promotion.

Paul Gallagher had the first – and what proved the only – effort on target during a cagey opening period, but Neil Sullivan held on to the striker's fierce drive.

The second-half began brightly and Gallagher was again at the centre of things as he fired in a free-kick, which deflected just wide after substitute Hannes Sigurdsson was hauled down on the edge of the box. Rob Hulse's snapshot then forced Steve Simonsen into his first meaningful save of the match after 50 minutes, before David Healy tested the stopper's reflexes again, this time from long-range, moments later.

Leeds continued to look vulnerable on the break, and they were again indebted to Sullivan on 70 minutes as he flew across goal to pluck Darel Russell's fierce drive out of the top corner.

The home side applied heavy late pressure in search of a winner and Robbie Blake curled wide before Simonsen saved the day, clawing Hulse's downward header onto the post.

Quote

● **Johan Boskamp**

We worked very hard and we see today that the mentality in the group is very high. I don't think Leeds created one clear chance, which showed our defence played well.

Championship Milestone

► **75**

Darel Russell made his 75th appearance in the Championship.

Form Coming into Fixture

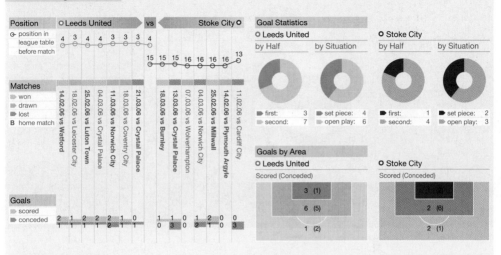

Team Statistics

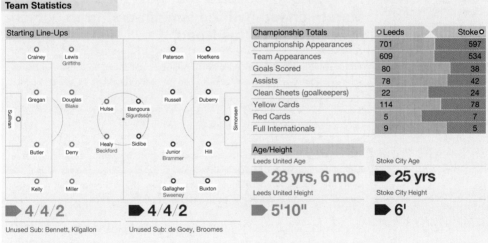

Championship Totals

Championship Totals	Leeds	Stoke
Championship Appearances	701	597
Team Appearances	609	534
Goals Scored	80	38
Assists	78	42
Clean Sheets (goalkeepers)	22	24
Yellow Cards	114	78
Red Cards	5	7
Full Internationals	9	5

Age/Height

	Leeds United	Stoke City
Age	28 yrs, 6 mo	25 yrs
Height	5'10"	6'

Starting Line-Ups formations: Leeds United 4/4/2, Stoke City 4/4/2

Unused Sub: Bennett, Kilgallon
Unused Sub: de Goey, Broomes

Match Statistics

League Table after Fixture

		Played	Won	Drawn	Lost	For	Against	Pts
● 4	Leeds	40	20	12	8	54	33	72
...		...	...	...	...	...	...	...
● 15	Stoke	39	14	6	19	40	53	48
● 16	Leicester	40	11	14	15	45	52	47
● 17	Burnley	39	13	7	19	43	51	46
↑ 18	Derby	40	9	18	13	50	56	45
↓ 19	Hull	40	11	12	17	44	50	45
↓ 20	Southampton	39	8	18	13	36	44	42
● 21	Sheff Wed	40	10	11	19	33	49	41

Statistics

Statistics	Leeds	Stoke
Goals	0	0
Shots on Target	6	6
Shots off Target	3	6
Hit Woodwork	0	0
Possession %	54	46
Corners	9	5
Offsides	0	3
Fouls	14	24
Disciplinary Points	8	4

1-2

Queens Park Rangers ○
Stoke City ○

▶ Dave Brammer battles with Steve Lomas

Event Line

7 ○ ⊕ Nygaard / RF / OP / IA	
Assist: Youssouf	
15 ○ ⇄ Moore > Youssouf	
25 ○ ▪ Bangoura	
Half time 1-0	
69 ○ ▪ Wilkinson	
71 ○ ⇄ Sidibe > Bangoura	
71 ○ ⇄ Gallagher > Sweeney	
73 ○ ⊕ Hoefkens / RF / P / IA	
Assist: Russell	
78 ○ ⇄ Langley > Bircham	
79 ○ ⊕ Sigurdsson / LF / OP / IA	
Assist: Gallagher	
80 ○ ⇄ Furlong > Ainsworth	
88 ○ ⇄ Buxton > Chadwick	
Full time 1-2	

Hannes Sigurdsson's first goal for City ensured March ended with a smash-and-grab victory over QPR at Loftus Road.

The Icelandic striker pounced with ten minutes remaining to cap an enthralling fightback after Carl Hoefkens' penalty had cancelled out Marc Nygaard's opener.

But the game's real turning point was in the 25th minute, when Steve Simonsen saved a penalty from Gareth Ainsworth.

Simonsen was the busier of the two 'keepers before Nygaard capitalised on some static defending to fire Rangers ahead. And they should have increased their lead soon after when Dave Brammer tripped Cook inside the area, but Simonsen guessed right and comfortably gathered Ainsworth's weak spot-kick.

Dan Shittu's foul on Darel Russell gave Hoefkens an opportunity to equalise from the spot, and the Belgian star duly obliged by sending Jones the wrong way.

As Rangers wobbled, Sigurdsson went in pursuit of a winner and just moments after forcing Jones into a smart double save, the striker buried Paul Gallagher's cutback to earn a first away win since December 17.

Quote

● **Gerry Taggart**

I'm very proud of the lads, especially after giving away a sloppy goal. We picked ourselves up, got the goals after the break and I thought we deserved to win.

Championship Milestone

▶ **First Goal**

Hannes Sigurdsson netted his first goal in the Championship.

Form Coming into Fixture

Position   ○ Queens Park Rangers vs   Stoke City ○

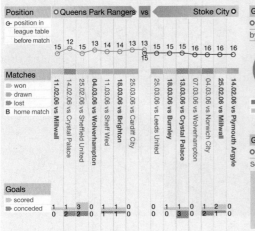

G- position in league table before match

Matches
- won
- drawn
- lost
- B home match

Queens Park Rangers matches:
- 11.02.06 vs Millwall
- 14.02.06 vs Crystal Palace
- 25.02.06 vs Sheffield United
- 04.03.06 vs Wolverhampton
- 11.03.06 vs Sheff Wed
- 18.03.06 vs Brighton
- 25.03.06 vs Cardiff City

Stoke City matches:
- 25.03.06 vs Leeds United
- 18.03.06 vs Burnley
- 13.03.06 vs Crystal Palace
- 07.03.06 vs Wolverhampton
- 04.03.06 vs Norwich City
- 25.02.06 vs Millwall
- 14.02.06 vs Plymouth Argyle

Goals
- scored
- conceded

1	1	3	0	1	1	0		0	1	1	0	1	2	0
0	2	2	0	1	1	0		0	0	3	0	2	1	0

Goal Statistics

○ Queens Park Rangers

by Half | by Situation

- first: 3
- second: 4
- set piece: 1
- open play: 5
- own goals: 1

○ Stoke City

by Half | by Situation

- first: 1
- second: 4
- set piece: 2
- open play: 3

Goals by Area

○ Queens Park Rangers
Scored (Conceded)

| 4 (1) |
| 3 (5) |
| 0 (0) |

○ Stoke City
Scored (Conceded)

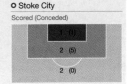

| 1 (0) |
| 2 (5) |
| 2 (0) |

Team Statistics

Starting Line-Ups

Queens Park Rangers:
- Milanese
- Cook
- Evatt
- Bircham (Langley)
- Youssouf (Moore)
- Bangoura (Sidibe)
- Jones P
- Shittu
- Lomas
- Nygaard
- Sigurdsson
- Bignot
- Ainsworth (Furlong)

Stoke City:
- Chadwick (Buxton)
- Hoefkens
- Brammer
- Duberry
- Simonsen
- Russell
- Broomes
- Sweeney (Gallagher)
- Wilkinson

▶ 4/4/2   ▶ 4/4/2

Unused Sub: Cole, Santos   Unused Sub: de Goey, Junior

Championship Totals

Championship Totals	○QPR	Stoke○
Championship Appearances	641	661
Team Appearances	558	555
Goals Scored	63	41
Assists	56	49
Clean Sheets (goalkeepers)	9	25
Yellow Cards	80	88
Red Cards	5	6
Full Internationals	6	5

Age/Height

Queens Park Rangers Age
▶ **29 yrs, 9 mo**

Stoke City Age
▶ **25 yrs, 5 mo**

Queens Park Rangers Height
▶ **6'**

Stoke City Height
▶ **6'**

Match Statistics

League Table after Fixture

		Played	Won	Drawn	Lost	For	Against	Pts
●	6 Preston	40	15	19	6	49	28	64
●	7 Wolverhampton	40	14	17	9	44	34	59
●	8 Cardiff	40	16	11	13	52	45	59
●	9 Norwich	40	15	8	17	49	57	53
●	10 Ipswich	40	13	14	13	47	55	53
●	11 Luton	40	15	7	18	59	61	52
●	12 Coventry	40	13	13	14	53	59	52
↑	13 Stoke	40	15	6	19	42	54	51
↓	14 QPR	40	12	13	15	44	54	49

Statistics

Statistics	○QPR	Stoke○
Goals	1	2
Shots on Target	2	5
Shots off Target	6	2
Hit Woodwork	0	1
Possession %	52	48
Corners	7	2
Offsides	2	3
Fouls	14	11
Disciplinary Points	0	8

1-1

Stoke City ○
Sheffield United ○

▶ Junior keeps the ball moving

Event Line

16 ○ ⊕ Skoko / H / IFK / OA	
18 ○ ▨ Morgan	
Half time 1-0	
57 ○ ⇄ Akinbiyi > Shipperley	
58 ○ ⇄ Kabba > Ifill	
70 ○ ⇄ Buxton > Hill	
70 ○ ⇄ Brammer > Junior	
77 ○ ⇄ Sigurdsson > Gallagher	
83 ○ ⊕ Webber / RF / OP / IA	
Assist: Short	
85 ○ ▨ Hoefkens	
Full time 1-1	

One of the best home performances of the season sadly earned just a point against promotion-chasing Sheffield United.

Josip Skoko's strike had United reeling, but a late equaliser from Danny Webber snatched a share of the spoils for the Blades as City paid the price for missing several chances.

Skoko opened the scoring in the 16th minute, heading over a stranded Paddy Kenny after the goalkeeper's tame clearance fell into his path. Mamady Sidibe almost added a second moments before the break when he fired over from 10-yards after twisting free of his marker.

Darel Russell forced Kenny into a smart save early on in the second-half before Steve Simonsen denied Michael Tonge and the lively Webber lashed wide.

The result should have been put beyond doubt with ten minutes remaining, but Kenny's outstretched boot did just enough to divert Skoko's snapshot against the post. The visitors made the most of that let-off and Webber showed great strength to outmuscle Lewis Buxton and debutant Carl Dickinson before coolly slotting beyond Simonsen to snatch a share of the spoils.

Quote	Championship Milestone
● **Johan Boskamp**	▶ **75**
There were moments when we played really good football, but the goal against us was poor because I think it was Sheffield's only good chance in the game.	Mamady Sidibe made his 75th appearance in the Championship.

Venue:	Britannia Stadium	Referee:	A.Marriner - 05/06		**Stoke City**
Attendance:	17,544	Matches:	22		**Sheffield United**
Capacity:	28,218	Yellow Cards:	69		
Occupancy:	62%	Red Cards:	7		

Form Coming into Fixture

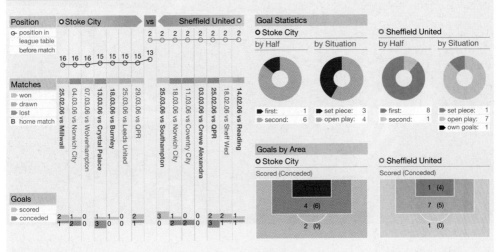

Position
○ Stoke City   vs   Sheffield United ○

Stoke City positions: 16, 16, 16, 15, 15, 15, 15, 13
Sheffield United positions: 2, 2, 2, 2, 2, 2, 2, 2

Matches: 25.02.06 vs Millwall, 04.03.06 vs Norwich City, 07.03.06 vs Wolverhampton, 13.03.06 vs Crystal Palace, 18.03.06 vs Burnley, 25.03.06 vs Leeds United, 29.03.06 vs QPR | 25.03.06 vs Southampton, 18.03.06 vs Norwich City, 11.03.06 vs Coventry City, 03.03.06 vs Crewe Alexandra, 25.02.06 vs QPR, 18.02.06 vs Sheff Wed, 14.02.06 vs Reading

Goals
scored: 2 1 0 1 1 0 2 | 3 1 0 0 2 2 1
conceded: 1 2 0 3 0 0 1 | 0 2 2 2 0 3 1 1

Goal Statistics

○ Stoke City
by Half / by Situation
- first: 1
- second: 6
- set piece: 3
- open play: 4

○ Sheffield United
by Half / by Situation
- first: 8
- second: 1
- set piece: 1
- open play: 7
- own goals: 1

Goals by Area
○ Stoke City — Scored (Conceded): 1 (0), 4 (6), 2 (0)
○ Sheffield United — Scored (Conceded): 1 (4), 7 (5), 1 (0)

Team Statistics

Starting Line-Ups

Stoke City: Simonsen; Dickinson, Gallagher/Sigurdsson, Broomes, Hill/Buxton, Hoefkens; Skoko, Junior/Brammer, Sidibe, Russell, Chadwick; Shipperley/Akinbiyi, Webber

Sheffield United: Kenny; Ifill, Kozluk, Kabba, Tonge, Short, Jagielka, Morgan, Armstrong, Unsworth

4/5/1
Unused Sub: de Goey, Kopteff

4/4/2
Unused Sub: Lucketti, Gillespie, Montgomery

Championship Totals

	○ Stoke	Sheff Utd ○
Championship Appearances	611	683
Team Appearances	533	552
Goals Scored	34	105
Assists	44	77
Clean Sheets (goalkeepers)	25	28
Yellow Cards	77	68
Red Cards	5	6
Full Internationals	5	4

Age/Height

Stoke City Age	Sheffield United Age
25 yrs, 7 mo	**28 yrs**
Stoke City Height	Sheffield United Height
6'	**6'**

Match Statistics

League Table after Fixture

		Played	Won	Drawn	Lost	For	Against	Pts
●	2 Sheff Utd	41	23	10	8	69	42	79
...		...	...	...	...	...	...	...
●	13 Stoke	41	15	7	19	43	55	52
↑	14 Plymouth	41	12	15	14	35	41	51
↓	15 QPR	41	12	13	16	45	56	49
↑	16 Hull	41	12	12	17	45	50	48
●	17 Burnley	41	13	9	19	44	52	48
↓	18 Leicester	41	11	14	16	46	54	47
↑	19 Southampton	41	9	19	13	40	47	46

Statistics

	○ Stoke	Sheff Utd ○
Goals	1	1
Shots on Target	5	4
Shots off Target	4	5
Hit Woodwork	1	0
Possession %	45	55
Corners	2	4
Offsides	0	1
Fouls	10	8
Disciplinary Points	4	4

1-4

Ipswich Town ○
Stoke City ○

▶ Sambegou Bangoura finds the back of the net

Event Line
Half time 0-0

46 ○ ⇄	Sito > Casement	
51 ○ ⊕	Wilnis / LF / OG / 6Y	
	Assist: Brammer	
53 ○ ▪	Garvan	
55 ○ ⇄	Haynes > Bowditch	
55 ○ ⇄	Magilton > Garvan	
66 ○ ⇄	Chadwick > Kopteff	
67 ○ ⊕	Haynes / LF / OP / 6Y	
	Assist: Lee	
82 ○ ⊕	Bangoura / RF / OP / IA	
	Assist: Gallagher	
85 ○ ⇄	Broomes > Hoefkens	
90 ○ ▪	Gallagher	
90 ○ ⊕	Chadwick / RF / OP / IA	
	Assist: Junior	
90 ○ ⊕	Russell / RF / OP / IA	
	Assist: Chadwick	
90 ○ ⇄	Garrett > Brammer	

Full time 1-4

An emphatic late flourish secured a comprehensive victory over Ipswich.

Sam Bangoura fired home the game's decisive goal eight minutes from time before Luke Chadwick and Darel Russell wrapped up the points in the dying seconds.

A Fabian Wilnis own goal put Ipswich on the back foot shortly after half-time, but Danny Haynes levelled matters before the late goal surge.

Paul Gallagher, Peter Kopteff and Darel Russell all went close during the opening exchanges before Wilnis bundled Dave Brammer's cross into his own net under pressure from Carl Hoefkens. Gallagher should have then made it two, but skewed wide from close range, and the home side drew level in the 67th minute when Steve Simonsen spilled Jimmy Juan's drive and Haynes made no mistake from five yards.

Bangoura led the fightback and saw an effort blocked on the line by Richard Naylor before springing the offside trap to volley clinically past Shane Supple for his first goal since December.

Substitute Chadwick's mazy run and confident finish ended any fears of an Ipswich reprieve and Russell scrambled home at the second attempt.

Quote
● Johan Boskamp

The last two games we have played is how we want to play, with our players strong on the ball and our midfielders applying pressure at the right moments.

Championship Milestone
▶ Debut

Robert Garrett made his Championship debut.

Form Coming into Fixture

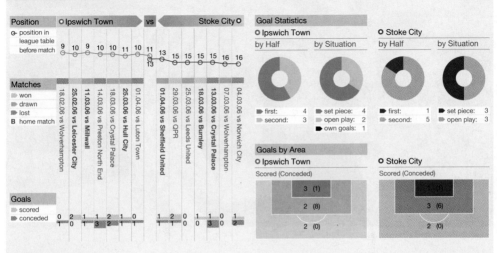

Position
- position in league table before match

Ipswich Town vs Stoke City

Ipswich: 9, 10, 9, 10, 10, 11, 10, 11, 13 / 13
Stoke: 15, 15, 15, 15, 16, 16

Matches
- won
- drawn
- lost
- B home match

18.02.06 vs Wolverhampton
25.02.06 vs Leicester City
11.03.06 vs Millwall
14.03.06 vs Preston North End
18.03.06 vs Crystal Palace
25.03.06 vs Hull City
01.04.06 vs Luton Town

01.04.06 vs Sheffield United
29.03.06 vs QPR
25.03.06 vs Leeds United
18.03.06 vs Burnley
13.03.06 vs Crystal Palace
07.03.06 vs Wolverhampton
04.03.06 vs Norwich City

Goals
- scored
- conceded

Ipswich: scored 0 2 1 1 2 1 0 / conceded 1 0 1 3 2 1 1
Stoke: scored 1 2 0 1 1 0 1 / conceded 1 1 0 0 3 0 2

Goal Statistics

Ipswich Town

by Half — first: 4, second: 3
by Situation — set piece: 4, open play: 2, own goals: 1

Stoke City

by Half — first: 1, second: 5
by Situation — set piece: 3, open play: 3

Goals by Area

Ipswich Town — Scored (Conceded)
3 (1)
2 (8)
2 (0)

Stoke City — Scored (Conceded)
1 (0)
3 (6)
2 (0)

Team Statistics

Starting Line-Ups

Ipswich Town
Wilnis, Richards
De Vos, Garvan Magilton, Bowditch Haynes
Supple
Bangoura
Naylor, Juan, Lee
Casement Sito, Currie

4/4/2

Unused Sub: Price, Barron

Stoke City
Kopteff, Hoefkens
Chadwick, Broomes
Russell
Duberry
Junior
Simonsen
Hill
Brammer Garrett
Gallagher, Wilkinson

4/5/1

Unused Sub: de Goey, Sweeney

Championship Totals

	Ipswich	Stoke
Championship Appearances	703	564
Team Appearances	608	517
Goals Scored	60	33
Assists	71	38
Clean Sheets (goalkeepers)	3	25
Yellow Cards	68	81
Red Cards	7	8
Full Internationals	3	4

Age/Height

Wolverhampton Wanderers Age	Stoke City Age
27 yrs, 11 mo	**26 yrs, 9 mo**
Wolverhampton Wanderers Height	Stoke City Height
6'	**6'**

Match Statistics

League Table after Fixture

		Played	Won	Drawn	Lost	For	Against	Pts
↑ 5	Preston	42	17	19	6	52	28	70
↓ 6	Crystal Palace	42	20	10	12	63	44	70
• 7	Wolverhampton	42	14	18	10	46	38	60
• 8	Cardiff	42	16	11	15	56	53	59
• 9	Norwich	42	16	8	18	51	60	56
• 10	Luton	41	16	7	18	60	61	55
↑ 11	Stoke	42	16	7	19	47	56	55
• 12	Coventry	42	13	14	15	55	62	53
↓ 13	Ipswich	42	13	14	15	48	60	53

Statistics

	Ipswich	Stoke
Goals	1	4
Shots on Target	7	9
Shots off Target	5	13
Hit Woodwork	0	0
Possession %	44	56
Corners	5	4
Offsides	1	4
Fouls	10	16
Disciplinary Points	4	4

1-2

Stoke City ○
Southampton ○

▶ Carl Dickinson sends over a cross

Event Line

22 ○ ⇄ Sweeney > Chadwick	
24 ○ ⊕ Rasiak / LF / P / IA	
Assist: Rasiak	
31 ○ ⊕ Rasiak / LF / IFK / IA	
Assist: Wright	
36 ○ ▦ Gallagher	
Half time 0-2	
46 ○ ⇄ Dyer > Belmadi	
46 ○ ⇄ Ostlund > Chaplow	
46 ○ ⇄ Dickinson > Wilkinson	
59 ○ ▦ Wright	
81 ○ ⇄ Rooney > Russell	
83 ○ ⊕ Gallagher / RF / OP / OA	
Assist: Rooney	
Full time 1-2	

Paul Gallagher scored a brilliant late goal but it wasn't enough to stop Southampton halting a four-match unbeaten run.

The Scot slammed home a blistering 12th goal of the season seven minutes from time to set up an exciting finish, but the game was lost in a lacklustre first-half.

Grzegorz Rasiak scored twice during a six-minute spell to put the Saints in the driving seat, and they remained comfortably in control until a frantic last ten minutes.

Claus Lundekvam sent an early warning of things to come when he scuffed wide from close-range before Rasiak opened the scoring from the penalty spot after being tripped by Marlon Broomes in the area. With the home side still reeling from that blow, the Polish striker doubled his tally on the half hour, nipping ahead of Broomes to steer Jermaine Wright's free-kick past Steve Simonsen.

As the game threatened to peter out, Gallagher brought it to life by exchanging passes with substitute Adam Rooney before rifling an unstoppable drive into the top corner of Kevin Miller's net from 25-yards.

Quote

● **Johan Boskamp**

It was a terrible game for us. We conceded two goals and made things hard for ourselves. We didn't create one chance and it was not good enough for us or the fans.

Venue:	Britannia Stadium	Referee:	J.P.Robinson - 05/06	**Stoke City**
Attendance:	16,501	Matches:	29	**Southampton**
Capacity:	28,218	Yellow Cards:	55	
Occupancy:	58%	Red Cards:	4	

Form Coming into Fixture

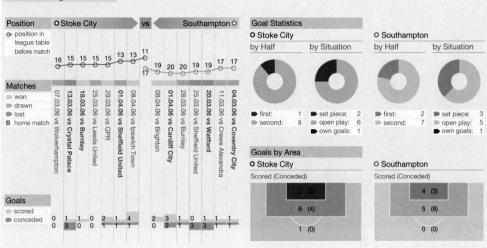

Position
⊙ position in league table before match

Stoke City vs **Southampton** ⊙

16 15 15 15 13 13 11 / 17 19 20 20 19 19 17 17

Matches
- won
- drawn
- lost
- B home match

07.03.06 vs Wolverhampton
13.03.06 vs Crystal Palace
18.03.06 vs Burnley
25.03.06 vs Leeds United
29.03.06 vs QPR
01.04.06 vs Sheffield United
08.04.06 vs Ipswich Town

08.04.06 vs Brighton
01.04.06 vs Cardiff City
28.03.06 vs Burnley
25.03.06 vs Sheffield United
20.03.06 vs Watford
11.03.06 vs Crewe Alexandra
04.03.06 vs Coventry City

Goals
- scored
- conceded

Stoke: scored 0 1 1 0 2 1 4 ; conceded 0 3 0 0 1 1 1
Southampton: scored 2 3 1 0 1 1 1 ; conceded 0 2 1 3 3 1 1

Goal Statistics

⊙ Stoke City

by Half — first: 1, second: 8
by Situation — set piece: 2, open play: 6, own goals: 1

⊙ Southampton

by Half — first: 2, second: 7
by Situation — set piece: 3, open play: 5, own goals: 1

Goals by Area

⊙ Stoke City — Scored (Conceded)
2 (2)
6 (4)
1 (0)

⊙ Southampton — Scored (Conceded)
4 (3)
5 (8)
0 (0)

Team Statistics

Starting Line-Ups

Stoke City:
Simonsen; Wilkinson, Dickinson, Gallagher; Brammer, Broomes, Junior, Bangoura, Fuller; Duberry, Russell/Rooney, Hoefkens, Chadwick/Sweeney

Southampton:
Chaplow/Ostlund, Baird; Wright, Lundekvam, Miller; Potter, Powell; Rasiak, Belmadi/Dyer, Brennan

▶ 4/5/1

▶ 4/4/2

Unused Sub: de Goey, Henry

Unused Sub: Smith, McGoldrick, Jones

Championship Totals

	⊙ Stoke	Southampton ⊙
Championship Appearances	572	331
Team Appearances	501	183
Goals Scored	37	45
Assists	43	40
Clean Sheets (goalkeepers)	25	1
Yellow Cards	80	32
Red Cards	7	2
Full Internationals	3	7

Age/Height

Stoke City Age
▶ **24 yrs, 8 mo**

Southampton Age
▶ **27 yrs, 5 mo**

Stoke City Height
▶ **6'**

Southampton Height
▶ **6'**

Match Statistics

League Table after Fixture

		Played	Won	Drawn	Lost	For	Against	Pts
●	7 Wolverhampton	43	14	19	10	47	39	61
●	8 Cardiff	43	16	11	16	56	54	59
●	9 Luton	43	16	8	19	62	64	56
↑	10 Coventry	43	14	14	15	57	63	56
↓	11 Norwich	43	16	8	19	51	61	56
↓	12 Stoke	43	16	7	20	48	58	55
↑	13 Plymouth	43	12	17	14	36	42	53
↓	14 Ipswich	43	13	14	16	49	62	53
↑	15 Southampton	43	11	19	13	44	48	52

Statistics

	⊙ Stoke	Southampton ⊙
Goals	1	2
Shots on Target	1	5
Shots off Target	1	3
Hit Woodwork	0	0
Possession %	54	46
Corners	4	12
Offsides	2	2
Fouls	13	15
Disciplinary Points	4	4

3-1

Reading ○
Stoke City ○

▶ Adam Rooney reels away after netting his first senior goal

Event Line

25 ○ ⊕ Sidwell / H / IFK / 6Y	
Assist: Ingimarsson	
Half time 1-0	
46 ○ ⇄ Rooney > Kopteff	
51 ○ ⇄ Gallagher > Sweeney	
54 ○ ⇄ Dobson > Sidwell	
56 ○ ⊕ Doyle / RF / P / IA	
Assist: Doyle	
59 ○ ⊕ Rooney / LF / OP / 6Y	
62 ○ ⊕ Halls / RF / OP / 6Y	
Assist: Hunt	
64 ○ ⇄ Golbourne > Shorey	
71 ○ ⇄ Henry > Bangoura	
71 ○ ⇄ Cox > Doyle	
Full time 3-1	

Adam Rooney's first career goal couldn't stop a forgettable Easter ending in defeat as league champions Reading broke through the 100-point barrier at the Madejski Stadium.

The young striker restored hope after Steve Sidwell and a Kevin Doyle put the home side 2-0 up, but former Potter John Halls pounced to put the result beyond doubt.

Reading began strongly and took a deserved lead when Sidwell strode in unmarked to head past Steve Simonsen midway through the first-half. Darel Russell went close to equalising shortly after the break, drilling a fierce effort straight at Graham Stack. But no sooner had attack turned to defence and the home side were awarded a penalty after Carl Hoefkens pulled back Doyle, who picked himself up to bury the spot-kick.

Rooney led the fight-back, slamming in a rebound from close-range after Ivar Ingimarsson headed against his own post. The resurgence was short-lived though, as Reading killed the game on the hour when Halls prodded home Stephen Hunt's teasing cross.

Quote

● **Johan Boskamp**

My biggest disappointment is that we let in two goals from set-pieces, that's been the story of our season.

Championship Milestone

▶ **First Goal**

Adam Rooney netted his first goal in the Championship.

Form Coming into Fixture

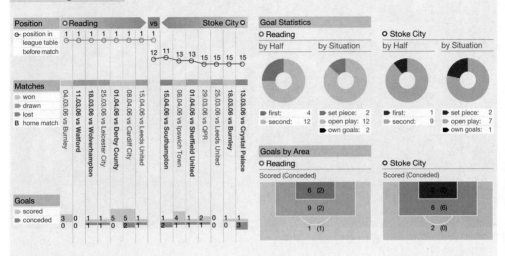

Position — O Reading vs Stoke City

position in league table before match

Reading: 1 1 1 1 1 1 1 1
Stoke City: 12 11 13 13 15 15 15 15

Matches
- won
- drawn
- lost
- B home match

Reading matches:
04.03.06 vs Burnley
11.03.06 vs Watford
18.03.06 vs Wolverhampton
25.03.06 vs Leicester City
01.04.06 vs Derby County
08.04.06 vs Cardiff City
15.04.06 vs Leeds United

Stoke City matches:
15.04.06 vs Southampton
08.04.06 vs Ipswich Town
01.04.06 vs Sheffield United
29.03.06 vs QPR
25.03.06 vs Leeds United
18.03.06 vs Burnley
13.03.06 vs Crystal Palace

Goals
- scored: 3 0 1 1 5 5 1 | 1 4 1 2 0 1 1
- conceded: 0 0 1 1 0 2 1 | 2 1 1 1 0 0 3

Goal Statistics

O Reading

by Half
- first: 4
- second: 12

by Situation
- set piece: 2
- open play: 12
- own goals: 2

O Stoke City

by Half
- first: 1
- second: 9

by Situation
- set piece: 2
- open play: 7
- own goals: 1

Goals by Area

O Reading — Scored (Conceded)

6 (2)
9 (2)
1 (1)

O Stoke City — Scored (Conceded)

2 (2)
6 (6)
2 (0)

Team Statistics

Starting Line-Ups

Reading:
Stack, Shorey (Golbourne), Ingimarsson, Sonko, Makin, Sidwell (Dobson), Hunt, Gunnarsson, Doyle (Cox), Halls, Long

Stoke City:
Simonsen, Kopteff (Rooney), Hoefkens, Russell, Duberry, Hill, Brammer, Bangoura (Henry), Junior, Dickinson, Sweeney (Gallagher)

Reading: **4/3/3**

Stoke City: **4/5/1**

Unused Sub: Hahnemann, Kitson

Unused Sub: de Goey, Broomes

Championship Totals

	O Reading	Stoke O
Championship Appearances	577	565
Team Appearances	446	537
Goals Scored	58	34
Assists	51	36
Clean Sheets (goalkeepers)	9	25
Yellow Cards	48	75
Red Cards	4	7
Full Internationals	3	4

Age/Height

	Reading	Stoke City
Age	24 yrs, 6 mo	24 yrs, 10 mo
Height	5'11"	6'

Match Statistics

League Table after Fixture

		Played	Won	Drawn	Lost	For	Against	Pts
●	1 Reading	44	30	12	2	96	30	102
...		...	...	...	...	...	...	...
↓	13 Stoke	44	16	7	21	49	61	55
↑	14 Burnley	44	14	11	19	45	52	53
↓	15 Plymouth	44	12	17	15	37	44	53
↓	16 Ipswich	44	13	14	17	50	64	53
●	17 Leicester	44	12	15	17	50	57	51
↑	18 Hull	44	12	14	18	48	54	50
↑	19 Derby	44	10	20	14	53	63	50

Statistics

	O Reading	Stoke O
Goals	3	1
Shots on Target	4	3
Shots off Target	4	5
Hit Woodwork	0	0
Possession %	55	45
Corners	3	6
Offsides	3	3
Fouls	8	16
Disciplinary Points	0	0

0-1

Stoke City ○
Coventry City ○

▶ Michael Duberry cannot hide his frustration

Event Line	
13 ○ ■ Brammer	
Half time 0-0	
46 ○ ⇄ Henry > Brammer	
64 ○ ⇄ Adebola > Hutchison	
68 ○ ⇄ Hazley > Paterson	
80 ○ ⇄ Morrell > McSheffrey	
85 ○ ⊕ Adebola / LF / OP / IA	
Assist: Thornton	
89 ○ ⇄ Turner > John	
Full time 0-1	

Dele Adebola stole in for a late winner to ensure the season at the Britannia Stadium ended on a disappointing note.

An uninspiring game was heading for a draw until the former Crewe striker drilled a low effort past Steve Simonsen in the 86th minute.

Johan Boskamp used the occasion to showcase some of his Academy starlets and saw Dave Brammer and full debutant Adam Rooney force Marton Fulop into a double save early on.

At the other end, Simonsen denied Stern John and Gary McSheffrey before Mamady Sidibe missed a golden opportunity to break open the deadlock when he fired wide with only Fulop to beat.

The arrival of substitute Adebola livened up the Sky Blues in the final 20 minutes and Kevin Thornton wrong-footed Simonsen with a shot which trundled wide.

Skipper Michael Duberry then hooked an Adebola effort away from goal as the home campaign looked set to end as it began, with a no-score draw, but Adebola had other ideas.

Quote

● Johan Boskamp

Noel Blake and his Academy staff have produced five or six players who have played in the first-team this season and that has to be encouraging for the future.

Championship Milestone

▶ Debut

Matthew Hazley made his Championship debut.

Venue:	Britannia Stadium	Referee:	P.Walton - 05/06	**Stoke City**
Attendance:	13,385	Matches:	40	**Coventry City**
Capacity:	28,218	Yellow Cards:	122	
Occupancy:	47%	Red Cards:	6	

Form Coming into Fixture

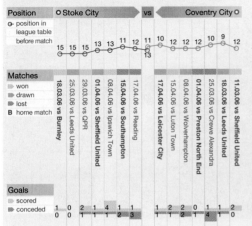

Position
- position in league table before match

O Stoke City vs Coventry City

15 15 15 13 13 11 12 11 10 12 12 12 10 9 12
13

Matches
- won
- drawn
- lost
- B home match

18.03.06 vs Burnley
25.03.06 vs Leeds United
29.03.06 vs QPR
01.04.06 vs Sheffield United
15.04.06 vs Southampton
17.04.06 vs Reading
17.04.06 vs Leicester City
15.04.06 vs Luton Town
08.04.06 vs Wolverhampton
01.04.06 vs Preston North End
25.03.06 vs Crewe Alexandra
18.03.06 vs Leeds United
11.03.06 vs Sheffield United

Goals
- scored
- conceded

| 1 | 0 | 2 | 1 | 4 | 1 | 1 | | 1 | 2 | 2 | 0 | 1 | 1 | 2 |
| 0 | 0 | 1 | 1 | 1 | 2 | 3 | | 1 | 1 | 2 | 1 | 4 | 1 | 0 |

Goal Statistics

O Stoke City — by Half — by Situation

- first: 1
- second: 9
- set piece: 2
- open play: 7
- own goals: 1

O Coventry City — by Half — by Situation

- first: 8
- second: 1
- set piece: 1
- open play: 8

Goals by Area

O Stoke City — Scored (Conceded)

2 (3)
6 (5)
2 (0)

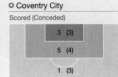

O Coventry City — Scored (Conceded)

3 (3)
5 (4)
1 (3)

Team Statistics

Starting Line-Ups

Stoke City:
Simonsen
Dickinson, Gallagher
Hill, Brammer (Henry), Sidibe, John Turner
Duberry, Russell, Rooney, Hutchison (Adebola)
Hoefkens, Paterson (Hazley)

Coventry City:
Fulop
Thornton, Whing
Hughes, Heath
Doyle, Hall
McSheffrey (Morrell), Giddings

▶ 4/4/2   ▶ 4/4/2

Unused Sub: de Goey, Broomes, Kopteff

Unused Sub: Williams, Osbourne

Championship Totals

	O Stoke	Coventry O
Championship Appearances	569	666
Team Appearances	530	601
Goals Scored	31	88
Assists	38	66
Clean Sheets (goalkeepers)	25	8
Yellow Cards	69	74
Red Cards	6	3
Full Internationals	3	4

Age/Height

Stoke City Age
▶ **24 yrs, 3 mo**

Coventry City Age
▶ **25 yrs, 11 mo**

Stoke City Height
▶ **6'**

Coventry City Height
▶ **6'**

Match Statistics

League Table after Fixture

		Played	Won	Drawn	Lost	For	Against	Pts
●	11 Coventry	45	15	15	15	59	64	60
↑	12 Ipswich	45	14	14	17	52	64	56
↓	13 Southampton	45	12	19	14	47	50	55
↓	14 Stoke	45	16	7	22	49	62	55
↑	15 Leicester	45	13	15	17	51	57	54
↓	16 Burnley	45	14	11	20	45	53	53
↓	17 Plymouth	45	12	17	16	37	45	53
●	18 Hull	45	12	15	18	49	55	51
●	19 Derby	45	10	20	15	53	65	50

Statistics

	O Stoke	Coventry O
Goals	0	1
Shots on Target	8	6
Shots off Target	10	3
Hit Woodwork	0	0
Possession %	51	49
Corners	7	4
Offsides	2	2
Fouls	13	11
Disciplinary Points	4	0

1-5

Brighton & Hove Albion ○
Stoke City ○

▶ Mamady Sidibe rises highest

Event Line

6 ○ ⊕ Rooney / RF / OP / IA	
	Assist: Sidibe
7 ○ ▣ Henderson	
22 ○ ⊕ Rooney / RF / OP / IA	
	Assist: Skoko
40 ○ ⊕ Sidibe / RF / OP / IA	
	Assist: Skoko
Half time 0-3	
58 ○ ⇄ Loft > Frutos	
63 ○ ⊕ Rooney / RF / OP / IA	
	Assist: Sidibe
70 ○ ⇄ Garrett > Brammer	
77 ○ ⇄ Sweeney > Rooney	
82 ○ ⊕ Sweeney / LF / OP / IA	
83 ○ ⇄ Kopteff > Skoko	
84 ○ ⊕ Loft / LF / OP / IA	
Full time 1-5	

Adam Rooney's first hat-trick in senior football capped a clinical final day display against already-relegated Brighton.

The young Irishman's treble came among further strikes from Mamady Sidibe and Peter Sweeney to run up the biggest win of the season in Johan Boskamp's last match in charge. Doug Loft's late consolation did little to lift the Seagulls, who were forced on to the back foot as early as the sixth minute.

Rooney, making only his second first-team start, latched onto a Sidibe pass and showed great composure to coolly slot beyond Wayne Henderson from eight yards. The Dubliner was celebrating his second on 22 minutes when he tucked away Josip Skoko's inviting cross before Darel Russell sent a long-range effort crashing back off the underside of the crossbar. But from the resulting move, Skoko found Sidibe and he turned superbly before volleying powerfully past Henderson.

The second-half began in identical fashion to the first – with a Rooney goal. The Academy starlet exchanged passes with Sidibe and slammed the ball home to complete a magnificent hat-trick. Sweeney's smart finish after a costly error in the Brighton defence completed the rout, but the home side finally had something to cheer six minutes from time when Loft beat Steve Simonsen from 12 yards.

Quote

● **Johan Boskamp**

Adam Rooney is only 18 and to score three goals on your second appearance is fantastic. His performance shows we should put the money into our Academy

Championship Milestone

▶ **First Goal**

Peter Sweeney netted his first goal in the Championship for Stoke.

Venue:	Withdean Stadium	Referee:	K.Wright - 05/06	
Attendance:	5,859	Matches:	32	
Capacity:	7,999	Yellow Cards:	100	
Occupancy:	73%	Red Cards:	9	

Brighton & Hove Albion
Stoke City

Form Coming into Fixture

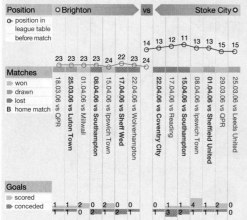

Position   Brighton   vs   Stoke City
- position in league table before match

Positions: 23 23 23 23 24 22 23 24 | 14 13 12 11 13 13 15 15

Matches
- won
- drawn
- lost
- B home match

18.03.06 vs QPR | 25.03.06 vs Luton Town | 01.04.06 vs Millwall | 08.04.06 vs Southampton | 15.04.06 vs Ipswich Town | 17.04.06 vs Sheff Wed | 22.04.06 vs Wolverhampton | 22.04.06 vs Coventry City | 17.04.06 vs Reading | 15.04.06 vs Southampton | 08.04.06 vs Ipswich Town | 01.04.06 vs Sheffield United | 29.03.06 vs QPR | 25.03.06 vs Leeds United

Goals
- scored
- conceded

Brighton: 1 1 2 0 2 0 0 | 1 1 0 2 1 2 1

Stoke: 0 1 1 4 1 2 0 | 1 3 2 1 1 1 0

Goal Statistics

Brighton & Hove Albion

by Half	by Situation
first: 4	set piece: 2
second: 2	open play: 3
	own goals: 1

Stoke City

by Half	by Situation
first: 1	set piece: 2
second: 8	open play: 6
	own goals: 1

Goals by Area

Brighton & Hove Albion
Scored (Conceded)

| 2 (4) |
| 4 (4) |
| 0 (0) |

Stoke City
Scored (Conceded)

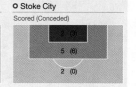

| 2 (3) |
| 5 (6) |
| 2 (0) |

Team Statistics

Starting Line-Ups

Lynch, Frutos (Loft), Brammer (Garrett), Buxton
Butters, Nicolas, Noel-Williams, Sidibe, Junior, Duberry
Henderson | Simonsen
Hinshelwood, Carpenter, Kazim-Richards (Sweeney), Rooney, Russell, Hill
Reid, Carole, Skoko (Kopteff), Dickinson

▶ 4/4/2   ▶ 4/4/2

Unused Sub: Chaigneau, El-Abd, Mayo, Gatting

Unused Sub: de Goey, Broomes

Championship Totals	Brighton	Stoke
Championship Appearances	554	558
Team Appearances	479	495
Goals Scored	42	22
Assists	37	33
Clean Sheets (goalkeepers)	7	25
Yellow Cards	43	65
Red Cards	3	7
Full Internationals	1	3

Age/Height

Brighton & Hove Albion Age	Stoke City Age
▶ 24 yrs, 9 mo	▶ 24 yrs, 11 mo

Brighton & Hove Albion Height	Stoke City Height
▶ 5'11"	▶ 6'

Match Statistics

League Table after Fixture

		Played	Won	Drawn	Lost	For	Against	Pts
●	7 Wolverhampton	46	16	19	11	50	42	67
↑	8 Coventry	46	16	15	15	62	65	63
↓	9 Norwich	46	18	8	20	56	65	62
●	10 Luton	46	17	10	19	66	67	61
↓	11 Cardiff	46	16	12	18	58	59	60
↑	12 Southampton	46	13	19	14	49	50	58
↑	13 Stoke	46	17	7	22	54	63	58
...	...	...	...	...	...	...	...	...
●	24 Brighton	46	7	17	22	39	71	38

Statistics	Brighton	Stoke
Goals	1	5
Shots on Target	6	9
Shots off Target	5	1
Hit Woodwork	0	1
Possession %	43	57
Corners	4	8
Offsides	5	2
Fouls	9	19
Disciplinary Points	4	0

Review of 2005/06

▶ Bangoura opens his City account in the 2-0 win over Crewe

When referee Kevin Wright blew the final whistle on City's season at Brighton's Withdean Stadium on Sunday, April 30, the biggest stories of a headline-making campaign were still to come.

With the future of manager Johan Boskamp unclear, and takeover talk rife, the summer of 2006 promised to be no ordinary close-season. And so it proved.

Three months later, with a new manager in place and the club under new ownership, everything points to a fresh start. Anticipation is keen, optimism is high and expectations are great.

The 2005/06 season will not go down as a memorable one on the field, but off it there was always enough going on to keep the club firmly in the news.

The departure of manager Tony Pulis – to return only 12 months later – for, in the words of the club's

previous owners, 'not signing enough foreign players' raised a few eyebrows as much for its timing as it's reasoning.

With barely a month to go before the new campaign, Dutchman Johan Boskamp was ushered into his first-ever job in English football with a major squad-rebuilding job as well as a steep learning curve ahead of him.

To the manager's credit he quickly built a side capable of holding it's own in the Championship and the struggle against relegation predicted by some pundits never materialised.

Unfortunately, behind-the-scenes harmony proved a more elusive goal and the season became remembered from November onwards for the breakdown of Boskamp's working relationship with his assistant Jan De Koning and Director of Football John Rudge after a dispute centred on a mysterious piece of paper during the 2-1 win at Coventry.

■ Hoefkens puts in another player of the year perfomance

From that point on the only regular winners were the media, who were regularly handed opportunities to feed on a juicy supply of headline-making titbits right up until the Dutchman's departure in May.

Just occasionally, events on the field eclipsed all else. City made a relatively solid start after the damp squib of an opening day 0-0 home draw with newly-promoted Sheffield Wednesday and the cavalier nature of the 4-2 defeat at Leicester three days later promised plenty of colourful football ahead.

That colour was often orange, with the manager – an international footballer who represented Holland in the 1978 World Cup finals – striving to inject some of his native footballing philosophy into City's play.

Sometimes it worked, sometimes not. A style developed which became more effective away from home and the early habit of gleaning more points on their travels was something which would stick with the players for the whole season, right up to that 5-1 romp on the South Coast on the final day.

By the end of September, away wins at Millwall, Hull and Preston offset home defeats to Watford, Wolves and Cardiff. The back-to-front pattern was established.

October proved a tougher month, with four defeats from five games, but there was the bonus – finally - of the arrival of club record signing Sambegou Bangoura from Belgian outfit Standard Liege and he scored on his home debut in the 2-0 win over Crewe.

November would be remembered only for the problems which arose between the manager and members of his backroom staff, which was a pity because despite all that on the field results improved and continued to do so right up until Christmas.

Indeed, when City met Burnley at Turf Moor on Boxing Day it was quite rightly billed as a clash between two potential promotion contenders with both teams on the very brink of the play-off zone.

▶ Championship status Is assured thanks to victory at Loftus Road.

City lost that, as they were to lose four of their next five league games in a debilitating run over the festive period and well into the New Year.

By the time the home game against Preston came around at the start of February, talk was more of relegation than promotion with the side bereft of confidence and belief as well as a goal output.

What made the difference? Those who blamed the spat between the manager and his staff couldn't have been right, as results after that watershed evening at Coventry in November actually improved afterwards.

Those who blamed the absence of Sam Bangoura, whisked away at the start of January to assist in Guinea's African Cup of Nations bid, could not have been right because even thought the African contributed eight goals in nine games during his purple patch in the run-up to Christmas, his absence alone could not explain the loss of form and confidence in the team as a whole.

However, it is true to say the manager had a game Plan A based around Bangoura as the focal point of the attack and when he departed – not to return until the middle of February and then not the player he had been before – Plans B, C and even D proved less than convincing as the team were asked to mix their previously more expressive style of play with a more regimented, more defensive, approach.

In truth, the players were caught between a rock and a hard place and the end product was not beautiful.

A series of grim 0-0 draws against the likes of Preston, Plymouth, Wolves and Leeds kept the points trickling in.

It needed a 2-1 win at QPR in a re-arranged game at the end of March to finally erase any lingering fears of a late flirtation with relegation.

After that, the more expressive football of early season returned and City ran up two huge away wins, 4-1 at

Rooney ends season in style firing In the first of his three in 5-1 win at Brighton

Ipswich three weeks' ahead of the Brighton thrashing, to leave supporters again scratching their heads while trying to figure out just what their team was all about.

A mid-table finish in 13th place was not as unlucky as it might seem, and as a bonus fans were able to enjoy the increasingly excellent form of Belgian defender Carl Hoefkens, the buy of the season who became the undisputed Player of the Year, as well as the emergence of some of the club's promising youngsters during the latter stages of the campaign – none more so than Irish teenager Adam Rooney, whose hat-trick at Brighton firmly marked him as one to watch in the future. And was there ever a better loan signing than Paul Gallagher, unwanted by Blackburn but whose 11 Championship and face-saving FA Cup goal at Tamworth made him leading scorer and hero at the same time?

Turning to the cups, fortunes were again mixed. City went out of the Carling Cup in the first round at Mansfield on penalties, needed penalties to knock non-league Tamworth out of the FA Cup after a nerve-jangling third round replay at The Lamb, then crept past Walsall in the fourth round to make the last sixteen for only the second time in nearly 20 years.

A fifth round home tie against Premiership strugglers Birmingham looked ripe for an upset, even given City's poor league form at the time, but the Blues sneaked away with a 1-0 win courtesy of a Mikkael Forssell goal just after half-time and two brilliant saves by Maik Taylor.

It was a strange cup run, one which should have engendered confidence and bred excitement throughout the club, the players and fans but somehow never did. It was, in truth, low-key passage into the last 16 of the competition and once there it fizzled out.

If fans were left wondering how to assess the FA Cup run, then much the same could be said of the league campaign.

It wasn't bad, but it wasn't good; there were good performances and some very bad ones; the team changed direction in mid-season and ended up treading water; another manager came and went; the players' wage bill was increased but the team finished no higher in the table.

It was, all-in-all, a season spent treading water and in years to come people may still wonder what, exactly, it all meant.

With a new manager, new ownership, and new ambitions, the 2006/07 season has the potential to be far more defining in the future of Stoke City.

Lowest On-Site Price Guaranteed!
SAVE 35% OFF PARKING
and we'll donate £1 to
THE NATIONAL FOREST
Book parking on-line
www.nottinghamema.com
Nottingham East Midlands Airport

1

Steve Simonsen
Goalkeeper

Season Review 05/06

City's undisputed number one missed just one game during another superb season, which ended with him being voted the Players' Player of the Year.

A former England Youth and under-21 international, he began his career at Tranmere before moving across the Mersey to join Premiership side Everton in 1998 for a fee £3.3 million – a British record for a goalkeeper.

However, a change of managers at Goodison Park hindered his progress and a free transfer to the Potters followed in 2004. Steve quickly established himself at the Britannia Stadium and, under contract until the summer of 2008, looks set be City's first choice goalkeeper for many years to come.

Player Details:

Date of Birth:	03.04.1979
Place of Birth:	South Shields
Nationality:	English
Height:	6'2"
Weight:	13st 2lb
Foot:	Right

Player Performance 05/06

League Performance

Percentage of total possible time player was on pitch   ⊖ position in league table at end of month

Month:	Aug	Sep	Oct	Nov	Dec	Jan	Feb	Mar	Apr	Total
	100%	76%	100%	100%	100%	100%	100%	100%	100%	98%
	8	9	14	8	12	15	16	13	13	
Team Pts:	10/18	6/15	3/15	12/15	6/18	1/9	5/12	8/18	7/18	58/138
Team Gls F:	8	3	4	10	8	2	2	5	12	54
Team Gls A:	8	9	7	4	10	6	4	6	9	63
Total mins:	540	340	450	450	540	270	360	540	540	4,030
Starts (sub):	6	4	5	5	6	3	4	6	6	45
Goals:	0	0	0	0	0	0	0	0	0	0
Assists:	0	0	0	0	0	0	0	0	0	0
Clean sheets:	2	1	1	2	0	0	2	3	0	11
Cards (Y/R):	1	0/1	0	0	0	0	0	0	0	1/1

League Performance Totals

Clean Sheets

▶ Simonsen:	11
▷ Team-mates:	1
Total:	**12**

Assists

▶ Simonsen:	0
▷ Team-mates:	48
Total:	**48**

Cards

▶ Simonsen:	2
▷ Team-mates:	75
Total:	**77**

Cup Games

	Apps	CS	Cards
FA Cup	4	1	1
Carling Cup	1	0	0
Total	**5**	**1**	**1**

Career History

Career Milestones

Club Debut:

vs Oldham (A), L 2-1, League Cup

 **24.08.04**

Time Spent at the Club:

 2 Seasons

First Goal Scored for the Club:

—

▶ —

Full International:

▶ —

Championship Totals

04-06

Appearances	76
Clean Sheets	25
Assists	0
Yellow Cards	3
Red Cards	1

Clubs

Year	Club	Apps	CS
04-06	Stoke	83	26
98-04	Everton	37	9
96-98	Tranmere	41	17

Off the Pitch

Age:

▶ Simonsen: 27 years, 1 month
▷ Team: 25 years, 7 months
❘ League: 26 years, 1 month

Height:

▶ Simonsen: 6'2"
▷ Team: 5'11"
❘ League: 5'11"

Weight:

▶ Simonsen: 13st 2lb
▷ Team: 12st 3lb
❘ League: 11st 13lb

33

Robert Duggan
Goalkeeper

Season Review 05/06

An agile young goalkeeper signed from Irish outfit Lourdes Celtic on scholarship terms in 2004, Robert gained valuable experience on the substitute's bench in 2005/06.

Although yet to make a first-team appearance, the Dubliner was awarded with a squad number for the first time and became a prominent fixture between the sticks at both Academy and reserve levels.

He has over a dozen Republic of Ireland at schoolboy levels and earned a professional contract in 2005 before penning new deal in May 2006, which will keep him at the club for at least another year.

Player Details:

Date of Birth:	01.04.1987
Place of Birth:	Dublin
Nationality:	Irish
Height:	6'1"
Weight:	12st 7lb
Foot:	Left

www.stokecityfc.com
Follow the action all the way to the net!

2

Carl Hoefkens
Defence

Season Review 05/06

Carl capped a magnificent debut season in English football by picking up the Fans' Player of the Year Award.

The arrival in the summer of 2005 of the cultured Belgian international from Germinal Beerschot for an undisclosed fee increased an already healthy competition in defence.

Equally adaptable at centre-back and full-back, his attacking outlook and excellent ball-playing ability proved a key to City's season - as did his expertise from the penalty spot.

Carl, who began his career in his homeland with Lierse, is a regular fixture in the Belgian national squad and, at 27, is set to enter his prime with City.

Player Details:

Date of Birth:	06.10.1978
Place of Birth:	Lierse
Nationality:	Belgian
Height:	6'1"
Weight:	12st 13lb
Foot:	Right/Left

Player Performance 05/06

League Performance

Percentage of total possible time player was on pitch   ⊙ position in league table at end of month

Month:	Aug	Sep	Oct	Nov	Dec	Jan	Feb	Mar	Apr	Total
	100%	100%	100%	100%	100%	100%	100%	71%	82%	94%
	8	9	14	8	12	15	16	13	13	
Team Pts:	10/18	6/15	3/15	12/15	6/18	1/9	5/12	8/18	7/18	58/138
Team Gls F:	8	3	4	10	8	2	2	5	12	54
Team Gls A:	8	9	7	4	10	6	4	6	9	63
Total mins:	540	450	450	450	540	270	360	385	445	3,890
Starts (sub):	6	5	5	5	6	3	4	5	5	44
Goals:	0	0	1	0	0	0	1	1	0	3
Assists:	1	0	0	1	0	0	1	0	0	3
Clean sheets:	2	2	1	2	0	0	2	3	0	12
Cards (Y/R):	1	1	1	0	0	0	0	0	1	4

League Performance Totals

Goals

▶ Hoefkens:	3
▨ Team-mates:	49
Total:	**52**
● own goals:	2

Assists

▶ Hoefkens:	3
▨ Team-mates:	45
Total:	**48**

Cards

▶ Hoefkens:	4
▨ Team-mates:	73
Total:	**77**

Cup Games

	Apps	Goals	Cards
FA Cup	4	0	2
Carling Cup	1	0	0
Total	**5**	**0**	**2**

Career History

Career Milestones

Club Debut:

vs Sheff Wed (H), D 0-0, Championship

▶ **06.08.05**

Time Spent at the Club:

▶ **1 Season**

First Goal Scored for the Club:

vs Derby (A), L 2-1, Championship

▶ **15.10.05**

Full International:

▶ **Belgium**

Championship Totals

04-06

Appearances	44
Goals	3
Assists	3
Yellow Cards	4
Red Cards	0

Clubs

Year	Club	Apps	Gls
05-06	Stoke	49	3
	Germinal Beerschot		
	Lierse		

Off the Pitch

Age:

- ▶ Hoefkens: 27 years, 7 months
- ▨ Team: 25 years, 7 months
- | League: 26 years, 1 month

Height:

- ▶ Hoefkens: 6'1"
- ▨ Team: 5'11"
- | League: 5'11"

Weight:

- ▶ Hoefkens: 12st 13lb
- ▨ Team: 12st 3lb
- | League: 11st 13lb

3

Marlon Broomes
Defence

A former England U21 international defender who proved a useful addition to the squad after signing from Preston in a swap deal involving Lewis Neal on the eve of last season.

Marlon was groomed by Blackburn Rovers from a trainee but made his league debut while on loan at Swindon in 1996.

He went on to enjoy four seasons at Ewood Park, punctuated by further loan spells at QPR and Grimsby, before linking up with Sheffield Wednesday and then moving on to Preston.

Even though his preferred position is centre-back, Marlon proved a reliable outlet at left-back for much of the campaign.

Player Details:

Date of Birth:	28.11.1977
Place of Birth:	Meriden
Nationality:	English
Height:	6'
Weight:	12st 12lb
Foot:	Right/Left

Player Performance 05/06

League Performance

Percentage of total possible time player was on pitch ⊙ position in league table at end of month

Month:	Aug	Sep	Oct	Nov	Dec	Jan	Feb	Mar	Apr	Total
	100%	100%	89%	20%	82%	84%	94%	75%	34%	76%
position	8	9	14	8	12	15	16	13	13	
Team Pts:	10/18	6/15	3/15	12/15	6/18	1/9	5/12	8/18	7/18	58/138
Team Gls F:	8	3	4	10	8	2	2	5	12	54
Team Gls A:	8	9	7	4	10	6	4	6	9	63
Total mins:	540	450	400	90	442	226	338	406	185	3,077
Starts (sub):	6	5	5	1	5	3	4	5	2 (1)	36 (1)
Goals:	2	0	0	0	0	0	0	0	0	2
Assists:	0	0	0	0	1	0	0	0	0	1
Clean sheets:	2	2	1	1	0	0	2	1	0	9
Cards (Y/R):	2	0	0/1	1	0	2	0	2	0	7/1

League Performance Totals

Goals

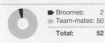

▶ Broomes:	2
▷ Team-mates:	50
Total:	**52**
● own goals:	2

Assists

▶ Broomes:	1
▷ Team-mates:	47
Total:	**48**

Cards

▶ Broomes:	8
▷ Team-mates:	69
Total:	**77**

Cup Games

	Apps	Goals	Cards
FA Cup	4	0	0
Carling Cup	1	0	0
Total	**5**	**0**	**0**

Career History

Career Milestones

Club Debut:

vs Sheff Wed (H), D 0-0, Championship

▶ **06.08.05**

First Goal Scored for the Club:

vs Leicester (A), L 4-2, Championship

▶ **09.08.05**

Time Spent at the Club:

▶ **1 Season**

Full International:

▶ **—**

Championship Totals

04-06

Appearances	48
Goals	2
Assists	2
Yellow Cards	8
Red Cards	1

Clubs

Year	Club	Apps	Gls
05-06	Stoke	42	2
02-05	Preston	77	0
01-02	Sheff Wed	20	0
01-01	Grimsby	18	2
00-00	QPR	5	0
97-97	Swindon	12	1
94-01	Blackburn	39	2

Off the Pitch

Age:

- ▶ Broomes: 28 years, 6 months
- ▷ Team: 25 years, 7 months
- | League: 26 years, 1 month

Height:

- ▶ Broomes: 6'
- ▷ Team: 5'11"
- | League: 5'11"

Weight:

- ▶ Broomes: 12st 12lb
- ▷ Team: 12st 3lb
- | League: 11st 13lb

5

Michael Duberry
Defence

Season Review 05/06

Michael began his first full season in City colours by being named club captain by former manager Johan Boskamp.

The experienced central defender initially arrived at the Britannia Stadium on loan from Leeds before making the move permanent in February 2005.

A strong, powerful presence at the heart of the City rearguard the 30-year-old is a former England U21 international and boasts Premiership experience with Chelsea and Leeds, who splashed out £4.5 million for his services in 1999.

First-team opportunities were always limited at Elland Road, but a fresh start in the Potteries has since seen him amass close to 100 appearances for the club.

Player Details:

Date of Birth:	14.10.1975
Place of Birth:	Enfield
Nationality:	English
Height:	6'1"
Weight:	14st
Foot:	Right

Player Performance 05/06

League Performance

Percentage of total possible time player was on pitch   ⊖ position in league table at end of month

Month:	Aug	Sep	Oct	Nov	Dec	Jan	Feb	Mar	Apr	Total
	83%	100%	60%	80%	100%	100%	100%	100%	83%	89%
	8	9	14	8	12	15	16	13	13	
Team Pts:	10/18	6/15	3/15	12/15	6/18	1/9	5/12	8/18	7/18	58/138
Team Gls F:	8	3	4	10	8	2	2	5	12	54
Team Gls A:	8	9	7	4	10	6	4	6	9	63
Total mins:	450	450	270	360	540	270	360	540	450	3,690
Starts (sub):	5	5	3	4	6	3	4	6	5	41
Goals:	0	0	1	0	0	0	0	0	0	1
Assists:	0	0	0	0	1	0	0	0	0	1
Clean sheets:	1	2	1	2	0	0	2	3	0	11
Cards (Y/R):	1	1	0/1	2	1	1	0	0	0	6/1

League Performance Totals

Goals

▶ Duberry:	1
▒ Team-mates:	51
Total:	**52**
▶ own goals:	2

Assists

▶ Duberry:	1
▒ Team-mates:	47
Total:	**48**

Cards

▶ Duberry:	7
▒ Team-mates:	70
Total:	**77**

Cup Games

	Apps	Goals	Cards
FA Cup	3	0	0
Carling Cup	1	0	0
Total	**4**	**0**	**0**

Career History

Career Milestones

Club Debut:

vs West Ham (A), L 2-0, Championship

 19.10.04

Time Spent at the Club:

▶ **1.5 Seasons**

First Goal Scored for the Club:

vs Crewe (H), W 2-0, Championship

 18.10.05

Full International:

▶ —

Championship Totals

04-06

Appearances	70
Goals	1
Assists	2
Yellow Cards	10
Red Cards	3

Clubs

Year	Club	Apps	Gls
04-06	Stoke	70	1
99-05	Leeds	77	4
95-95	Bournemouth	8	0
93-99	Chelsea	116	3

Off the Pitch

Age:

▶ Duberry: 30 years, 7 months
▒ Team: 25 years, 7 months
| League: 26 years, 1 month

Height:

▶ Duberry: 6'1"
▒ Team: 5'11"
| League: 5'11"

Weight:

▶ Duberry: 14st
▒ Team: 12st 3lb
| League: 11st 13lb

6

Clint Hill
Defence

Season Review 05/06

Clint's determination was rewarded in 2005/06 as he shrugged off a long-term knee injury to play a major role in City's finish to the season.

Having risen through the ranks at Tranmere, the defender moved to Oldham in 2002 before joining the Potters for £120,000 in the summer of 2003.

His Potters career was initially hampered by an ankle injury, but his no-nonsense style immediately endeared him as a firm crowd favourite and the 2004/05 season ended with Clint being crowned Fans' Player of the Year. Unfortunately, injury struck again in April 2005, but he was still handed a new contract until 2008 before returning to action in February 2006.

Player Details:

Date of Birth:	19.10.1978
Place of Birth:	Liverpool
Nationality:	English
Height:	6'
Weight:	12st
Foot:	Left/Right

Player Performance 05/06

League Performance

Percentage of total possible time player was on pitch   ⊖ position in league table at end of month

Month:	Aug	Sep	Oct	Nov	Dec	Jan	Feb	Mar	Apr	Total
	0%	0%	0%	0%	0%	0%	56%	83%	80%	26%
Team Pts:	10/18	6/15	3/15	12/15	6/18	1/9	5/12	8/18	7/18	58/138
Team Gls F:	8	3	4	10	8	2	2	5	12	54
Team Gls A:	8	9	7	4	10	6	4	6	9	63
Total mins:	0	0	0	0	0	0	202	450	430	1,082
Starts (sub):	0	0	0	0	0	0	2 (1)	5	5	12 (1)
Goals:	0	0	0	0	0	0	0	0	0	0
Assists:	0	0	0	0	0	0	0	0	0	0
Clean sheets:	0	0	0	0	0	0	1	3	0	4
Cards (Y/R):	0	0	0	0	0	0	0	0	0	0

Positions in league table: 8, 9, 14, 8, 12, 15, 16, 13, 13

League Performance Totals

Goals
- Hill: 0
- Team-mates: 52
- **Total: 52**
- own goals: 2

Assists
- Hill: 0
- Team-mates: 48
- **Total: 48**

Cards
- Hill: 0
- Team-mates: 77
- **Total: 77**

Cup Games

	Apps	Goals	Cards
FA Cup	1	0	0
Carling Cup	0	0	0
Total	**1**	**0**	**0**

Career History

Career Milestones

Club Debut:
vs Wigan (A), L 2-1, Championship
➡ **14.10.03**

Time Spent at the Club:
➡ **3 Seasons**

First Goal Scored for the Club:
vs Cardiff (H), L 1-3, Championship
➡ **05.04.05**

Full International:
➡ **—**

Championship Totals

04-06

Appearances	45
Goals	1
Assists	2
Yellow Cards	6
Red Cards	1

Clubs

Year	Club	Apps	Gls
03-06	Stoke	59	1
02-03	Oldham	25	1
97-02	Tranmere	170	20

Off the Pitch

Age:
- Hill: 27 years, 7 months
- Team: 25 years, 7 months
- League: 26 years, 1 month

Height:
- Hill: 6'
- Team: 5'11"
- League: 5'11"

Weight:
- Hill: 12st
- Team: 12st 3lb
- League: 11st 13lb

22 Lewis Buxton
Defence

Season Review 05/06

Lewis continued to make steady progress on the first-team stage in 2005/06 with several dependable displays at both right and left full-back.

A promising young defender signed from Portsmouth in December 2004, despite his tender years he wasted no time in making his mark at the Britannia Stadium by quickly holding down a place in the side.

Handed his professional debut aged just seventeen at Pompey under Graham Rix, further loan spells at Exeter and Bournemouth have since seen him build up a reputation as a steady performer, capable of filling in anywhere across the defence. Lewis also registered his first senior goal in September 2005 against Wolves.

Player Details:

Date of Birth:	10.12.1983
Place of Birth:	Newport
Nationality:	English
Height:	6'1"
Weight:	13st 10lb
Foot:	Right/Left

Player Performance 05/06

League Performance

Percentage of total possible time player was on pitch   ⊕ position in league table at end of month

Month:	Aug	Sep	Oct	Nov	Dec	Jan	Feb	Mar	Apr	Total
	47%	100%	80%	80%	53%	67%	50%	54%	20%	60%
Team Pts:	10/18	6/15	3/15	12/15	6/18	1/9	5/12	8/18	7/18	58/138
Team Gls F:	8	3	4	10	8	2	2	5	12	54
Team Gls A:	8	9	7	4	10	6	4	6	9	63
Total mins:	256	450	360	360	285	180	180	291	110	2,472
Starts (sub):	2 (1)	5	4	4 (1)	3 (1)	2	2	2 (3)	1 (1)	25 (7)
Goals:	0	1	0	0	0	0	0	0	0	1
Assists:	0	0	0	0	0	0	0	0	0	0
Clean sheets:	1	2	1	1	0	0	1	1	0	7
Cards (Y/R):	0	1	3	0	0	0	0	1	0	5

League Performance Totals

Goals

- ► Buxton: 1
- ► Team-mates: 51
- **Total: 52**
- ► own goals: 2

Assists

- ► Buxton: 0
- ► Team-mates: 48
- **Total: 48**

Cards

- ► Buxton: 5
- ► Team-mates: 72
- **Total: 77**

Cup Games

	Apps	Goals	Cards
FA Cup	3	0	0
Carling Cup	1	0	1
Total	**4**	**0**	**1**

Career History

Career Milestones

Club Debut:
vs Preston (H), D 0-0, Championship
► **26.12.04**

Time Spent at the Club:
► **1.5 Seasons**

First Goal Scored for the Club:
vs Wolves (H), L 1-3, Championship
► **24.09.05**

Full International:
► —

Championship Totals

04-06

Appearances	48
Goals	1
Assists	0
Yellow Cards	9
Red Cards	0

Clubs

Year	Club	Apps	Gls
04-06	Stoke	53	1
03-04	Bournemouth	46	0
02-02	Exerter	6	0
00-04	Portsmouth	30	0

Off the Pitch

Age:

- ► Buxton: 22 years, 5 months
- ► Team: 25 years, 7 months
- | League: 26 years, 1 month

Height:

- ► Buxton: 6'1"
- ► Team: 5'11"
- | League: 5'11"

Weight:

- ► Buxton: 13st 10lb
- ► Team: 12st 3lb
- | League: 11st 13lb

28 Andy Wilkinson
Defence

Player Details:

Date of Birth:	06.08.1984
Place of Birth:	Stone
Nationality:	English
Height:	5'11"
Weight:	11st
Foot:	Right

Season Review 05/06

Andy's influence on the first-team may have been even greater had it not been for some unfortunate injuries.

The Stone-born youngster broke into the side at the start of last season before suffering tendonitis of the knee, which forced him out of action for nearly four months.

He returned in March to make three more starts before missing the rest of the campaign after sustaining ankle ligament damage during a clash against Southampton on April 15.

A strong and competitive Academy graduate, Andy has also enjoyed loan spells at Telford, Partick Thistle and Shrewsbury Town respectively.

Player Performance 05/06

League Performance

Percentage of total possible time player was on pitch   ○- position in league table at end of month

Month:	Aug	Sep	Oct	Nov	Dec	Jan	Feb	Mar	Apr	Total
		8	9	14	8	12	15	16	13	13	
	1%	0%	21%	0%	0%	0%	0%	17%	25%	8%
Team Pts:	10/18	6/15	3/15	12/15	6/18	1/9	5/12	8/18	7/18	58/138
Team Gls F:	8	3	4	10	8	2	2	5	12	54
Team Gls A:	8	9	7	4	10	6	4	6	9	63
Total mins:	4	0	93	0	0	0	0	90	136	323
Starts (sub):	0 (1)	0	1 (1)	0	0	0	0	1	2	4 (2)
Goals:	0	0	0	0	0	0	0	0	0	0
Assists:	0	0	0	0	0	0	0	0	0	0
Clean sheets:	0	0	0	0	0	0	0	0	0	0
Cards (Y/R):	0	0	0	0	0	0	0	1	0	1

League Performance Totals

Goals

▶ Wilkinson:	0
▷ Team-mates:	52
Total:	**52**
▶ own goals:	2

Assists

▶ Wilkinson:	0
▷ Team-mates:	48
Total:	**48**

Cards

▶ Wilkinson:	1
▷ Team-mates:	76
Total:	**77**

Cup Games

	Apps	Goals	Cards
FA Cup	0	0	0
Carling Cup	0	0	0
Total	**0**	**0**	**0**

Career History

Career Milestones

Club Debut:

vs Blackpool (A), L 2-3, FT LG Trophy

▶ **16.10.01**

Time Spent at the Club:

▶ **5 Seasons**

First Goal Scored for the Club:

—

 —

Full International:

▶ **—**

Championship Totals

04-06

Appearances	7
Goals	0
Assists	0
Yellow Cards	1
Red Cards	0

Clubs

Year	Club	Apps	Gls
05-05	Shrewsbury	9	0
04-05	Partick Thistle	11	0
03-04	Telford	9	0
01-06	Stoke	12	0

Off the Pitch

Age:

- ▶ Wilkinson: 21 years, 9 months
- ▷ Team: 25 years, 7 months
- | League: 26 years, 1 month

Height:

- ▶ Wilkinson: 5'11"
- ▷ Team: 5'11"
- | League: 5'11"

Weight:

- ▶ Wilkinson: 11st
- ▷ Team: 12st 3lb
- | League: 11st 13lb

31 Carl Dickinson
Defence

Season Review 05/06

An encouraging addition to the first-team squad last season, Carl shrugged off the agony of a broken leg to make five senior appearances for City.

Signed from Derby County's academy in 2002, he is a versatile player who can play in a variety of positions.

A mainstay for the under 19's and reserves over the past three seasons, he is a physical and determined player, who is comfortable at left-back, left midfield or central midfield.

Earned rave reviews after an impressive full-debut against Sheffield United in April and continued his progression over the summer after linking-up with Icelandic Premier Division outfit Vikingur FK on loan.

Player Details:

Date of Birth:	31.03.1987
Place of Birth:	Swadlincote
Nationality:	English
Height:	6'1"
Weight:	10st 7lb
Foot:	Left

Player Performance 05/06

League Performance

Percentage of total possible time player was on pitch   ⊙ position in league table at end of month

Month:	Aug	Sep	Oct	Nov	Dec	Jan	Feb	Mar	Apr	Total
position	8	9	14	8	12	15	16	13	75% / 13	
	0%	0%	0%	0%	0%	0%	0%	0%		10%
Team Pts:	10/18	6/15	3/15	12/15	6/18	1/9	5/12	8/18	7/18	58/138
Team Gls F:	8	3	4	10	8	2	2	5	12	54
Team Gls A:	8	9	7	4	10	6	4	6	9	63
Total mins:	0	0	0	0	0	0	0	0	404	404
Starts (sub):	0	0	0	0	0	0	0	0	4 (1)	4 (1)
Goals:	0	0	0	0	0	0	0	0	0	0
Assists:	0	0	0	0	0	0	0	0	0	0
Clean sheets:	0	0	0	0	0	0	0	0	0	0
Cards (Y/R):	0	0	0	0	0	0	0	0	0	0

League Performance Totals

Goals

- Dickinson: 0
- Team-mates: 52

Total: 52

- own goals: 2

Assists

- Dickinson: 0
- Team-mates: 48

Total: 48

Cards

- Dickinson: 0
- Team-mates: 77

Total: 77

Cup Games

	Apps	Goals	Cards
FA Cup	0	0	0
Carling Cup	0	0	0
Total	**0**	**0**	**0**

Career History

Career Milestones

Club Debut:
vs Coventry (H), W 1-0, Championship

➡ **11.12.04**

First Goal Scored for the Club:
—

➡ **—**

Time Spent at the Club:

➡ **2 Seasons**

Full International:

➡ **—**

Championship Totals

04-06

Appearances	6
Goals	0
Assists	0
Yellow Cards	0
Red Cards	0

Clubs

Year	Club	Apps	Gls
04-06	Stoke	6	0

Off the Pitch

Age:

- Dickinson: 19 years, 2 months
- Team: 25 years, 7 months
- League: 26 years, 1 month

Height:

- Dickinson: 6'1"
- Team: 5'11"
- League: 5'11"

Weight:

- Dickinson: 10st 7lb
- Team: 12st 3lb
- League: 11st 13lb

4

John Eustace
Midfield

Player Details:

Date of Birth:	03.11.1979
Place of Birth:	Solihull
Nationality:	English
Height:	5'11"
Weight:	11st 12lb
Foot:	Right

Season Review 05/06

A long-term knee problem forced the influential midfielder to watch the whole of the 2005/06 campaign from the sidelines.

Injuries have no doubt halted the progress of the 28-year-old star, who joined the Potters from Coventry City via a loan spell at Middlesbrough in July 2003.

He visited the renowned Richard Steadman clinic in America in his latest bid to get his City career back on track and has targeted a return to action this coming season.

A tough-tackling, goalscoring, midfield player by nature, John played a pivotal role during the 2003/04 season, weighing in with some important goals during City's mid-season rich vein of form.

Player Performance 05/06

League Performance

Percentage of total possible time player was on pitch   ⊖ position in league table at end of month

Month:	Aug	Sep	Oct	Nov	Dec	Jan	Feb	Mar	Apr	Total
	8	9	14	8	12	15	16	13	13	
	0%	0%	0%	0%	0%	0%	0%	0%	0%	0%
Team Pts:	10/18	6/15	3/15	12/15	6/18	1/9	5/12	8/18	7/18	58/138
Team Gls F:	8	3	4	10	8	2	2	5	12	54
Team Gls A:	8	9	7	4	10	6	4	6	9	63
Total mins:	0	0	0	0	0	0	0	0	0	0
Starts (sub):	0	0	0	0	0	0	0	0	0	0
Goals:	0	0	0	0	0	0	0	0	0	0
Assists:	0	0	0	0	0	0	0	0	0	0
Clean sheets:	0	0	0	0	0	0	0	0	0	0
Cards (Y/R):	0	0	0	0	0	0	0	0	0	0

League Performance Totals

Goals

▶ Eustace:	0
⇨ Team-mates:	52
Total:	**52**
▶ own goals:	2

Assists

▶ Eustace:	0
⇨ Team-mates:	48
Total:	**48**

Cards

▶ Eustace:	0
⇨ Team-mates:	77
Total:	**77**

Cup Games

	Apps	Goals	Cards
FA Cup	0	0	0
Carling Cup	0	0	0
Total	**0**	**0**	**0**

Career History

Career Milestones

Club Debut:

vs Derby Cty (A), W 3-0, Champ.

 09.08.03

Time Spent at the Club:

▶ **3 Seasons**

First Goal Scored for the Club:

vs Bradford C. (H), W 1-0, Champ.

 22.11.03

Full International:

 —

Championship Totals

04-06

Appearances	7
Goals	0
Assists	0
Yellow Cards	2
Red Cards	0

Clubs

Year	Club	Apps	Gls
03-06	Stoke	38	6
03-03	Middlesbrough	1	0
99-99	Dundee Utd		
96-03	Coventry City	98	10

Off the Pitch

Age:

- ▶ Eustace: 26 years, 6 months
- ⇨ Team: 25 years, 7 months
- | League: 26 years, 1 month

Height:

- ▶ Eustace: 5'11"
- ⇨ Team: 5'11"
- | League: 5'11"

Weight:

- ▶ Eustace: 11st 12lb
- ⇨ Team: 12st 3lb
- | League: 11st 13lb

8 Dave Brammer
Midfield

Player Details:

Date of Birth:	28.02.1975
Place of Birth:	Bromborough
Nationality:	English
Height:	5'8"
Weight:	12st
Foot:	Right

Season Review 05/06

A match winning 30-yard thunderbolt against Luton last August saw Dave scoop the City 'Goal of the Season' for the second successive campaign. The vastly-experienced midfield lynchpin was once again a permanent fixture in the Potters engine room.

The Merseyside-born star started off his career at Wrexham and moved to Port Vale in 1999 before switching to Crewe Alexandra for a fee of £500,000 two years later.

A move back to the Potteries to join City (thus making him a member of the small and exclusive group to have played for Stoke, Vale and Crewe) followed in 2004, and Dave's wide range of passing and eye for goal has since gone on to make him a mainstay in midfield.

Player Performance 05/06

League Performance

Percentage of total possible time player was on pitch   ⊖ position in league table at end of month

Month:	Aug	Sep	Oct	Nov	Dec	Jan	Feb	Mar	Apr	Total
	100%	75%	80%	80%	100%	67%	71%	72%	75%	81%
	8	9	14	8	12	15	16	13	13	
Team Pts:	10/18	6/15	3/15	12/15	6/18	1/9	5/12	8/18	7/18	58/138
Team Gls F:	8	3	4	10	8	2	2	5	12	54
Team Gls A:	8	9	7	4	10	6	4	6	9	63
Total mins:	540	336	360	360	540	180	257	389	406	3,368
Starts (sub):	6	4	4	4	6	2	3	4 (1)	5 (1)	38 (2)
Goals:	1	0	0	0	0	0	0	0	0	1
Assists:	0	0	0	1	2	1	0	1	1	6
Clean sheets:	2	2	1	2	0	0	1	2	0	10
Cards (Y/R):	0	1	1	1	2	0	0	0	1	6

League Performance Totals

Goals

- Brammer: 1
- Team-mates: 51
- **Total: 52**
- own goals: 2

Assists

- Brammer: 6
- Team-mates: 42
- **Total: 48**

Cards

- Brammer: 6
- Team-mates: 71
- **Total: 77**

Cup Games

	Apps	Goals	Cards
FA Cup	4	0	1
Carling Cup	1	1	0
Total	**5**	**1**	**1**

Career History

Career Milestones

Club Debut:
vs Wolves (H), W 2-1, Championship

08.08.04

Time Spent at the Club:
2 Seasons

First Goal Scored for the Club:
vs Leicester (H), W 3-2, Championship
22.02.05

Full International:
—

Championship Totals

04-06

Appearances	83
Goals	2
Assists	9
Yellow Cards	14
Red Cards	0

Clubs

Year	Club	Apps	Gls
04-06	Stoke	89	3
01-04	Crewe	103	6
99-01	Port Vale	85	4
93-99	Wrexham	170	14

Off the Pitch

Age:
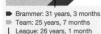

- Brammer: 31 years, 3 months
- Team: 25 years, 7 months
- League: 26 years, 1 month

Height:

- Brammer: 5'8"
- Team: 5'11"
- League: 5'11"

Weight:

- Brammer: 12st
- Team: 12st 3lb
- League: 11st 13lb

11 Kevin Harper
Midfield

Player Details:

Date of Birth:	15.01.1976
Place of Birth:	Oldham
Nationality:	Scottish
Height:	5'6"
Weight:	12st
Foot:	Right/Left

Season Review 05/06

A series of injuries disrupted the Scottish winger's progress throughout 2005/06.

The versatile utility man, who joined City from Portsmouth for a small fee in January 2005, saw his pre-season cut short by a hamstring problem before a dislocated shoulder at the start of the year ended his campaign.

A former Scotland under-21 international, Kevin is widely recognised as a midfielder, but his great pace also makes him well adaptable either at full-back or wing-back.

He made his professional debut in his homeland with Hibernian before moving on to Derby and Portsmouth, collecting Premiership experience along the way.

Player Performance 05/06

League Performance

Percentage of total possible time player was on pitch   ⊙ position in league table at end of month

Month:	Aug	Sep	Oct	Nov	Dec	Jan	Feb	Mar	Apr	Total
	34%	71%	0%	0%	8%	47%	0%	0%	0%	16%
	8	9	14	8	12	15	16	13	13	
Team Pts:	10/18	6/15	3/15	12/15	6/18	1/9	5/12	8/18	7/18	58/138
Team Gls F:	8	3	4	10	8	2	2	5	12	54
Team Gls A:	8	9	7	4	10	6	4	6	9	63
Total mins:	183	321	0	0	44	128	0	0	0	676
Starts (sub):	1 (4)	3 (2)	0	0	0 (1)	1 (2)	0	0	0	5 (9)
Goals:	1	0	0	0	0	0	0	0	0	1
Assists:	0	1	0	0	0	0	0	0	0	1
Clean sheets:	0	1	0	0	0	0	0	0	0	1
Cards (Y/R):	0	0	0	0	0	0	0	0	0	0

League Performance Totals

Goals
- Harper: 1
- Team-mates: 51
- **Total: 52**
- own goals: 2

Assists
- Harper: 1
- Team-mates: 47
- **Total: 48**

Cards
- Harper: 0
- Team-mates: 77
- **Total: 77**

Cup Games

	Apps	Goals	Cards
FA Cup	2	0	1
Carling Cup	1	0	0
Total	**3**	**0**	**1**

Career History

Career Milestones

Club Debut:
vs Millwall (A), W 0-1, Championship
▶ **19.02.05**

Time Spent at the Club:
▶ **1.5 Seasons**

First Goal Scored for the Club:
vs Norwich (H), W 3-1, Championship
▶ **29.08.05**

Full International:
▶ —

Championship Totals
04-06

Appearances	25
Goals	1
Assists	7
Yellow Cards	1
Red Cards	0

Clubs

Year	Club	Apps	Gls
05-06	Stoke	26	1
04-04	Leicester	2	0
03-03	Norwich	9	0
00-05	Portsmouth	128	9
99-00	Walsall	9	1
98-00	Derby	41	2
92-98	Hibernian	96	15
	Hutchison Vale		

Off the Pitch

Age:
- Harper: 30 years, 4 months
- Team: 25 years, 7 months
- League: 26 years, 1 month

Height:
- Harper: 5'6"
- Team: 5'11"
- League: 5'11"

Weight:
- Harper: 12st
- Team: 12st 3lb
- League: 11st 13lb

12

Peter Sweeney
Midfield

Season Review 05/06

A back problem delayed the start of Peter's career with City last season.

Signed from Millwall in a deal worth up to £250,000 in the summer, he missed the first three months of the campaign before returning to establish himself as an important part of the squad. A talented left-footed winger, Peter came through the ranks at The New Den and has a London background, but is actually an ex-Scotland under-21 international having been born in Glasgow.

He made his Lions debut in 2002, but had to wait another year for his real breakthrough, when he played a major role in Millwall's march to the FA Cup final and started against Manchester United at the Millennium Stadium.

Player Details:

Date of Birth:	25.09.1984
Place of Birth:	Glasgow
Nationality:	Scottish
Height:	6'
Weight:	12st 1lb
Foot:	Left

Player Performance 05/06

League Performance

Percentage of total possible time player was on pitch — ⊖ position in league table at end of month

Month:	Aug	Sep	Oct	Nov	Dec	Jan	Feb	Mar	Apr	Total
	0%	0%	11%	0%	29%	33%	47% 16	18%	24%	17%
	8	9	14	8	12	15		13	13	
Team Pts:	10/18	6/15	3/15	12/15	6/18	1/9	5/12	8/18	7/18	58/138
Team Gls F:	8	3	4	10	8	2	2	5	12	54
Team Gls A:	8	9	7	4	10	6	4	6	9	63
Total mins:	0	0	48	0	154	90	169	97	132	690
Starts (sub):	0	0	0 (3)	0	2 (1)	1	3 (1)	1 (2)	1 (2)	8 (9)
Goals:	0	0	0	0	0	0	0	0	1	1
Assists:	0	0	0	0	1	0	0	0	0	1
Clean sheets:	0	0	0	0	0	0	0	0	0	0
Cards (Y/R):	0	0	0	0	1	0	0	0	0	1

League Performance Totals

Goals
- Sweeney: 1
- Team-mates: 51
- **Total: 52**
- own goals: 2

Assists
- Sweeney: 1
- Team-mates: 47
- **Total: 48**

Cards
- Sweeney: 1
- Team-mates: 76
- **Total: 77**

Cup Games

	Apps	Goals	Cards
FA Cup	3	0	0
Carling Cup	0	0	0
Total	**3**	**0**	**0**

Career History

Career Milestones

Club Debut:
vs Crewe (H), W 2-0, Championship
➤ **18.10.05**

Time Spent at the Club:
➤ **1 Season**

First Goal Scored for the Club:
vs Brighton (A), W 1-5, Championship
➤ **30.04.06**

Full International:
➤ —

Championship Totals

04-06

Appearances	41
Goals	3
Assists	3
Yellow Cards	3
Red Cards	0

Clubs

Year	Club	Apps	Gls
05-06	Stoke	20	1
01-05	Millwall	67	5

Off the Pitch

Age:
- Sweeney: 21 years, 8 months
- Team: 25 years, 7 months
- League: 26 years, 1 month

Height:
- Sweeney: 6'
- Team: 5'11"
- League: 5'11"

Weight:
- Sweeney: 12st 1lb
- Team: 12st 3lb
- League: 11st 13lb

17

Darel Russell
Midfield

Darel surpassed 100 appearances for the Potters with another energetic season at the heart of midfield.

The former England Youth international, signed from Norwich City for £125,000 during the summer of 2003, weighed in with three goals and cemented a permanent spot in Johan Boskamp's side.

A tireless worker, Darel is strong in the tackle, good on the ball and extremely versatile, being able to fill in at central and right-sided midfield roles as well as at wing-back.

At 25, his best years are still ahead of him and he should reach his peak with City after signing a new contract, which keeps him at the club until the summer of 2008.

Player Details:

Date of Birth:	22.10.1980
Place of Birth:	Mile End
Nationality:	English
Height:	5'10"
Weight:	12st
Foot:	Right

Player Performance 05/06

League Performance

Percentage of total possible time player was on pitch   ⊙ position in league table at end of month

Month:	Aug	Sep	Oct	Nov	Dec	Jan	Feb	Mar	Apr	Total
	8	70% 9	100% 14	100% 8	83% 12	67% 15	16 18%	95% 13	98% 13	73%
	10%									
Team Pts:	10/18	6/15	3/15	12/15	6/18	1/9	5/12	8/18	7/18	58/138
Team Gls F:	8	3	4	10	8	2	2	5	12	54
Team Gls A:	8	9	7	4	10	6	4	6	9	63
Total mins:	54	314	450	450	450	180	65	512	531	3,006
Starts (sub):	2	3 (1)	5	5	5	2	1 (1)	6	6	35 (2)
Goals:	0	0	0	1	0	1	0	0	1	3
Assists:	0	0	1	0	0	0	0	1	0	2
Clean sheets:	0	1	1	2	0	0	1	2	0	7
Cards (Y/R):	0	2	1	2	1	0	0/1	2	0	8/1

League Performance Totals

Goals

- ▶ Russell: 3
- ▦ Team-mates: 49
- **Total: 52**
- ● own goals: 2

Assists

- ▶ Russell: 2
- ▦ Team-mates: 46
- **Total: 48**

Cards

- ▶ Russell: 9
- ▦ Team-mates: 68
- **Total: 77**

Cup Games

	Apps	Goals	Cards
FA Cup	1	0	0
Carling Cup	1	0	0
Total	**2**	**0**	**0**

Career History

Career Milestones

Club Debut:

vs Derby (A), W 0-3, Championship

 09.08.03

First Goal Scored for the Club:

vs Sunderland (H), W 3-1, Championship

▶ **16.09.03**

Time Spent at the Club:

▶ **3 Seasons**

Full International:

▶ —

Championship Totals

04-06

Appearances	82
Goals	5
Assists	2
Yellow Cards	15
Red Cards	1

Clubs

Year	Club	Apps	Gls
03-06	Stoke	136	9
97-03	Norwich	147	9

Off the Pitch

Age:

- ▶ Russell: 25 years, 7 months
- ▦ Team: 25 years, 7 months
- | League: 26 years, 1 month

Height:

- ▶ Russell: 5'10"
- ▦ Team: 5'11"
- | League: 5'11"

Weight:

- ▶ Russell: 12st
- ▦ Team: 12st 3lb
- | League: 11st 13lb

19 Luke Chadwick
Midfield

Season Review 05/06

After heavily impressing during a six-month loan spell from West Ham, Luke joined the Potters for £100,000 in January 2006, signing a two-and-a-half year contract at the Britannia Stadium. A speedy and exciting right-sided winger, the 25-year-old began his career at Arsenal as a youth before linking up with Manchester United, where he made his Premiership debut in 2000.

He gained Champions League experience during his time with the Reds and added a further 53 appearances to his name during loan spells with Reading and Burnley respectively. A tricky player who likes to run at opponents with the ball at his feet, Luke helped himself to three goals from 40 games in 2005/06.

Player Details:

Date of Birth:	18.11.1980
Place of Birth:	Cambridge
Nationality:	English
Height:	5'11"
Weight:	11st 8lb
Foot:	Right/Left

Player Performance 05/06

League Performance

Percentage of total possible time player was on pitch   ⊖ position in league table at end of month

Month:	Aug	Sep	Oct	Nov	Dec	Jan	Feb	Mar	Apr	Total
	99%	58%	65%	65%	75%	81%	75%	47%	25%	64%
Team Pts:	10/18	6/15	3/15	12/15	6/18	1/9	5/12	8/18	7/18	58/138
Team Gls F:	8	3	4	10	8	2	2	5	12	54
Team Gls A:	8	9	7	4	10	6	4	6	9	63
Total mins:	536	260	292	292	403	220	270	252	136	2,661
Starts (sub):	6	4	4	3 (1)	5	3	3	3 (1)	2 (1)	33 (3)
Goals:	0	0	1	0	0	0	0	0	1	2
Assists:	1	0	1	0	0	0	1	0	1	4
Clean sheets:	2	0	1	1	0	0	2	0	0	6
Cards (Y/R):	0	0	0	0	1	1	2	1	0	5

League Performance Totals

Goals

► Chadwick:	2
▒ Team-mates:	50
Total:	**52**
● own goals:	2

Assists

► Chadwick:	4
▒ Team-mates:	44
Total:	**48**

Cards

► Chadwick:	5
▒ Team-mates:	72
Total:	**77**

Cup Games

	Apps	Goals	Cards
FA Cup	4	1	0
Carling Cup	0	0	0
Total	**4**	**1**	**0**

Career History

Career Milestones

Club Debut:
vs Sheff Wed (H), D 0-0, Championship

► **06.08.05**

Time Spent at the Club:

► **1 Season**

First Goal Scored for the Club:
vs Plymouth (A), L 2-1, Championship

► **01.10.05**

Full International:

► **—**

Championship Totals

04-06

Appearances	68
Goals	3
Assists	9
Yellow Cards	7
Red Cards	0

Clubs

Year	Club	Apps	Gls
05-06	Stoke	40	3
04-05	West Ham	36	1
03-04	Burnley	40	6
03-03	Reading	17	1
99-00	Royal Antwerp		
99-04	Man Utd	39	2

Off the Pitch

Age:

► Chadwick: 25 years, 6 months
▒ Team: 25 years, 7 months
| League: 26 years, 1 month

Height:

► Chadwick: 5'11"
▒ Team: 5'11"
| League: 5'11"

Weight:

► Chadwick: 11st 8lb
▒ Team: 12st 3lb
| League: 11st 13lb

23

Karl Henry
Midfield

Player Details:

Date of Birth:	26.11.1982
Place of Birth:	Wolverhampton
Nationality:	English
Height:	6'
Weight:	12st
Foot:	Right

Player Performance 05/06

League Performance

Percentage of total possible time player was on pitch   ⊖ position in league table at end of month

Month:	Aug	Sep	Oct	Nov	Dec	Jan	Feb	Mar	Apr	Total
	55% / 8	9 / 10%	14 / 2%	8 / 25%	12 / 34%	83% / 15	50% 16	13 / 0%	13 / 12%	27%
Team Pts:	10/18	6/15	3/15	12/15	6/18	1/9	5/12	8/18	7/18	58/138
Team Gls F:	8	3	4	10	8	2	2	5	12	54
Team Gls A:	8	9	7	4	10	6	4	6	9	63
Total mins:	299	46	9	114	184	224	180	0	63	1,119
Starts (sub):	3 (2)	1	0 (2)	1 (4)	2 (2)	2 (1)	2	0	0 (2)	11 (13)
Goals:	0	0	0	0	0	0	0	0	0	0
Assists:	1	0	0	0	0	0	0	0	0	1
Clean sheets:	1	0	0	0	0	1	0	0	0	2
Cards (Y/R):	0	1	0	0	0	0	0	0	0	1

League Performance Totals

Goals

▶ Henry:	0
▨ Team-mates:	52
Total:	**52**
▶ own goals:	2

Assists

▶ Henry:	1
▨ Team-mates:	47
Total:	**48**

Cards

▶ Henry:	1
▨ Team-mates:	76
Total:	**77**

Cup Games

	Apps	Goals	Cards
FA Cup	3	0	1
Carling Cup	1	0	0
Total	**4**	**0**	**1**

Career History

Career Milestones

Club Debut:
vs Walsall (H), W 4-0, FT LG Trophy
▶ **07.02.01**

Time Spent at the Club:
▶ **7 Seasons**

First Goal Scored for the Club:
vs Bradford (A), L 4-2, Championship
▶ **26.12.02**

Full International:
▶ **—**

Championship Totals

04-06

Appearances	58
Goals	0
Assists	1
Yellow Cards	4
Red Cards	0

Clubs

Year	Club	Apps	Gls
04-04	Cheltenham	9	1
99-06	Stoke	136	1

Off the Pitch

Age:

- ▶ Henry: 23 years, 6 months
- ▨ Team: 25 years, 7 months
- | League: 26 years, 1 month

Height:

- ▶ Henry: 6'
- ▨ Team: 5'11"
- | League: 5'11"

Weight:
- ▶ Henry: 12st
- ▨ Team: 12st 3lb
- | League: 11st 13lb

25

Peter Kopteff
Midfield

Season Review 05/06

City fought off stiff competition to land the Finnish international star on a free transfer from Norwegian side Viking Stavanger in December 2005.

A regular in Finland's national side with nearly 40 caps to his name, Peter is starting to adapt to the physical demands of the English game after a slow start.

A quick and skilful predominately left-sided winger of considerable experience, he made his name in his homeland with HJK Helsinki before moving to Stavanger in 2002.

He went on to score 12 goals in just over 100 appearances for the Nordic outfit and is looking to reproduce that kind of form with the Potters in the future.

Player Details:

Date of Birth:	10.04.1979
Place of Birth:	Helsinki
Nationality:	Finnish
Height:	5'11"
Weight:	11st 9lb
Foot:	Left

Player Performance 05/06

League Performance

Percentage of total possible time player was on pitch   ⊖ position in league table at end of month

Month:	Aug	Sep	Oct	Nov	Dec	Jan	Feb	Mar	Apr	Total
	8	9	14	8	12	15	16 31%	13	13 22%	
	0%	0%	0%	0%	0%	7%		0%		6%
Team Pts:	10/18	6/15	3/15	12/15	6/18	1/9	5/12	8/18	7/18	58/138
Team Gls F:	8	3	4	10	8	2	2	5	12	54
Team Gls A:	8	9	7	4	10	6	4	6	9	63
Total mins:	0	0	0	0	0	20	111	0	119	250
Starts (sub):	0	0	0	0	0	0 (1)	1 (1)	0	2 (1)	3 (3)
Goals:	0	0	0	0	0	0	0	0	0	0
Assists:	0	0	0	0	0	0	0	0	0	0
Clean sheets:	0	0	0	0	0	0	0	0	0	0
Cards (Y/R):	0	0	0	0	0	0	0	0	0	0

League Performance Totals

Goals
- Kopteff: 0
- Team-mates: 52
- **Total: 52**
- own goals: 2

Assists
- Kopteff: 0
- Team-mates: 48
- **Total: 48**

Cards
- Kopteff: 0
- Team-mates: 77
- **Total: 77**

Cup Games

	Apps	Goals	Cards
FA Cup	3	0	0
Carling Cup	0	0	0
Total	**3**	**0**	**0**

Career History

Career Milestones

Club Debut:
vs Ipswich (H), D 2-2, Championship
▶ **02.01.06**

Time Spent at the Club:
▶ **0.5 Seasons**

First Goal Scored for the Club:
—
▶ **—**

Full International:
▶ **Finland**

Championship Totals

04-06

Appearances	6
Goals	0
Assists	0
Yellow Cards	0
Red Cards	0

Clubs

Year	Club	Apps	Gls
06-06	Stoke	9	0
	Viking Stavanger	129	12
	HJK Helsinki	66	4

Off the Pitch

Age:

- Kopteff: 27 years, 1 month
- Team: 25 years, 7 months
- League: 26 years, 1 month

Height:

- Kopteff: 5'11"
- Team: 5'11"
- League: 5'11"

Weight:
- Kopteff: 11st 9lb
- Team: 12st 3lb
- League: 11st 13lb

35

Robert Garrett
Midfield

Season Review 05/06

A feisty young Ulsterman snapped up from St. Andrews FC in 2004, Robert made two first-team appearances, both as a second-half substitute, in 2005/06.

Having captained the Academy side and established himself as a regular in the reserves, he also forced his way into the Northern Ireland international set-up, representing his country at under-19 level.

A tough-tackling central midfield player with an eye for goal, Rob pledged his long-term future to the Potters by signing a new contract at the club, which will keep him tied to the Britannia Stadium until the summer of 2007.

Player Details:

Date of Birth:	05.05.1988
Place of Birth:	Belfast
Nationality:	Northern Irish
Height:	5'7"
Weight:	10st 8lb
Foot:	Right

Player Performance 05/06

League Performance

Percentage of total possible time player was on pitch   ↺ position in league table at end of month

Month:	Aug	Sep	Oct	Nov	Dec	Jan	Feb	Mar	Apr	Total
	8	9	14	8	12	15	16	13	13	
	0%	0%	0%	0%	0%	0%	0%	0%	4%	0%
Team Pts:	10/18	6/15	3/15	12/15	6/18	1/9	5/12	8/18	7/18	58/138
Team Gls F:	8	3	4	10	8	2	2	5	12	54
Team Gls A:	8	9	7	4	10	6	4	6	9	63
Total mins:	0	0	0	0	0	0	0	0	20	20
Starts (sub):	0	0	0	0	0	0	0	0	0 (2)	0 (2)
Goals:	0	0	0	0	0	0	0	0	0	0
Assists:	0	0	0	0	0	0	0	0	0	0
Clean sheets:	0	0	0	0	0	0	0	0	0	0
Cards (Y/R):	0	0	0	0	0	0	0	0	0	0

League Performance Totals

Goals

- Garrett: 0
- Team-mates: 52
- **Total: 52**
- own goals: 2

Assists

- Garrett: 0
- Team-mates: 48
- **Total: 48**

Cards

- Garrett: 0
- Team-mates: 77
- **Total: 77**

Cup Games

	Apps	Goals	Cards
FA Cup	0	0	0
Carling Cup	0	0	0
Total	**0**	**0**	**0**

Career History

Career Milestones

Club Debut:
vs Ipswich (A), W 1-4, Championship

➡ **08.04.06**

Time Spent at the Club:

➡ **2 Seasons**

First Goal Scored for the Club:
—

➡ **—**

Full International:

➡ **—**

Championship Totals

04-06

Appearances	2
Goals	0
Assists	0
Yellow Cards	0
Red Cards	0

Clubs

Year	Club	Apps	Gls
04-06	Stoke	2	0

Off the Pitch

Age:
- Garrett: 18 years
- Team: 25 years, 7 months
- League: 26 years, 1 month

Height:
- Garrett: 5'7"
- Team: 5'11"
- League: 5'11"

Weight:
- Garrett: 10st 8lb
- Team: 12st 3lb
- League: 11st 13lb

36 Matthew Hazley
Midfield

Season Review 05/06

Talented left-sided midfielder Matthew made his first senior appearance as a second-half substitute against Coventry in April.

A second-year scholarship player recruited from Northern Irish outfit Glenavon in 2004, he has represented Northern Ireland at all youth levels and forfeited the chance of playing against Italy to be available for City's FA Youth Cup victory over Manchester United in 2004.

A tricky winger who possesses bags of potential, Matthew is a regular at both Academy and reserve level and will be hoping to make a further breakthrough in the first-team this coming season.

Player Details:

Date of Birth:	30.12.1987
Place of Birth:	Banbridge
Nationality:	Northern Irish
Height:	5'7"
Weight:	11st 4lb
Foot:	Left

Off the Pitch

Age:

- Hazley: 18 years, 5 months
- Team: 25 years, 7 months
- League: 26 years, 1 month

Height:

- Hazley: 5'7"
- Team: 5'11"
- League: 5'11"

Weight:

- Hazley: 11st 4lb
- Team: 12st 3lb
- League: 11st 13lb

26 Anthony Pulis
Midfield

Season Review 05/06

Anthony ended 2005/06 on loan at Plymouth Argyle after struggling to break into the City first-team.

The former Portsmouth youngster, son of ex-Potters manager Tony Pulis, penned a two-and-a-half year at the Britannia Stadium after joining the club in December 2004.

A skilful central midfielder, he also enjoyed a loan spell with Torquay United shortly after signing for City and has since established himself as a regular in the reserves.

He is also a Welsh under-21 international, and is hoping to make further progress with both club and country next season.

Player Details:

Date of Birth:	21.07.1984
Place of Birth:	Bristol
Nationality:	Welsh
Height:	5'10"
Weight:	11st 10lb
Foot:	Right

Off the Pitch

Age:

- Pulis: 21 years, 10 months
- Team: 25 years, 7 months
- League: 26 years, 1 month

Height:

- Pulis: 5'10"
- Team: 5'11"
- League: 5'11"

Weight:

- Pulis: 11st 10lb
- Team: 12st 3lb
- League: 11st 13lb

7

Sambegou Bangoura
Forward

Player Details:

Date of Birth:	03.04.1982
Place of Birth:	Conakry
Nationality:	Guinean
Height:	6'
Weight:	12st 1lb
Foot:	Right/Left

Player Performance 05/06

League Performance

Percentage of total possible time player was on pitch   ⊙ position in league table at end of month

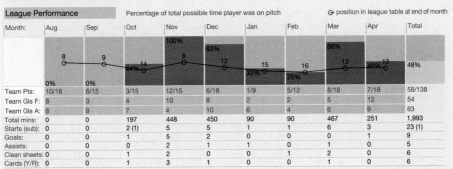

Month:	Aug	Sep	Oct	Nov	Dec	Jan	Feb	Mar	Apr	Total
Team Pts:	10/18	6/15	3/15	12/15	6/18	1/9	5/12	8/18	7/18	58/138
Team Gls F:	8	3	4	10	8	2	2	5	12	54
Team Gls A:	8	9	7	4	10	6	4	6	9	63
Total mins:	0	0	197	448	450	90	90	467	251	1,993
Starts (sub):	0	0	2 (1)	5	5	1	1	6	3	23 (1)
Goals:	0	0	1	5	2	0	0	0	1	9
Assists:	0	0	0	2	1	1	0	1	0	5
Clean sheets:	0	0	1	2	0	0	1	2	0	6
Cards (Y/R):	0	0	1	3	1	0	0	1	0	6

League Performance Totals

Goals

► Bangoura: 9
▒ Team-mates: 43
Total: 52
► own goals: 2

Assists

► Bangoura: 5
▒ Team-mates: 43
Total: 48

Cards

► Bangoura: 6
▒ Team-mates: 71
Total: 77

Cup Games

	Apps	Goals	Cards
FA Cup	1	0	0
Carling Cup	0	0	0
Total	**1**	**0**	**0**

Career History

Career Milestones

Club Debut:

vs Derby (A), L 2-1, Championship

► **15.10.05**

Time Spent at the Club:

► **1 Season**

First Goal Scored for the Club:

vs Crewe (H), W 2-0, Championship

► **18.10.05**

Full International:

► **Guinea**

Championship Totals

04-06

Appearances	24
Goals	9
Assists	5
Yellow Cards	6
Red Cards	0

Clubs

Year	Club	Apps	Gls
05-06	Stoke	25	9
	Standard Liege		
	Lokeren		

Off the Pitch

Age:

► Bangoura: 24 years, 1 month
▒ Team: 25 years, 7 months
| League: 26 years, 1 month

Height:

► Bangoura: 6'
▒ Team: 5'11"
| League: 5'11"

Weight:

► Bangoura: 12st 1lb
▒ Team: 12st 3lb
| League: 11st 13lb

34 Adam Rooney
Forward

Season Review 05/06

Striker Adam capped a remarkable season by netting his first senior hat-trick on the final day of the 2005/06 campaign against Brighton. The young Dubliner's treble came on only his second start for the club and after he had opened his first-team account with a solitary strike against champions Reading just a fortnight before.

He made his City debut as a substitute at Tamworth in the FA Cup in January, having arrived at the Britannia Stadium on trial in the summer of 2005.

A physical striker with a powerful right-foot, the teenager will be looking to carry on where he left off this coming season.

Player Details:

Date of Birth:	21.04.1988
Place of Birth:	Dublin
Nationality:	Irish
Height:	6'
Weight:	12st 3lb
Foot:	Right

Player Performance 05/06

League Performance

Percentage of total possible time player was on pitch   ⊖ position in league table at end of month

Month:	Aug	Sep	Oct	Nov	Dec	Jan	Feb	Mar	Apr	Total
	8	9	14	8	12	15	16	13	13 41%	
	0%	0%	0%	0%	0%	4%	0%	0%		6%
Team Pts:	10/18	6/15	3/15	12/15	6/18	1/9	5/12	8/18	7/18	58/138
Team Gls F:	8	3	4	10	8	2	2	5	12	54
Team Gls A:	8	9	7	4	10	6	4	6	9	63
Total mins:	0	0	0	0	0	12	0	0	220	232
Starts (sub):	0	0	0	0	0	0 (1)	0	0	2 (2)	2 (3)
Goals:	0	0	0	0	0	0	0	0	4	4
Assists:	0	0	0	0	0	0	0	0	1	1
Clean sheets:	0	0	0	0	0	0	0	0	0	0
Cards (Y/R):	0	0	0	0	0	1	0	0	0	1

League Performance Totals

Goals
- Rooney: 4
- Team-mates: 48
- **Total: 52**
- own goals: 2

Assists
- Rooney: 1
- Team-mates: 47
- **Total: 48**

Cards
- Rooney: 1
- Team-mates: 76
- **Total: 77**

Cup Games

	Apps	Goals	Cards
FA Cup	2	0	0
Carling Cup	0	0	0
Total	**2**	**0**	**0**

Career History

Career Milestones

Club Debut:
vs Tamworth (A), D 1-1, FA Cup

 **17.01.06**

Time Spent at the Club:

▶ **1 Season**

First Goal Scored for the Club:
vs Reading (A), L 3-1, Championship

▶ **17.04.06**

Full International:

▶ —

Championship Totals

04-06

Appearances	5
Goals	4
Assists	1
Yellow Cards	1
Red Cards	0

Clubs

Year	Club	Apps	Gls
05-06	Stoke	7	4

Off the Pitch

Age:
- ▶ Rooney: 18 years, 1 month
- ▶ Team: 25 years, 7 months
- League: 26 years, 1 month

Height:
- ▶ Rooney: 6'
- ▶ Team: 5'11"
- League: 5'11"

Weight:
- ▶ Rooney: 12st 3lb
- ▶ Team: 12st 3lb
- League: 11st 13lb

9

Mamady Sidibe
Forward

Season Review 05/06

A powerful, imposing striker, Mama weighed in with seven goals on his debut season at the Britannia Stadium.

The Mali international, signed on a free transfer from Gillingham in the summer of 2005, missed only a handful of games and proved an excellent foil for main goalgetters Paul Gallagher and Sam Bangoura.

Standing at 6' 5" tall, the 26-year-old is a deceptive player. Despite his obvious aerial ability, Mama is extremely comfortable with the ball at his feet, which makes him an effective target man both in the air and on the ground.

Player Details:

Date of Birth:	18.12.1979
Place of Birth:	Bamako
Nationality:	Malian
Height:	6'4"
Weight:	12st 2lb
Foot:	Right

Player Performance 05/06

League Performance

Percentage of total possible time player was on pitch

position in league table at end of month

Month:	Aug	Sep	Oct	Nov	Dec	Jan	Feb	Mar	Apr	Total
	100%	91%	68%	90%	100%	100%	80%	62%	50%	81%
	8	9	14	8	12	15	16	13	13	
Team Pts:	10/18	6/15	3/15	12/15	6/18	1/9	5/12	8/18	7/18	58/138
Team Gls F:	8	3	4	10	8	2	2	5	12	54
Team Gls A:	8	9	7	4	10	6	4	6	9	63
Total mins:	540	411	307	404	540	270	288	333	270	3,363
Starts (sub):	6	5	3 (2)	4 (1)	6	3	4	3 (2)	3	37 (5)
Goals:	1	0	0	1	2	1	0	0	1	6
Assists:	2	0	0	2	2	0	0	0	2	8
Clean sheets:	2	1	0	1	0	0	1	2	0	7
Cards (Y/R):	0	1	0	0	0	0	1	0	0	2

League Performance Totals

Goals

- Sidibe: 6
- Team-mates: 46
- **Total: 52**
- own goals: 2

Assists

- Sidibe: 8
- Team-mates: 40
- **Total: 48**

Cards

- Sidibe: 2
- Team-mates: 75
- **Total: 77**

Cup Games

	Apps	Goals	Cards
FA Cup	4	1	0
Carling Cup	1	0	1
Total	**5**	**1**	**1**

Career History

Career Milestones

Club Debut:

vs Sheff Wed (H), D 0-0, Championship

06.08.05

Time Spent at the Club:

1 Season

First Goal Scored for the Club:

vs Norwich (H), W 3-1, Championship

29.08.05

Full International:

Mali

Championship Totals

04-06

Appearances	77
Goals	8
Assists	14
Yellow Cards	3
Red Cards	0

Clubs

Year	Club	Apps	Gls
05-06	Stoke	47	7
02-05	Gillingham	115	13
01-02	Swansea	35	8

Off the Pitch

Age:

- Sidibe: 26 years, 5 months
- Team: 25 years, 7 months
- League: 26 years, 1 month

Height:

- Sidibe: 6'4"
- Team: 5'11"
- League: 5'11"

Weight:

- Sidibe: 12st 2lb
- Team: 12st 3lb
- League: 11st 13lb

10 Hannes Sigurdsson
Forward

Season Review 05/06

Troublesome injury problems hampered and prematurely ended Hannes' first season at City.

The Icelandic international striker was snapped up on loan from Norwegian outfit Viking Stavanger in the summer before penning a permanent deal in January.

A tall and powerful target man, he is perfectly suited to the demands of the English game and bagged his first goal for the Potters against QPR in March.

But even though a hernia operation cut short his season, at 23 Hannes has youth on his side and is expected to play a major part in the club's future.

Player Details:

Date of Birth:	10.04.1983
Place of Birth:	Reykjavik
Nationality:	Icelandic
Height:	6'2"
Weight:	13st 12lb
Foot:	Left/Right

Player Performance 05/06

League Performance

Percentage of total possible time player was on pitch   ⊙ position in league table at end of month

Month:	Aug	Sep	Oct	Nov	Dec	Jan	Feb	Mar	Apr	Total
	8 / 0%	9 / 0%	65% / 14	8 / 46% / 31%	12	15 / 0%	82% / 16	13 / 30%	13 / 2%	28%
Team Pts:	10/18	6/15	3/15	12/15	6/18	1/9	5/12	8/18	7/18	58/138
Team Gls F:	8	3	4	10	8	2	2	5	12	54
Team Gls A:	8	9	7	4	10	6	4	6	9	63
Total mins:	0	0	293	207	168	0	296	162	13	1,139
Starts (sub):	0	0	3 (1)	3 (2)	1 (4)	0	2 (2)	1 (3)	0 (1)	10 (13)
Goals:	0	0	0	0	0	0	0	1	0	1
Assists:	0	0	1	0	0	0	0	0	0	1
Clean sheets:	0	0	1	0	0	0	0	0	0	1
Cards (Y/R):	0	0	0	0	1	0	0	0	0	1

League Performance Totals

Goals

▶ Sigurdsson: 1
▶ Team-mates: 51
Total: 52
▶ own goals: 2

Assists

▶ Sigurdsson: 1
▶ Team-mates: 47
Total: 48

Cards

▶ Sigurdsson: 1
▶ Team-mates: 76
Total: 77

Cup Games

	Apps	Goals	Cards
FA Cup	3	0	0
Carling Cup	0	0	0
Total	**3**	**0**	**0**

Career History

Career Milestones

Club Debut:
vs Plymouth (A), L 2-1, Championship
▶ 01.10.05
Time Spent at the Club:
▶ 1 Season

First Goal Scored for the Club:
vs QPR (A), W 1-2, Championship
▶ 29.03.06
Full International:
▶ Iceland

Championship Totals

04-06

Appearances	23
Goals	1
Assists	1
Yellow Cards	1
Red Cards	0

Clubs

Year	Club	Apps	Gls
05-06	Stoke	26	1
	Viking Stavanger	22	15

Off the Pitch

Age:

▶ Sigurdsson: 23 years, 1 month
▷ Team: 25 years, 7 months
| League: 26 years, 1 month

Height:

▶ Sigurdsson: 6'2"
▷ Team: 5'11"
| League: 5'11"

Weight:

▶ Sigurdsson: 13st 12lb
▷ Team: 12st 3lb
| League: 11st 13lb

30

Martin Paterson
Forward

Season Review 05/06

Promising young striker Martin graduated through the City schoolboy and Academy ranks to make his senior debut as a substitute in April 2005.

Two first-team starts against Leeds and Coventry followed in 2005/06 for a player who boasts a prolific scoring record at both Academy and reserve team levels.

A quick and decisive striker who wears his heart on his sleeve, Martin grabbed 11 goals in just 14 appearances for City's under-18's and averaged a goal every other game for the reserves.

He also captained the Potters to victory over Manchester United in the FA Youth Cup in 2004, netting the only goal in a superb 1-0 win.

Player Details:

Date of Birth:	10.05.1987
Place of Birth:	Morecambe
Nationality:	English
Height:	5'10"
Weight:	10st
Foot:	Right

Off the Pitch

Age:

- Paterson: 19 years
- Team: 25 years, 7 months
- League: 26 years, 1 month

Height:

- Paterson: 5'10"
- Team: 5'11"
- League: 5'11"

Weight:

- Paterson: 10st
- Team: 12st 3lb
- League: 11st 13lb

Vincent Péricard
Forward

Season Review 05/06

A quick and powerful striker who became Tony Pulis' first signing since returning as City manager when he agreed a three-year deal in June 2006. Born in Cameroon, the 23-year-old former France under-21 international began his professional career with Saint Etienne before joining Italian outfit Juventus in 2000, aged just 17. He gained Champions League experience during his time in Turin and moved to England with Portsmouth, originally on a year-long loan in 2002. After bagging ten goals in his first season, the move was made permanent, but a serious knee injury restricted him to just six appearances during the next two years. He spent most of 2005/06 on loan, firstly at Sheffield United and then under Pulis at Plymouth Argyle. He scored four goals while at Home Park and impressed enough for the new City manager to pursue his interest following his release from Pompey.

Player Details:

Date of Birth:	03.10.1982
Place of Birth:	Efko, Cameroon
Nationality:	French
Height:	6'1"
Weight:	13st 8lbs
Foot:	Right

Off the Pitch

Age:

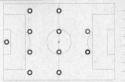

- Péricard: 23 years, 7 months
- Team: 25 years, 7 months
- League: 26 years, 1 month

Height:

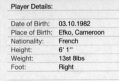

- Péricard: 6'1"
- Team: 5'11"
- League: 5'11"

Weight:

- Péricard: 13st 8lb
- Team: 12st 3lb
- League: 11st 13lb

Barnsley

Nickname:	The Tykes	Telephone:	01226 211 211
Manager:	Andy Ritchie	Ticket Office:	01226 211 200
Chairman:	Gordon Shepherd	Club Shop:	01226 211 400
Website:	www.barnsleyfc.co.uk		

Season Review 05/06

Barnsley gained promotion via the Playoffs after seeing off Huddersfield and then Swansea. Despite having been a striker himself, boss Andy Ritchie put together a defence that kept 19 clean sheets over the course of the League One season.

The Tykes were far from being defensively-minded, however, winning many admirers with some of their inventive attacking displays.

Points / Position

won drawn lost H home A away

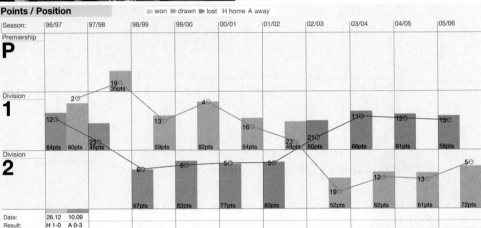

Season:	96/97	97/98	98/99	99/00	00/01	01/02	02/03	03/04	04/05	05/06
Premiership **P**										
Division **1**	12○ 64pts	2○ 80pts	19○ 35pts / 23○ 46pts	13○ 59pts	4○ 82pts	16○ 54pts	23○ 48pts / 21○ 50pts	11○ 66pts	12○ 61pts	13○ 58pts
Division **2**			8○ 67pts	6○ 82pts	5○ 77pts	5○ 80pts	52pts / 19○	12○ 62pts	13○ 61pts	5○ 72pts
Date:	26.12	10.09								
Result:	H 1-0	A 0-3								

Champ. Head-to-Head

Facts	○ Stoke	Barnsley ○
Games		
Points	0	0
Won	0	0
Drawn	0	0
Goals		
For	0	0
Clean Sheets	0	0
Shots on Target	0	0
Disciplinary		
Fouls	0	0
Yellow Cards	0	0
Red Cards	0	0

Goals by Area

○ Stoke   ○ Barnsley

0		0
0		0
0		0

Goals by Position

○ Stoke   ○ Barnsley

	Stoke	Barnsley
forward:	0	forward: 0
midfield:	0	midfield: 0
defence:	0	defence: 0

Goals Scored by Period

0	0	0	0	0	0	
0	15	30	45	60	75	90
0	0	0	0	0	0	

Average Attendance

All-Time Records

Total Championship Record	○ Stoke	Barnsley ○
Played	92	0
Points	119	0
Won	34	0
Drawn	17	0
Lost	41	0
For	90	0
Against	101	0
Players Used	48	0

All-Time Record vs Stoke						
Competition	Played	Won	Drawn	Lost	For	Against
League	50	19	12	19	62	67
FA Cup	3	2	1	0	7	5
League Cup	1	0	0	1	2	3
Other	0	0	0	0	0	0
Total	54	21	13	20	71	75

Oakwell Stadium

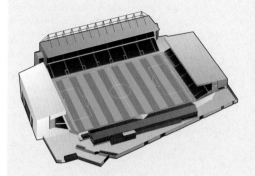

Stadium History

The Oakwell of today is unrecognisable from the place that Barnsley called home prior to the 1990's. Three of the four stands were knocked down and replaced, whilst the original West Stand was made all-seater. Furthermore, disabled facilities were significantly improved with the building of the Corner Stand in 1997.

Completion of the East Stand in 1993 enabled the Tykes to proudly boast that they were the first club in South Yorkshire to have executive boxes built in their stadium.

Stadium Statistics 05/06

Highest attendance
13,063 v Huddersfield Town 31.12.05

Lowest attendance
6,996 v Tranmere Rovers 06.12.05

Average attendance
9,045

How to Get There

Travel Information

Car parking
There is space for around 500 vehicles in a visitors car park at the ground.

Train
Barnsley Station is located in the town centre, just a five minute walk away from Oakwell.

Bus
Fans arriving at Barnsley Bus Station face a 10 minute walk to the ground.

Area Map

Local Map

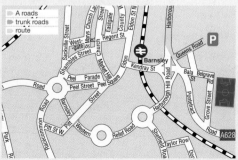

Birmingham City

Nickname:	The Blues	Telephone:	0871 226 1875
Manager:	Steve Bruce	Ticket Office:	0871 226 1875
Chairman:	David Gold	Club Shop:	0871 226 1875
Website:	www.bcfc.com		

Season Review 05/06

Injuries played a major part as Birmingham's four-season stay in the top-flight came to an end. Manager Steve Bruce was rarely able to pick a settled team with key players such as Matthew Upson, Mikael Forssell and David Dunn all missing large chunks of the campaign.

Goals proved particularly hard to come by, with only Sunderland managing less than the 28 netted by the Blues.

Points / Position

won ▶ drawn ▶ lost   H home A away

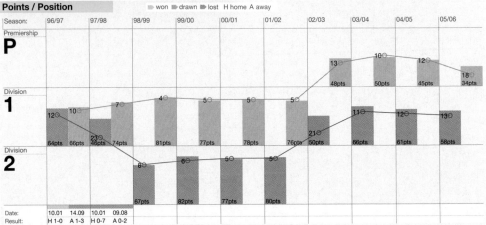

Season:	96/97	97/98	98/99	99/00	00/01	01/02	02/03	03/04	04/05	05/06
Premiership P							13○ 48pts	10○ 50pts	12○ 45pts	18○ 34pts
Division 1	12○ 64pts	10○ 66pts	23 46pts 7○ 74pts	4○ 81pts	5○ 77pts	5○ 78pts	5○ 76pts 21○ 50pts	11○ 66pts	12○ 61pts	13○ 58pts
Division 2			8○ 67pts	6○ 82pts	5○ 77pts	5○ 80pts				
Date:	10.01	14.09	10.01	09.08						
Result:	H 1-0	A 1-3	H 0-7	A 0-2						

Champ. Head-to-Head

Facts	○ Stoke	Birmingham ○
Games		
Points	0	0
Won	0	0
Drawn	0	0
Goals		
For	0	0
Clean Sheets	0	0
Shots on Target	0	0
Disciplinary		
Fouls	0	0
Yellow Cards	0	0
Red Cards	0	0

Goals by Area

○ Stoke   ○ Birmingham

0		0
0		0
0		0

Goals by Position

○ Stoke   ○ Birmingham

▶ forward:	0	▶ forward:	0
▶ midfield:	0	▶ midfield:	0
▶ defence:	0	▶ defence:	0

Goals Scored by Period

0	0	0	0	0	0
0	15	30	45	60	75	90
0	0	0	0	0	0

Average Attendance

▶ —

▶ —

All-Time Records

Total Championship Record	○ Stoke	Birmingham ○
Played	92	0
Points	119	0
Won	34	0
Drawn	17	0
Lost	41	0
For	90	0
Against	101	0
Players Used	48	0

All-Time Record vs Stoke

Competition	Played	Won	Drawn	Lost	For	Against
League	80	26	17	37	101	113
FA Cup	8	3	3	2	9	10
League Cup	0	0	0	0	0	0
Other	0	0	0	0	0	0
Total	**88**	**29**	**20**	**39**	**110**	**123**

St Andrew's Stadium

Stadium History

Birmingham moved to St Andrew's in 1906, attracting a crowd of 32,000 against Middlesbrough in the first game played at their new home.

The ground was heavily damaged by German bombers during the Second World War, and it wasn't until 1994 that it received major investment. Work began on the Kop Stand and Tilton Road End, with the Railway Stand having to wait until the 1998-99 season before it was given a facelift. The stadium is now an established footballing venue.

Seating Plan

Capacity
30,016

- family area
- away fans
- disabled

Stadium Statistics 05/06

Highest attendance
29,312 v Aston Villa 16.10.05

Lowest attendance
24,010 v West Ham United 05.12.05

Average attendance
27,392

How to Get There

Travel Information

Car parking

Apart from street parking, there is a small car park at the ground and one on Garrison Lane.

Train

The stations are Birmingham New Street or Birmingham Moor Street (20 minutes walk). A taxi will cost around £5 to the ground.

Area Map

Local Map

- A roads
- trunk roads
- route

Burnley

Nickname:	The Clarets	Telephone:	0870 443 1882
Manager:	Steve Cotterill	Ticket Office:	0870 443 1914
Chairman:	Barry Kilby	Club Shop:	0870 443 1882
Website:	www.burnleyfootballclub.com		

Season Review 05/06

It was a season of little excitement at Turf Moor, with a mid-season push for the Playoffs proving to be the only real highlight. The goals of much-maligned striker Ade Akinbiyi were badly missed after he left for Sheffield United in January.

A worrying end to the campaign saw Steve Cotterill's team win just two of their final 14 Championship matches.

Points / Position

won drawn lost H home A away

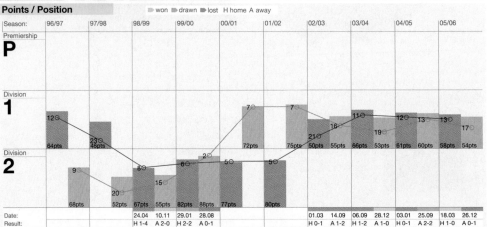

Season:	96/97	97/98	98/99	99/00	00/01	01/02	02/03	03/04	04/05	05/06
Date:			24.04	10.11	29.01	28.08	01.03	14.09	06.09	28.12	03.01	25.09	18.03	26.12
Result:			H 1-4	A 2-0	H 2-2	A 0-1		H 0-1	A 1-2	H 1-2	A 1-0	H 0-1	A 2-2	H 1-0	A 0-1

Champ. Head-to-Head

Facts	O Stoke	Burnley O
Games		
Points	4	7
Won	1	2
Drawn	1	1
Goals		
For	3	4
Clean Sheets	1	2
Shots on Target	20	14
Disciplinary		
Fouls	50	71
Yellow Cards	3	7
Red Cards	0	1

Goals by Area

O Stoke   O Burnley

1	2
2	2
0	0

Goals by Position

O Stoke   O Burnley

	Stoke		Burnley
forward:	3	forward:	3
midfield:	0	midfield:	0
defence:	0	defence:	1

Goals Scored by Period

0	0	1	2	0	0
0	15	30	45	60	75	90
1	1	0	1	0	1

Average Attendance

▶ **13,886**

▶ **15,447**

All-Time Records

Total Championship Record	O Stoke	Burnley O
Played	92	92
Points	119	114
Won	34	29
Drawn	17	27
Lost	41	36
For	90	84
Against	101	93
Players Used	48	42

All-Time Record vs Stoke						
Competition	Played	Won	Drawn	Lost	For	Against
League	84	30	17	37	120	142
FA Cup	7	3	1	3	9	15
League Cup	5	2	1	2	4	7
Other	2	0	1	1	0	2
Total	98	35	20	43	133	166

Turf Moor

Stadium History

Having been in existence for just nine months, Burnley moved to Turf Moor in February 1883. It is believed that the ground was the first to play host to royalty, as Prince Albert, the son of Queen Victoria, attended a game in October 1886.

Much development has taken place since then, most recently the building of two new stands during the mid-1990's. The James Hargreaves Stand was swiftly followed by the Jimmy McIlroy Stand, giving the Clarets a modern venue to be proud of.

Seating Plan

Capacity
22,546

- family area
- away fans
- disabled

Stadium Statistics 05/06

Highest attendance
17,912 v Stoke City 26.12.05

Lowest attendance
10,431 v Cardiff City 10.09.05

Average attendance
12,461

How to Get There

Travel Information

Car parking
Due to matchday parking restrictions, away fans are advised to use the cricket club on Belvedere Road

Train
The nearest stations are Burnley Central (20 minute walk) and Burnley Manchester Road (15 minute walk).

Bus
The main Bus Station is located just off Centenary Way, not far from Turf Moor.

Area Map

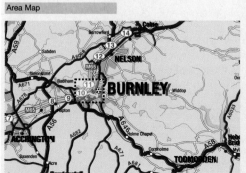

Local Map

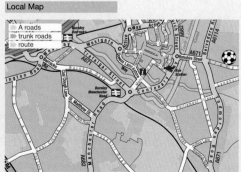

Cardiff City

Nickname:	The Bluebirds
Manager:	Dave Jones
Chairman:	Sam Hammam
Website:	www.cardiffcityfc.co.uk

Telephone:	02920 221 001
Ticket Office:	0845 345 1400
Club Shop:	0845 345 1485

Season Review 05/06

Cardiff spent the season on the fringes of a Playoff place, but ultimately fell away to finish 11th. On-loan midfielder Jason Koumas played a starring role, with Cameron Jerome demonstrating enough ability in attack to earn a summer move to Birmingham.

Producing consistent performances proved difficult for the Bluebirds, with back-to-back victories only achieved twice during the Championship campaign.

Points / Position

won drawn lost H home A away

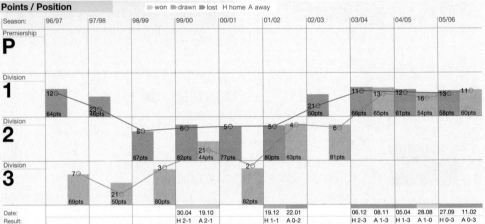

Season:	96/97	97/98	98/99	99/00	00/01	01/02	02/03	03/04	04/05	05/06

Premiership **P**

Division **1**: 12◯ 64pts | 23◯ 46pts | | | | | 21◯ 50pts | 66pts | 11◯ | 13◯ 65pts | 12◯ 61pts | 16◯ 54pts | 13◯ 58pts | 11◯ 60pts

Division **2**: | | 8◯ 67pts | 6◯ 82pts | 5◯ 77pts | 5◯ 80pts | 4◯ 83pts | 6◯ 81pts

Division **3**: | 7◯ 69pts | 21◯ 50pts | 3◯ 80pts | | 2◯ 82pts

Date:	30.04	19.10		19.12	22.01		06.12	08.11	05.04	28.08	27.09	11.02
Result:	H 2-1	A 2-1		H 1-1	A 0-2		H 2-3	A 1-3	H 1-3	A 1-0	H 0-3	A 0-3

Champ. Head-to-Head

Facts	◯ Stoke	Cardiff ◯
Games		
Points	3	9
Won	1	3
Drawn	0	0
Goals		
For	2	9
Clean Sheets	1	2
Shots on Target	12	20
Disciplinary		
Fouls	55	49
Yellow Cards	8	7
Red Cards	0	0

Goals by Area

◯ Stoke   ◯ Cardiff

0	1
1	5
1	3

Goals by Position

◯ Stoke   ◯ Cardiff

	Stoke		Cardiff
forward:	1	forward:	5
midfield:	0	midfield:	1
defence:	1	defence:	3

Goals Scored by Period

0	0	2	0	0	0
0	15	30	45	60	75	90
2	3	1	2	1	0

Average Attendance

▶ **12,513**

▶ **11,855**

All-Time Records

Total Championship Record	◯ Stoke	Cardiff ◯
Played	92	92
Points	119	114
Won	34	29
Drawn	17	27
Lost	41	36
For	90	106
Against	101	110
Players Used	48	48

All-Time Record vs Stoke

Competition	Played	Won	Drawn	Lost	For	Against
League	32	14	6	12	53	40
FA Cup	2	0	0	2	2	6
League Cup	0	0	0	0	0	0
Other	2	1	0	1	2	3
Total	**36**	**15**	**6**	**15**	**57**	**49**

Cardiff City

Ninian Park

Stadium History

Ninian Park, named after Lord Ninian Crichton-Stuart, became home to Cardiff in 1910. A 2-1 friendly defeat against Aston Villa on September 1 marked the first match played at the venue, and drew a crowd of over 7,000 spectators.

Much work had been required to turn land used primarily as a waste tip into a flat surface capable of staging football, with many volunteers playing a key role in the process. Nowadays, plans to build a new and improved stadium are in place.

Seating Plan

Popular Bank

Canton Stand

Grange Terrace

Grandstand

Capacity
20,000

▶ family area
▶ away fans
   disabled

Stadium Statistics 05/06

Highest attendance
16,403 v Plymouth Argyle 26.12.05

Lowest attendance
8,724 v Ipswich Town 28.11.05

Average attendance
11,720

How to Get There

Travel Information

Car parking
Spaces are available at a car park opposite the ground, and at the Leckwith Road Athletics Stadium.

Train
Ninian Park Halt is served by trains from Cardiff Central Station, and is just a 2-3 minute walk from the ground.

Bus
There are regular services to Ninian Park from Cardiff Central Bus Station.

Area Map

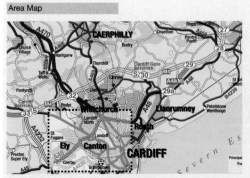

Local Map

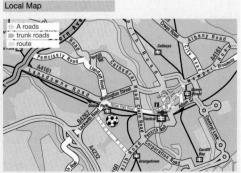

Colchester United

Nickname:	The U's	Telephone:	0871 226 2161
Manager:	—	Ticket Office:	0871 226 2161
Chairman:	Peter Heard	Club Shop:	01206 715 309
Website:	www.cu-fc.com		

Season Review 05/06

Phil Parkinson was the toast of Colchester after leading his side to a surprise promotion, but he could not resist the overtures of Hull during the summer. The unfashionable Layer Road club overcame a shaky start and even managed a run of nine straight League One wins at home.

Amazingly, no team in the division performed in front of a lower average gate than the men from Essex.

Points / Position

● won ● drawn ● lost H home A away

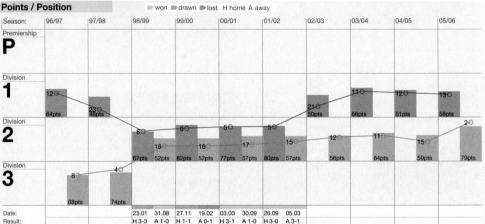

Season:	96/97	97/98	98/99	99/00	00/01	01/02	02/03	03/04	04/05	05/06
Premiership **P**										
Division **1**	12 / 64pts	23 / 46pts	8	8	5	5	21 / 50pts	11 / 66pts	12 / 61pts	13 / 58pts
Division **2**		18 / 67pts	18 / 52pts	17 / 82pts	15 / 52pts	12 / 77pts	11 / 57pts	15 / 80pts	57pts / 58pts	2 / 64pts / 59pts / 79pts
Division **3**	8 / 68pts	4 / 74pts								

Date:	23.01	31.08	27.11	19.02	03.03	30.09	26.09	05.03
Result:	H 3-3	A 1-0	H 1-1	A 0-1	H 3-1	A 1-0	H 3-0	A 3-1

Champ. Head-to-Head

Facts	○ Stoke	Colchester ○
Games		
Points	0	0
Won	0	0
Drawn	0	0
Goals		
For	0	0
Clean Sheets	0	0
Shots on Target	0	0
Disciplinary		
Fouls	0	0
Yellow Cards	0	0
Red Cards	0	0

Goals by Area

○ Stoke   ○ Colchester

0	0	0
0		0

Goals by Position

○ Stoke   ○ Colchester

	Stoke	Colchester
● forward:	0	● forward: 0
● midfield:	0	● midfield: 0
● defence:	0	● defence: 0

Goals Scored by Period

0	0	0	0	0	0	
0	15	30	45	60	75	90
0	0	0	0	0	0	

Average Attendance

All-Time Records

Total Championship Record	○ Stoke	Colchester ○
Played	92	0
Points	119	0
Won	34	0
Drawn	17	0
Lost	41	0
For	90	0
Against	101	0
Players Used	48	0

All-Time Record vs Stoke

Competition	Played	Won	Drawn	Lost	For	Against
League	8	1	2	5	7	15
FA Cup	0	0	0	0	0	0
League Cup	0	0	0	0	0	0
Other	0	0	0	0	0	0
Total	**8**	**1**	**2**	**5**	**7**	**15**

Colchester United

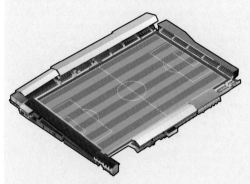

Stadium History

Layer Road opened its doors in August 1909, but it wasn't until 1937 that Colchester United were formed and took over the ground from previous occupants Colchester Town. In more recent times, ownership has changed hands between the local Borough council and the club on a couple of occasions.

It is hoped that a new 10,000-capacity community stadium at Cuckoo Farm will be constructed in time for the team to start playing there by the beginning of the 2007/08 season.

Seating Plan

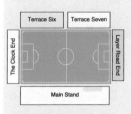

Capacity
6,200

- family area
- away fans
- disabled

Stadium Statistics 05/06

Highest attendance
5,920 v Southend United 04.03.06

Lowest attendance
2,721 v Barnsley 13.08.05

Average attendance
3,969

How to Get There

Travel Information

Car parking
Limited street parking is available in the area surrounding the ground.

Train
Away supporters are advised to use Colchester (North) Station.

Bus
The number 64 travels along Layer Road, and can be caught from the town centre.

Area Map

Local Map

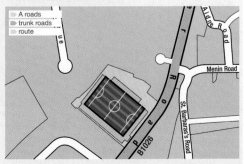

- A roads
- trunk roads
- route

Coventry City

Nickname:	The Sky Blues	Telephone:	0870 421 1987
Manager:	Micky Adams	Ticket Office:	0870 421 1987
Chairman:	Geoffrey Robinson	Club Shop:	0870 421 1987
Website:	www.ccfc.co.uk		

Season Review 05/06

Coventry made real progress over the course of the campaign, brushing aside a slow start to finish in a creditable eighth place. The brand new Ricoh Arena proved to be a happy hunting ground for the Sky Blues, with just four visiting teams emerging victorious.

Gary McSheffrey always looked dangerous, whilst Dele Adebola and Stern John struck up a decent partnership in attack.

Points / Position

won drawn lost H home A away

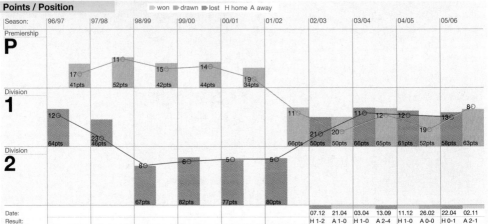

Season:	96/97	97/98	98/99	99/00	00/01	01/02	02/03	03/04	04/05	05/06
Premiership P	17 / 41pts	11 / 52pts	15 / 42pts	14 / 44pts	19 / 34pts					
Division 1	12 / 64pts	23 / 46pts					11 / 66pts	11 / 66pts	12 / 65pts	12 / 61pts	19 / 52pts	13 / 58pts	8 / 63pts
Division 2			8 / 67pts	6 / 82pts	5 / 77pts	5 / 80pts	21 / 50pts	20 / 50pts			

Date:	07.12	21.04	03.04	13.09	11.12	26.02	22.04	02.11
Result:	H 1-2	A 1-0	H 1-0	A 2-4	H 1-0	A 0-0	H 0-1	A 2-1

Champ. Head-to-Head

Facts	O Stoke	Coventry O
Games		
Points	7	4
Won	2	1
Drawn	1	1
Goals		
For	3	2
Clean Sheets	2	2
Shots on Target	24	16
Disciplinary		
Fouls	69	55
Yellow Cards	9	4
Red Cards	0	1

Goals by Area

O Stoke   O Coventry

	1	1	
		0	1
2			0

Goals Scored by Period

0	1	1	1	0	0
0	15	30	45	60	75	90
1	0	0	0	0	1

Goals by Position

O Stoke   O Coventry

	Stoke	Coventry
forward:	2	forward: 1
midfield:	0	midfield: 1
defence:	1	defence: 0

Average Attendance

14,565

15,244

All-Time Records

Total Championship Record	O Stoke	Coventry O
Played	92	92
Points	119	115
Won	34	29
Drawn	17	28
Lost	41	35
For	90	123
Against	101	138
Players Used	48	51

All-Time Record vs Stoke

Competition	Played	Won	Drawn	Lost	For	Against
League	50	20	7	23	61	77
FA Cup	1	1	0	0	1	0
League Cup	1	1	0	0	2	1
Other	0	0	0	0	0	0
Total	**52**	**22**	**7**	**23**	**64**	**78**

Coventry City

Ricoh Arena

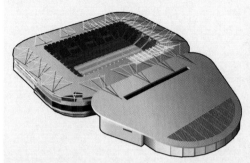

Stadium History

Coventry began the 2005-06 season in the impressive surroundings of the brand new Ricoh Arena. Having ended their 106-year stay at Highfield Road with a 6-2 demolition of Derby, the Sky Blues christened their new stadium with a 3-0 win against Q.P.R on August 20, 2005.

Built on a 70-acre site in the north of the city, the new ground is capable of housing 32,000 spectators. Football is not the only thing on offer at the venue, however, with the development also comprising a supermarket and casino.

Seating Plan

Capacity
32,000

➤ family area
➤ away fans
disabled

Stadium Statistics 05/06

Highest attendance
26,851 v Wolverhampton Wanderers 02.01.06

Lowest attendance
16,156 v Millwall 10.12.05

Average attendance
21,301

How to Get There

Travel Information

Car parking
The Ricoh Arena offers around 2000 parking spaces on site.

Train
Coventry Station is a five minute taxi ride away from the new ground.

Bus
Six members-only bus routes to the stadium have been created.

Area Map

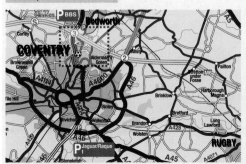

Local Map

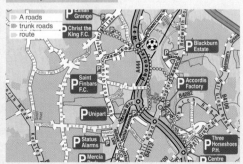

Crystal Palace

Nickname: The Eagles
Manager: Peter Taylor
Chairman: Simon Jordan
Website: www.cpfc.co.uk

Telephone: 0208 768 6000
Ticket Office: 0871 2000 071
Club Shop: 0208 768 6100

Season Review 05/06

A campaign that began with high hopes of a return to the Premiership ended in bitter Playoff disappointment. Manager Iain Dowie then left for Charlton, with key men Andy Johnson and Fitz Hall also moving on to pastures new.

The Eagles struggled to fulfill their potential and will be hoping that new boss Peter Taylor can remedy that next season.

Points / Position

won · drawn · lost H home A away

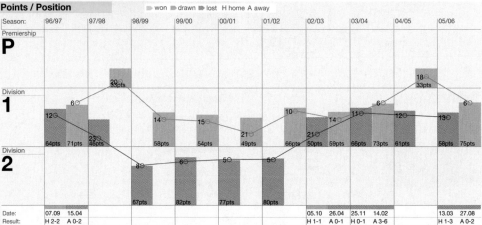

Season:	96/97	97/98	98/99	99/00	00/01	01/02	02/03	03/04	04/05	05/06
	64pts	71pts	46pts	58pts	54pts	49pts	66pts	50pts	59pts	66pts 73pts	61pts	58pts 75pts

| Date: | 07.09 | 15.04 | | | | | 05.10 | 26.04 | 25.11 | 14.02 | | 13.03 | 27.08 |
| Result: | H 2-2 | A 0-2 | | | | | H 1-1 | A 0-1 | H 0-1 | A 3-6 | | H 1-3 | A 0-2 |

Champ. Head-to-Head

Facts	Stoke	C. Palace
Games		
Points	0	6
Won	0	2
Drawn	0	0
Goals		
For	1	5
Clean Sheets	0	1
Shots on Target	10	10
Disciplinary		
Fouls	26	23
Yellow Cards	2	0
Red Cards	0	0

Goals by Area

Stoke · Crystal Palace

	Stoke	Palace
	1	1
	0	3
0		1

Goals Scored by Period

0	0	0	1	0	0
0	15	30	45	60	75	90
0	1	1	2	0	1

Goals by Position

Stoke · Crystal Palace

	Stoke		Crystal Palace
forward:	0	forward:	3
midfield:	1	midfield:	1
defence:	0	defence:	0
		own goals:	1

Average Attendance

10,121

17,637

All-Time Records

Total Championship Record	Stoke	C. Palace
Played	92	46
Points	119	75
Won	34	21
Drawn	17	12
Lost	41	13
For	90	67
Against	101	48
Players Used	48	23

All-Time Record vs Stoke

Competition	Played	Won	Drawn	Lost	For	Against
League	42	19	11	12	61	46
FA Cup	1	0	0	1	0	1
League Cup	0	0	0	0	0	0
Other	0	0	0	0	0	0
Total	43	19	11	13	61	47

Crystal Palace

Selhurst Park

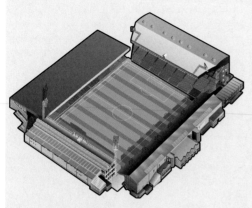

Stadium History

Having spent £2,570 on acquiring land and a further £30,000 on construction work, Crystal Palace moved into their new Selhurst Park home in 1924. Though the ground remained undeveloped until 1969, a friendly against Real Madrid in 1962 marked the installation of new floodlights mounted on pylons in each corner of the stadium.

In recent times, the venue has provided fellow London clubs Charlton Athletic and Wimbledon with temporary accommodation when they were without a home.

Seating Plan

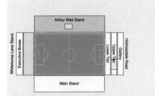

Capacity
26,309

- family area
- away fans
- disabled

Stadium Statistics 05/06

Highest attendance
23,843 v Leeds United 04.03.06

Lowest attendance
17,291 v Preston North End 24.09.05

Average attendance
19,457

How to Get There

Travel Information

Car parking
Plenty of street parking is available, while the local Sainsbury's car park can also be used.

Train
The nearest stations are Thornton Heath and Selhurst. Crystal Palace Station is nowhere near the stadium.

Bus
Buses from all the surrounding areas run past the ground.

Area Map

Local Map

Derby County

Nickname:	The Rams	Telephone:	0870 444 1884
Manager:	Billy Davies	Ticket Office:	0870 444 1884
Chairman:	Peter Gadsby	Club Shop:	01332 209 000
Website:	www.dcfc.co.uk		

Season Review 05/06

Derby failed to build on what had been an impressive season in 2004/05, with Phil Brown only lasting a few months in the managerial hotseat. Caretaker replacement Terry Westley then did just enough to keep the Rams out of the relegation picture.

The summer appointment of former Preston boss Billy Davies has given many fans hope of better times to come at Pride Park.

Points / Position

▶ won ▶ drawn ▶ lost H home A away

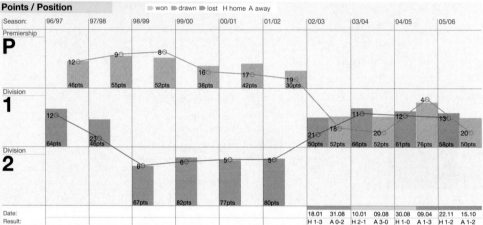

Season:	96/97	97/98	98/99	99/00	00/01	01/02	02/03	03/04	04/05	05/06
Premiership P	12 46pts	9 55pts	8 52pts	16 38pts	17 42pts	19 30pts				
Division 1	12 64pts	23 46pts					21 50pts / 18 52pts	11 66pts / 20 52pts	12 61pts / 4 76pts	13 58pts / 20 50pts
Division 2			8 67pts	6 82pts	5 77pts	5 80pts				

Date:							18.01	31.08	10.01	09.08	30.08	09.04	22.11	15.10
Result:							H 1-3	A 0-2	H 2-1	A 3-0	H 1-0	A 1-3	H 1-2	A 1-2

Champ. Head-to-Head

Facts	○ Stoke	Derby ○
Games		
Points	3	9
Won	1	3
Drawn	0	0
Goals		
For	4	7
Clean Sheets	1	0
Shots on Target	22	27
Disciplinary		
Fouls	47	43
Yellow Cards	5	6
Red Cards	0	0

Goals by Area

○ Stoke   ○ Derby

	1	2	
	2		3
1			2

Goals Scored by Period

1	0	1	1	0	1
0	15	30	45	60	75	90
1	0	2	0	2	2

Goals by Position

○ Stoke   ○ Derby

▶ forward: 1   ▶ forward: 2
▶ midfield: 0   ▶ midfield: 4
▶ defence: 3   ▶ defence: 1

Average Attendance

▶ **15,939**
▶ **24,935**

All-Time Records

Total Championship Record	○ Stoke	Derby ○
Played	92	92
Points	119	126
Won	34	32
Drawn	17	30
Lost	41	30
For	90	124
Against	101	127
Players Used	48	47

All-Time Record vs Stoke						
Competition	Played	Won	Drawn	Lost	For	Against
League	122	48	37	37	208	186
FA Cup	3	2	0	1	7	3
League Cup	0	0	0	0	0	0
Other	0	0	0	0	0	0
Total	125	50	37	38	215	189

Pride Park

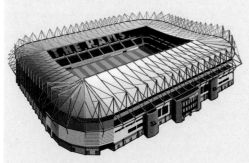

Stadium History

Her Majesty the Queen and the Duke of Edinburgh officially opened Pride Park, with a friendly against Sampdoria getting things underway on the pitch. That was in the summer of 1997, and two years later the capacity was increased to in excess of 33,000.

Having previously hosted an Under-21 match, the ground staged a full international as England defeated Mexico 4-0 in a May 2001 friendly. Despite no longer playing in the Premiership, Derby regularly attract crowds of around 25,000.

Seating Plan

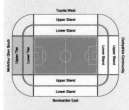

Capacity
33,597

▶ family area
▶ away fans
  disabled

Stadium Statistics 05/06

Highest attendance
30,391 v Sheffield Wednesday 30.04.06

Lowest attendance
21,434 v Reading 31.12.05

Average attendance
24,166

How to Get There

Travel Information

Car parking
Away fans are advised to park at Wilmorton College.

Train
It is a 15 minute walk from Derby Railway Station to Pride Park.

Bus
Shuttle buses run to the ground from the bus station in the city centre.

Area Map

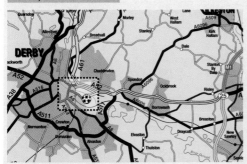

Local Map

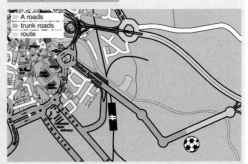

Hull City

Nickname:	The Tigers	Telephone:	0870 837 0003
Manager:	Phil Parkinson	Ticket Office:	0870 837 0004
Chairman:	Adam Pearson	Club Shop:	0870 837 0005
Website:	www.hullcityafc.premiumtv.co.uk		

Season Review 05/06

Hull enjoyed a fairly comfortable season back at Championship level and were never unduly troubled by the threat of relegation. Victory over local rivals Leeds in April was the undoubted highlight of a solid campaign.

The summer departure of popular manager Peter Taylor came as a massive blow to the club, but his youthful replacement, Phil Parkinson, has shown plenty of promise.

Points / Position

won drawn lost H home A away

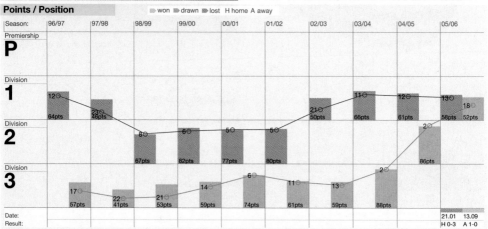

Season:	96/97	97/98	98/99	99/00	00/01	01/02	02/03	03/04	04/05	05/06
Premiership P										
Division 1	12 64pts	23 48pts					21 50pts	11 66pts	12 61pts	13 58pts / 18 52pts
Division 2			8 67pts	6 82pts	5 77pts	5 80pts			2 86pts	
Division 3	17 57pts	22 41pts	21 53pts	14 59pts	6 74pts	11 61pts	13 59pts	2 88pts		
Date:										21.01 13.09
Result:										H 0-3 A 1-0

Champ. Head-to-Head

Facts	○ Stoke	Hull ○
Games		
Points	3	3
Won	1	1
Drawn	0	0
Goals		
For	1	3
Clean Sheets	1	1
Shots on Target	13	17
Disciplinary		
Fouls	37	33
Yellow Cards	8	5
Red Cards	0	0

Goals by Area
○ Stoke   ○ Hull

1   1
0   1
0   1

Goals by Position
○ Stoke   ○ Hull

	Stoke		Hull
forward:	1	forward:	2
midfield:	0	midfield:	0
defence:	0	defence:	0
		own goals:	1

Goals Scored by Period

0	0	0	0	1	0
0	15	30	45	60	75	90
1	0	0	1	0	1

Average Attendance

▶ **13,444**

▶ **18,692**

All-Time Records

Total Championship Record	○ Stoke	Hull ○
Played	92	46
Points	119	52
Won	34	12
Drawn	17	16
Lost	41	18
For	90	49
Against	101	55
Players Used	48	33

All-Time Record vs Stoke

Competition	Played	Won	Drawn	Lost	For	Against
League	46	15	13	18	54	61
FA Cup	4	1	0	3	5	10
League Cup	0	0	0	0	0	0
Other	0	0	0	0	0	0
Total	**50**	**16**	**13**	**21**	**59**	**71**

Hull City

KC Stadium

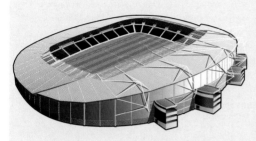

Stadium History

Constructed in 14 months, the KC Stadium opened for business with a friendly victory against Sunderland on December 18, 2002. Built at a cost of £43.5m, the stadium complex was the first in Britain to be located within a parkland setting.

Moving to this state-of-the-art venue has had a positive effect on the pitch, with Hull securing successive promotions and establishing themselves in the Championship. The ground is also home to the city's rugby league team, while other facilities such as a skate park can be found on the council-owned site.

Seating Plan

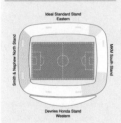

Capacity
25,504

- family area
- away fans
- disabled

Stadium Statistics 05/06

Highest attendance
23,486 v Leeds United 01.04.06

Lowest attendance
17,698 v Reading 18.10.05

Average attendance
19,841

How to Get There

Travel Information

Car parking
There is a car park at the ground costing £2.50.

Train
Paragon Station is around 10 minutes walk from the stadium.

Bus
A park and ride service operates from the Priory Park site on the way into Hull.

Area Map

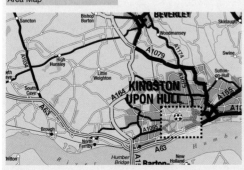

Local Map

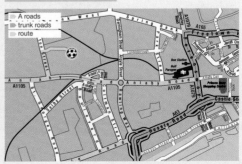

Ipswich Town

Nickname:	The Tractor Boys	Telephone:	01473 400 500
Manager:	Jim Magilton	Ticket Office:	0870 111 0555
Chairman:	David Sheepshanks	Club Shop:	01473 400 501
Website:	www.itfc.co.uk		

Season Review 05/06

Ipswich struggled to adapt to life without Darren Bent, Shefki Kuqi, Kelvin Davis and Tommy Miller. Manager Joe Royle had little choice but to put his faith in youth and saw the Tractor Boys slump to a disappointing 15th-place finish.

Legendary skipper Jim Magilton looked set for an emotional summer exit, but instead found himself succeeding Royle as boss.

Points / Position

won drawn lost H home A away

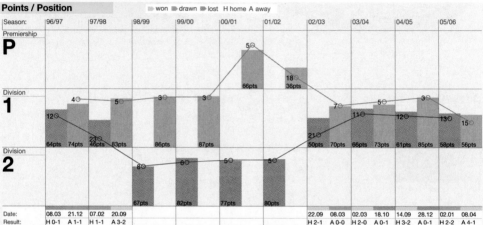

Season:	96/97	97/98	98/99	99/00	00/01	01/02	02/03	03/04	04/05	05/06
Date:	08.03	21.12	07.02	20.09			22.09	08.03	02.03	18.10	14.09	28.12	02.01	08.04
Result:	H 0-1	A 1-1	H 1-1	A 3-2			H 2-1	A 0-0	H 2-0	A 0-1	H 3-2	A 0-1	H 2-2	A 4-1

Champ. Head-to-Head

Facts

	Stoke	Ipswich
Games		
Points	7	4
Won	2	1
Drawn	1	1
Goals		
For	9	6
Clean Sheets	0	1
Shots on Target	27	31
Disciplinary		
Fouls	58	49
Yellow Cards	7	3
Red Cards	1	0

Goals by Area

Stoke   Ipswich

5	1
	5
0	0

Goals Scored by Period

	0	1	1	1	2	4
	0	15	30	45	60	75	90
	1	1	2	0	2	0

Goals by Position

Stoke   Ipswich

- forward: 3 | forward: 1
- midfield: 3 | midfield: 2
- defence: 2 | defence: 3
- own goals: 1

Average Attendance

18,761

24,905

All-Time Records

Total Championship Record

	Stoke	Ipswich
Played	92	92
Points	119	141
Won	34	38
Drawn	17	27
Lost	41	27
For	90	138
Against	101	122
Players Used	48	42

All-Time Record vs Stoke

Competition	Played	Won	Drawn	Lost	For	Against
League	64	26	16	22	100	88
FA Cup	5	1	2	2	2	3
League Cup	3	1	0	2	4	5
Other	0	0	0	0	0	0
Total	72	28	18	26	106	96

Ipswich Town

Portman Road

Stadium History

Having shared what is now the training pitch behind the Britannia Stand with the local cricket club for a number of years, Ipswich moved to the site of today's Portman Road in the early 1900's.

The Supporters' Association funded several developments in the 1950's, most notably raising £30,500 towards the building of a new West Stand. Since the turn of the Millennium, further work has taken place. The impressive Greene King and North stands cost around £22m to build.

Seating Plan

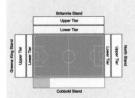

Capacity
30,300

- family area
- away fans
- disabled

Stadium Statistics 05/06

Highest attendance
29,184 v Norwich City 18.09.05

Lowest attendance
22,551 v Preston North End 29.08.05

Average attendance
24,252

How to Get There

Travel Information

Car parking
There are roughly 800 spaces available in car parks around the stadium.

Train
The ground is about 400 metres away from Ipswich Station.

Bus
Bus stops are located on nearby Princes Street, Civic Drive and Handford Road.

Area Map

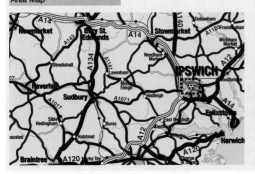

Local Map

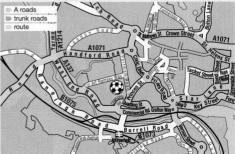

Leeds United

Nickname:	United	Telephone:	0113 367 6000
Manager:	Kevin Blackwell	Ticket Office:	0845 121 1992
Chairman:	Ken Bates	Club Shop:	0870 125 3337
Website:	www.leedsunited.com		

Season Review 05/06

A promising campaign ended in bitter disappointment for Leeds as they missed out on promotion against Watford in the Playoff Final. Kevin Blackwell's team were a permanent fixture in the top six, but rarely threatened to go up automatically.

Rob Hulse, David Healy and Robbie Blake all contributed a decent amount of goals, with Eddie Lewis providing a number of vital assists.

Points / Position

won drawn lost H home A away

Season:	96/97	97/98	98/99	99/00	00/01	01/02	02/03	03/04	04/05	05/06

Premiership P

- 11 — 46pts (96/97)
- 5 — 59pts (97/98)
- 4 — 67pts (98/99)
- 3 — 69pts (99/00)
- 4 — 68pts (00/01)
- 5 — 66pts (01/02)
- 15 — 47pts (02/03)
- 19 — 33pts (03/04)

Division 1

- 12 — 64pts (96/97)
- 23 — 46pts (97/98)
- 21 — 50pts (02/03)
- 11 — 66pts (03/04)
- 12 — 61pts (04/05)
- 14 — 60pts (04/05)
- 13 — 58pts (05/06)
- 5 — 78pts (05/06)

Division 2

- 8 — 67pts (98/99)
- 8 — 82pts (99/00)
- 5 — 77pts (00/01)
- 5 — 80pts (01/02)

Date:								22.01	28.09	28.12	25.03
Result:								H 0-1	A 0-0	H 0-1	A 0-0

Champ. Head-to-Head

Facts	O Stoke	Leeds O
Games		
Points	2	8
Won	0	2
Drawn	2	2
Goals		
For	0	2
Clean Sheets	2	4
Shots on Target	17	21
Disciplinary		
Fouls	61	50
Yellow Cards	7	6
Red Cards	0	0

Goals by Area

O Stoke   O Leeds

	1	
0		1
0		0

Goals Scored by Period

0	0	0	0	0	0
0	15	30	45	60	75	90
0	0	0	0	2	0

Goals by Position

O Stoke   O Leeds

- forward: 0
- midfield: 0
- defence: 0

- forward: 0
- midfield: 1
- defence: 0
- own goals: 1

Average Attendance

➤ **19,390**

➤ **23,606**

All-Time Records

Total Championship Record	O Stoke	Leeds O
Played	92	92
Points	119	138
Won	34	35
Drawn	17	33
Lost	41	24
For	90	106
Against	101	90
Players Used	48	46

All-Time Record vs Stoke

Competition	Played	Won	Drawn	Lost	For	Against
League	82	39	18	25	129	117
FA Cup	2	2	0	0	4	1
League Cup	3	2	0	1	6	3
Other	0	0	0	0	0	0
Total	**87**	**43**	**18**	**26**	**139**	**121**

Leeds United

Elland Road

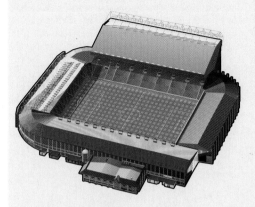

Stadium History

Having previously housed rugby and then Leeds City Football Club, Elland Road became home to the newly-formed Leeds United in 1919. A fire devastated the West Stand in September 1956, with damage estimated at £100,000. The stadium has recovered from that dark day, and can now boast a 17,000-capacity East Stand.

Unfortunately, recent financial problems forced the club to sell the ground on a 25-year sale and lease-back deal, though they do have the right to repurchase it at any time.

Seating Plan

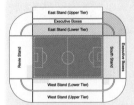

Capacity
40,204

- family area
- away fans
- disabled

Stadium Statistics 05/06

Highest attendance
27,843 v Sheffield Wednesday 21.01.06

Lowest attendance
18,353 v Derby County 28.09.05

Average attendance
22,354

How to Get There

Travel Information

Car parking
Visiting supporters are directed into Car Park A, at a cost of £3 per car.

Train
Elland Road is around a 35 minute walk from Leeds Station.

Bus
Shuttle buses start running from the railway station to the ground two hours before kick-off.

Area Map

Local Map

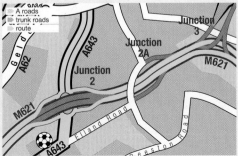

Leicester City

Nickname:	The Foxes	Telephone:	0870 040 6000
Manager:	Rob Kelly	Ticket Office:	0870 499 1884
Chairman:	Andrew Taylor	Club Shop:	0870 040 6000
Website:	www.lcfc.co.uk		

Season Review 05/06

The Foxes endured a disappointing campaign, only moving away from the relegation places following the departure of manager Craig Levein. A run of 28 points from the final 16 games then helped caretaker boss Rob Kelly secure the role on a permanent basis.

Midfielder Joey Gudjonsson was very much the star performer, even managing to score from the halfway line against Hull.

Points / Position

● won ● drawn ● lost H home A away

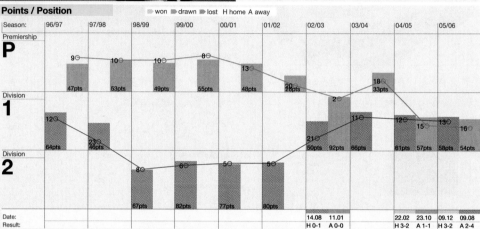

Season:	96/97	97/98	98/99	99/00	00/01	01/02	02/03	03/04	04/05	05/06

Premiership P — 9 (47pts), 10 (53pts), 10 (49pts), 8 (55pts), 13 (48pts), 20 (28pts), 18 (33pts)

Division 1 — 12 (64pts), 23 (46pts), 21/2 (50pts, 92pts, 66pts), 11 (61pts), 12 (57pts), 13/15 (58pts), 16 (54pts)

Division 2 — 8 (67pts), 6 (82pts), 5 (77pts), 5 (80pts)

| Date: | | | | | | | 14.08 | 11.01 | | 22.02 | 23.10 | 09.12 | 09.08 |
| Result: | | | | | | | H 0-1 | A 0-0 | | H 3-2 | A 1-1 | H 3-2 | A 2-4 |

Champ. Head-to-Head

Facts	○ Stoke	Leicester ○
Games		
Points	7	4
Won	2	1
Drawn	1	1
Goals		
For	9	9
Clean Sheets	0	0
Shots on Target	20	25
Disciplinary		
Fouls	60	52
Yellow Cards	4	6
Red Cards	1	0

Goals by Area
○ Stoke   ○ Leicester

7   6
1   2

Goals by Position
○ Stoke   ○ Leicester

	Stoke	Leicester
▶ forward:	5	5
▶ midfield:	1	3
▶ defence:	3	0
▶ own goals:		1

Goals Scored by Period

0	1	3	1	2	2
0	15	30	45	60	75	90
2	2	0	1	1	3

Average Attendance
▶ **12,601**
▶ **21,701**

All-Time Records

Total Championship Record	○ Stoke	Leicester ○
Played	92	92
Points	119	111
Won	34	25
Drawn	17	36
Lost	41	31
For	90	100
Against	101	105
Players Used	48	50

All-Time Record vs Stoke

Competition	Played	Won	Drawn	Lost	For	Against
League	74	25	23	26	99	94
FA Cup	9	3	4	2	16	14
League Cup	2	1	1	0	4	3
Other	2	1	1	0	1	0
Total	**87**	**30**	**29**	**28**	**120**	**111**

Walkers Stadium

Having beaten Tottenham 2-1 in a memorable final match at their legendary Filbert Street home, Leicester made the short journey to the Walkers Stadium. Former fox Gary Lineker was handed the honour of officially opening the state-of-the-art facility.

Promotion to the Premiership was achieved during the inaugural season at the new venue, but relegation swiftly followed. In June 2003, England defeated Serbia & Montenegro in the first full international to be staged in the city.

Seating Plan

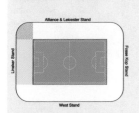

Stadium Statistics 05/06

Capacity
32,500

▷ family area
▷ away fans
☐ disabled

Highest attendance
25,578 v Reading 25.03.06

Lowest attendance
18,856 v Watford 22.11.05

Average attendance
22,233

How to Get There

Travel Information

Car parking
There is plenty of street parking available, particularly in the Upperton Road area.

Train
Leicester Station is located in the city centre, some 20-25 minutes walk from the ground.

Bus
Numbers 36, 52, 52a, 52b, 52c and 53 regularly go to and from the city centre.

Area Map

Local Map

Luton Town

Nickname:	The Hatters	Telephone:	01582 411 622
Manager:	Mike Newell	Ticket Office:	01582 416 976
Chairman:	Bill Tomlins	Club Shop:	01582 488 864
Website:	www.lutontown.co.uk		

Season Review 05/06

Luton burst onto the Championship scene in spectacular fashion, rarely dropping out of the top-six until mid-December. Though the Hatters eventually finished in tenth, they won many admirers for approaching the game in such a positive fashion.

The achievements of manager Mike Newell also attracted attention, with both Leicester and Crystal Palace expressing an interest in securing his services.

Points / Position

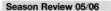
won drawn lost H home A away

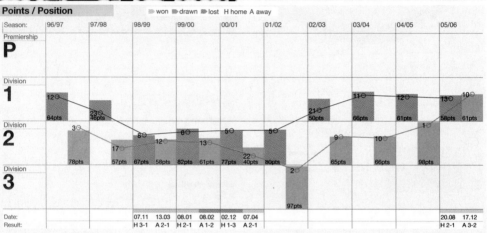

Season:	96/97	97/98	98/99	99/00	00/01	01/02	02/03	03/04	04/05	05/06
Premiership **P**										
Division **1**	12 64pts	23 46pts					21 50pts	11 66pts	12 61pts	13 58pts 10 61pts
Division **2**	3 78pts	17 57pts	8 67pts 12 58pts	6 82pts	13 61pts	5 77pts 22 40pts	5 80pts 2	9 65pts	10 66pts	1 98pts
Division **3**							97pts			

Date:			07.11	13.03	08.01	08.02	02.12	07.04			20.08	17.12
Result:			H 3-1	A 2-1	H 2-1	A 1-2	H 1-3	A 2-1			H 2-1	A 3-2

Champ. Head-to-Head

Facts

Facts	○ Stoke	Luton ○
Games		
Points	6	0
Won	2	0
Drawn	0	0
Goals		
For	5	3
Clean Sheets	0	0
Shots on Target	13	15
Disciplinary		
Fouls	34	22
Yellow Cards	3	3
Red Cards	0	1

Goals by Area
○ Stoke   ○ Luton

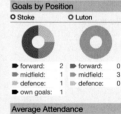

	Stoke	Luton
	0	
	3	3
	1	0

Goals by Position
○ Stoke   ○ Luton

	Stoke	Luton
▶ forward:	2	0
▶ midfield:	1	3
▶ defence:	1	0
▶ own goals:	1	

Goals Scored by Period

	0	0	1	0	1	3
	0	15	30	45	60	75	90
	1	1	0	0	0	1

Average Attendance

▶ **18,653**

▶ **8,296**

All-Time Records

Total Championship Record

Total Championship Record	○ Stoke	Luton ○
Played	92	46
Points	119	61
Won	34	17
Drawn	17	10
Lost	41	19
For	90	66
Against	101	67
Players Used	48	24

All-Time Record vs Stoke

Competition	Played	Won	Drawn	Lost	For	Against
League	36	9	11	16	51	55
FA Cup	2	1	1	0	4	3
League Cup	0	0	0	0	0	0
Other	0	0	0	0	0	0
Total	**38**	**10**	**12**	**16**	**55**	**58**

Luton Town

Kenilworth Road

Stadium History

Following spells playing at Dunstable Road and Dallow Lane, Luton moved to Kenilworth Road in 1905. One of the stands burnt down during a fire in 1920, and was replaced by the Main Stand of today. Having set a record attendance for the ground of 30,069 in the late 1950's, the capacity has since fallen to just over 10,000.

The club experimented with a plastic playing surface in more recent times, though this was removed and replaced with conventional grass in the early 1990's.

Seating Plan

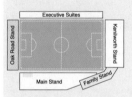

Capacity
10,300

- family area
- away fans
- disabled

Stadium Statistics 05/06

Highest attendance
10,248 v Wolverhampton Wanderers 10.09.05

Lowest attendance
7,474 v Crewe Alexandra 22.11.05

Average attendance
9,139

How to Get There

Travel Information

Car parking
There is limited street parking near the ground, with a multi-storey car park in the town centre.

Bus
Take the number 31 from opposite the railway station, and ask for the Oak Road stop.

Train
Luton Station is a 10 minute walk from Kenilworth Road.

Area Map

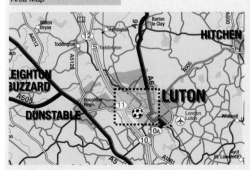

Local Map

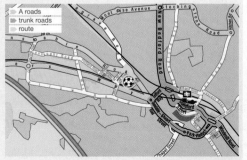

Norwich City

Nickname:	**The Canaries**
Manager:	**Nigel Worthington**
Chairman:	**Roger Munby**
Website:	**www.canaries.co.uk**

Telephone:	**01603 760 760**
Ticket Office:	**0870 444 1902**
Club Shop:	**0870 444 1902**

Season Review 05/06

The Canaries struggled to adjust to life back in the Championship, failing to recover from a sluggish start to the campaign. Manager Nigel Worthington came in for much criticism, particularly in light of some woeful displays away from Carrow Road.

Though the team could only manage a ninth-place finish, the club came top of the division in average attendance terms.

Points / Position

won ▶ drawn ▶ lost H home A away

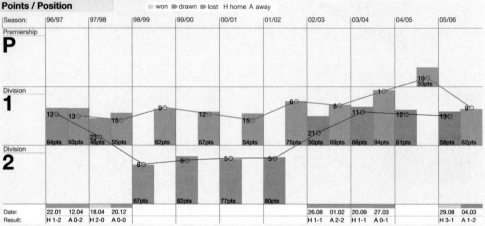

Season:	96/97	97/98	98/99	99/00	00/01	01/02	02/03	03/04	04/05	05/06
Premiership **P**										
Division **1**	12 / 64pts	13 / 63pts	15 / 23 / 46pts / 55pts	9 / 62pts	12 / 57pts	15 / 54pts	6 / 21 / 75pts / 50pts	8 / 11 / 69pts / 66pts	1 / 12 / 94pts / 61pts	19 / 33pts / 13 / 58pts / 9 / 62pts
Division **2**			8 / 67pts	6 / 82pts	5 / 77pts	5 / 80pts				

Date:	22.01	12.04	18.04	20.12			26.08	01.02	20.09	27.03		29.08	04.03
Result:	H 1-2	A 0-2	H 2-0	A 0-0			H 1-1	A 2-2	H 1-1	A 0-1		H 3-1	A 1-2

Champ. Head-to-Head

Facts	○ Stoke	Norwich ○
Games		
Points	3	3
Won	1	1
Drawn	0	0
Goals		
For	4	3
Clean Sheets	0	0
Shots on Target	11	8
Disciplinary		
Fouls	22	21
Yellow Cards	4	1
Red Cards	0	1

Goals by Area

○ Stoke   ○ Norwich

3	0 / 3
1	0

Goals by Position

○ Stoke   ○ Norwich

▶ forward:	2	▶ forward:	3
▶ midfield:	2	▶ midfield:	0
▶ defence:	0	▶ defence:	0

Goals Scored by Period

1	0	1	1	1	0
0	15	30	45	60	75	90
0	0	1	1	0	1

Average Attendance

▶ **14,249**

▶ **24,223**

All-Time Records

Total Championship Record	○ Stoke	Norwich ○
Played	92	46
Points	119	62
Won	34	18
Drawn	17	8
Lost	41	20
For	90	56
Against	101	65
Players Used	48	31

All-Time Record vs Stoke						
Competition	Played	Won	Drawn	Lost	For	Against
League	38	13	13	12	52	45
FA Cup	1	1	0	0	1	0
League Cup	2	0	0	2	2	4
Other	0	0	0	0	0	0
Total	**41**	**14**	**13**	**14**	**55**	**49**

Carrow Road

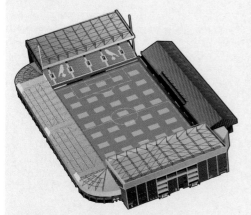

Norwich moved to Carrow Road in 1935, and the stadium has come a long way since then. Despite hosting the likes of European giants Bayern Munich and Inter Milan, the record attendance at the ground of 43,984 was set in a 1963 FA Cup tie with Leicester City.

The recently-constructed 8,000 capacity Jarrold Stand is a sign that the club is moving in the right direction, while Delia Smith's personal touch ensures that business is brisk on the catering front.

Seating Plan

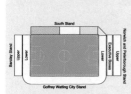

Capacity
27,470

▷ family area
▷ away fans
▷ disabled

Stadium Statistics 05/06

Highest attendance
27,470 v Hull City 27.09.05

Lowest attendance
23,838 v Cardiff City 01.11.05

Average attendance
24,952

How to Get There

Travel Information

Car parking
Norfolk County Hall offers around 2000 spaces, while there are plenty of car parks in the city centre.

Bus
No services run to, or near, the ground.

Train
Carrow Road is a five minute walk from Norwich Station.

Area Map

Local Map

▷ A roads
▷ trunk roads
▷ route

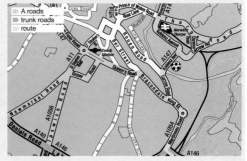

Plymouth Argyle

Nickname:	The Pilgrims
Manager:	Ian Holloway
Chairman:	Paul Stapleton
Website:	www.pafc.co.uk

Telephone:	01752 562 561
Ticket Office:	0871 222 1288
Club Shop:	01752 558 292

Season Review 05/06

Despite winning at eventual champions Reading on the opening day of the season, manager Bobby Williamson did not last much longer in the role. Tony Pulis was appointed as his successor and guided the Pilgrims to 14th place, before departing for Stoke in the summer.

Plymouth fans will be hoping that new boss Ian Holloway can bring a little more attacking flair to the team.

Points / Position

won drawn lost H home A away

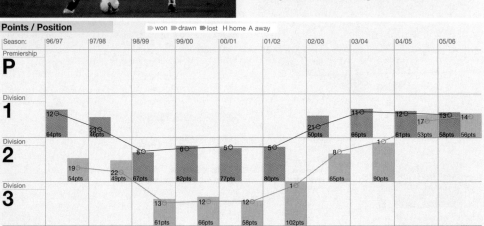

Date:	16.04	20.11	14.02	01.10
Result:	H 2-0	A 0-0	H 0-0	A 1-2

Champ. Head-to-Head

Facts	○Stoke	Plymouth○
Games		
Points	5	5
Won	1	1
Drawn	2	2
Goals		
For	3	2
Clean Sheets	3	2
Shots on Target	16	19
Disciplinary		
Fouls	58	43
Yellow Cards	7	3
Red Cards	0	0

Goals by Area

○ Stoke   ○ Plymouth

0		1
		1
1		0

Goals Scored by Period

0	1	1	1	0	0
0	15	30	45	60	75	90
0	0	0	1	0	1

Goals by Position

○ Stoke   ○ Plymouth

	Stoke	Plymouth
forward:	1	0
midfield:	2	1
defence:	0	0
own goals:		1

Average Attendance

▶ **11,630**

▶ **13,934**

All-Time Records

Total Championship Record	○Stoke	Plymouth○
Played	92	92
Points	119	109
Won	34	27
Drawn	17	28
Lost	41	37
For	90	91
Against	101	110
Players Used	48	44

All-Time Record vs Stoke

Competition	Played	Won	Drawn	Lost	For	Against
League	34	8	9	17	38	52
FA Cup	0	0	0	0	0	0
League Cup	2	1	1	0	4	2
Other	0	0	0	0	0	0
Total	**36**	**9**	**10**	**17**	**42**	**54**

Plymouth Argyle

Home Park

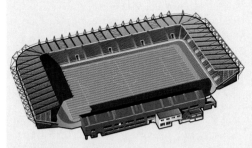

Stadium History

Originally home to Devonport Albion Rugby Club, the Home Park Recreation Ground was unused for three years prior to 1901. Football then began to take place at the venue, leading to Plymouth Argyle turning professional in 1903.

The stadium was badly damaged during a World War II air raid, but went on to play host to Pele and his Santos team in March 1973. Recent rebuilding work has seen development on three sides of the ground, raising the capacity to in excess of 20,000.

Seating Plan

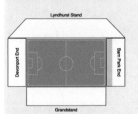

Capacity
20,922

- family area
- away fans
- disabled

Stadium Statistics 05/06

Highest attendance
17,726 v Leeds United 02.01.06

Lowest attendance
10,460 v Crewe Alexandra 13.09.05

Average attendance
13,776

How to Get There

Travel Information

Car parking
A large free car park is situated next to the ground.

Train
Plymouth North Road Station is a fair way from Home Park, but has direct links from all over the country.

Bus
Regular services run from the city centre to the required Milehouse area of Plymouth.

Area Map

Local Map

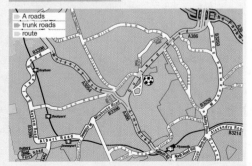

Preston North End

Nickname:	The Lilywhites	Telephone:	0870 442 1964
Manager:	Paul Simpson	Ticket Office:	0870 442 1966
Chairman:	Derek Shaw	Club Shop:	0870 442 1965
Website:	www.pnefc.co.uk		

Season Review 05/06

A 22-match unbeaten run midway through the season helped Preston reach the Playoffs, where they were beaten at the semi-final stage by Leeds. Manager Billy Davies then left for Derby, with Carlisle boss Paul Simpson replacing him at Deepdale.

The lilywhites kept 24 Championship clean sheets in 2005/06, but will be weakened by the departure of defender Claude Davis.

Points / Position

won drawn lost H home A away

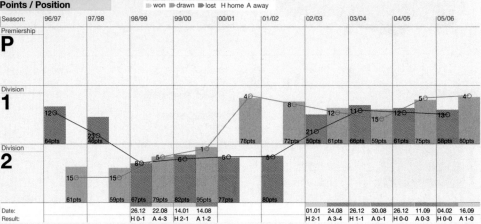

Season:	96/97	97/98	98/99	99/00	00/01	01/02	02/03	03/04	04/05	05/06
Premiership										
Division 1	12 / 64pts	23 / 46pts			4 / 78pts	8 / 72pts	21 / 50pts / 12 / 61pts	11 / 66pts / 15 / 59pts	12 / 61pts / 5 / 75pts	13 / 58pts / 4 / 80pts
Division 2	15 / 61pts	15 / 59pts	8 / 67pts / 5 / 79pts	6 / 82pts / 1 / 95pts	5 / 77pts	5 / 80pts				
Date:			26.12	22.08	14.01	14.08	01.01	24.08	26.12	30.08
Result:			H 0-1	A 4-3	H 2-1	A 1-2	H 2-1	A 3-4	H 1-1	A 0-1

Date:	26.12	11.09	04.02	16.09
Result:	H 0-0	A 0-3	H 0-0	A 1-0

Champ. Head-to-Head

Facts	Stoke	Preston
Games		
Points	5	5
Won	1	1
Drawn	2	2
Goals		
For	1	3
Clean Sheets	3	3
Shots on Target	14	19
Disciplinary		
Fouls	51	72
Yellow Cards	4	7
Red Cards	1	0

Goals by Area

Stoke   Preston

	1		1
0			1

Goals Scored by Period

0	0	0	0	0	1
0	15	30	45	60	75	90
0	1	0	0	0	2

Goals by Position

Stoke   Preston

- forward: 1
- midfield: 0
- defence: 0

- forward: 3
- midfield: 0
- defence: 0

Average Attendance

16,784

12,606

All-Time Records

Total Championship Record	Stoke	Preston
Played	92	92
Points	119	155
Won	34	41
Drawn	17	32
Lost	41	19
For	90	126
Against	101	88
Players Used	48	50

All-Time Record vs Stoke						
Competition	Played	Won	Drawn	Lost	For	Against
League	90	39	19	32	152	127
FA Cup	5	3	1	1	11	7
League Cup	2	1	0	1	5	2
Other	0	0	0	0	0	0
Total	**97**	**43**	**20**	**34**	**168**	**136**

Preston North End

Deepdale

Stadium History

Housing the National Football Museum, located in the Sir Tom Finney and Bill Shankly Kop stands, Deepdale is a ground steeped in history. The stadium is currently three-quarters of the way through a total redevelopment program that began in 1996, as the club look to turn their home into a 30,000-capacity arena.

During the summer of 2005 the venue played host to several matches in the Women's European Championships, further highlighting its modern capabilities.

Seating Plan

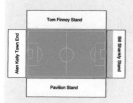

Capacity
22,225

- family area
- away fans
- disabled

Stadium Statistics 05/06

Highest attendance
19,350 v Leeds United 30.04.06

Lowest attendance
12,453 v Stoke City 16.09.05

Average attendance
14,619

How to Get There

Travel Information

Car parking
Moor Park High School and Deepdale Primary School charge £5 for parking.

Train
Preston Station is around 1.5 miles away from Deepdale.

Bus
Numbers 5, 6 and 19 stop at the bus station, and travel along Deepdale Road.

Area Map

Local Map

QPR

Nickname:	The Superhoops	Telephone:	020 8743 0262
Manager:	Gary Waddock	Ticket Office:	0870 112 1967
Chairman:	Gianni Paladini	Club Shop:	020 8749 6862
Website:	www.qpr.co.uk		

Season Review 05/06

Boardroom friction did little to help matters on the pitch at Loftus Road, with Rangers finishing the season just above the relegation places. Manager Ian Holloway had been sent on "gardening leave" in February and was replaced by coach Gary Waddock.

A return of just five points from the final 11 games of the campaign highlighted the sense of uncertainty at the club.

Points / Position

won drawn lost H home A away

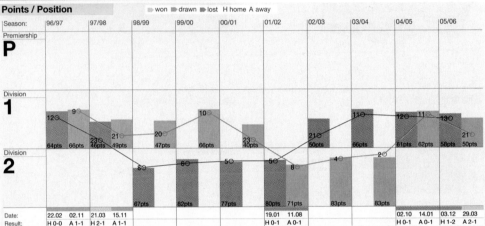

Season:	96/97	97/98	98/99	99/00	00/01	01/02	02/03	03/04	04/05	05/06

Premiership **P**

Division **1**

12 9 23 21 20 10 23 21 8 11 12 11 13 21
64pts 66pts 46pts 49pts 47pts 66pts 40pts 50pts 66pts 61pts 62pts 58pts 50pts

Division **2**

8 6 5 5 8 4 2
67pts 82pts 77pts 80pts 71pts 83pts 83pts

| Date: | 22.02 | 02.11 | 21.03 | 15.11 | | | 19.01 | 11.08 | | 02.10 | 14.01 | 03.12 | 29.03 |
| Result: | H 0-0 | A 1-1 | H 2-1 | A 1-1 | | | H 0-1 | A 0-1 | | H 0-1 | A 0-1 | H 1-2 | A 2-1 |

Champ. Head-to-Head

Facts	O Stoke	QPR O
Games		
Points	3	9
Won	1	3
Drawn	0	0
Goals		
For	3	5
Clean Sheets	0	2
Shots on Target	14	13
Disciplinary		
Fouls	54	64
Yellow Cards	9	9
Red Cards	2	0

Goals by Area

O Stoke   O QPR

0   0

3   4

0   1

Goals by Position

O Stoke   O QPR

	Stoke	QPR
forward:	1	3
midfield:	1	2
defence:	1	0

Goals Scored by Period

0	1	0	0	1	1
	15	30	45	60	75	90
2	1	0	1	1	0

Average Attendance

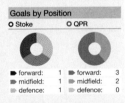

16,122

12,239

All-Time Records

Total Championship Record	O Stoke	QPR O
Played	92	92
Points	119	112
Won	34	29
Drawn	17	25
Lost	41	38
For	90	104
Against	101	123
Players Used	48	56

All-Time Record vs Stoke

Competition	Played	Won	Drawn	Lost	For	Against
League	24	13	5	6	35	22
FA Cup	1	1	0	0	3	0
League Cup	0	0	0	0	0	0
Other	0	0	0	0	0	0
Total	25	14	5	6	38	22

Loftus Road

Stadium History

The club led a somewhat nomadic existence for many years, occupying several grounds prior to arriving at Loftus Road and only settling there at the third time of asking in the early 1960's. Development was soon underway, with the South Africa Road Stand the first to be completed.

A plastic pitch was installed during the 1980's, and lasted seven seasons before being replaced with natural grass. More recently, the stadium offered a temporary two-year home to West London neighbours Fulham.

Seating Plan

Capacity
18,500

- family area
- away fans
- disabled

Stadium Statistics 05/06

Highest attendance
16,152 v Watford 22.04.06

Lowest attendance
10,901 v Preston North End 22.11.05

Average attendance
13,440

How to Get There

Travel Information

Car parking
Street parking is available near the ground.

Train
Acton Central Station is a bus ride away from Loftus Road.

Tube
The nearest stations are White City on the Central line and Shepherds Bush on the Hammersmith & City line.

Bus
Number 283 goes to nearby Bloemfontein Road.

Area Map

Local Map

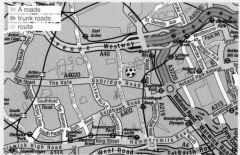

Sheff Wed

Nickname:	The Owls	Telephone:	0870 999 1867
Manager:	Paul Sturrock	Ticket Office:	0870 999 1867
Chairman:	Dave Allen	Club Shop:	0870 999 1867
Website:	www.swfc.co.uk		

Season Review 05/06

Paul Sturrock's team achieved their goal of Championship survival, helped in no small part by a terrific level of support. Things looked bleak during the early months of the campaign, but the Owls eventually found their feet.

Northern Ireland international Chris Brunt was particularly outstanding, weighing in with seven goals and six assists in the league.

Points / Position

won drawn lost H home A away

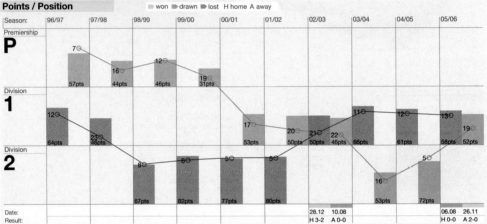

Season:	96/97	97/98	98/99	99/00	00/01	01/02	02/03	03/04	04/05	05/06
Premiership P		7 57pts	16 44pts	12 46pts	19 31pts					
Division 1	12 64pts	23 46pts				17 53pts	20 50pts / 21 50pts	22 46pts / 11 66pts	12 61pts	13 58pts / 19 52pts
Division 2			8 67pts	6 82pts	5 77pts	5 80pts		16 53pts	72pts	5

Date:							28.12 10.08		06.08 26.11
Result:							H 3-2 A 0-0		H 0-0 A 2-0

Champ. Head-to-Head

Facts	Stoke	Sheff Wed
Games		
Points	4	1
Won	1	0
Drawn	1	1
Goals		
For	2	0
Clean Sheets	2	1
Shots on Target	8	12
Disciplinary		
Fouls	20	21
Yellow Cards	5	4
Red Cards	1	0

Goals by Area

Stoke | Sheff Wed

```
        0
   1        0
0              0
```

Goals Scored by Period

```
0   1   0   0   0   1
0  15  30  45  60  75  90
0   0   0   0   0   0
```

Goals by Position

Stoke | Sheff Wed

	Stoke		Sheff Wed
forward:	2	forward:	0
midfield:	0	midfield:	0
defence:	0	defence:	0

Average Attendance

18,744

21,970

All-Time Records

Total Championship Record	Stoke	Sheff Wed
Played	92	46
Points	119	52
Won	34	13
Drawn	17	13
Lost	41	20
For	90	39
Against	101	52
Players Used	48	37

All-Time Record vs Stoke

Competition	Played	Won	Drawn	Lost	For	Against
League	74	31	15	28	110	95
FA Cup	6	2	2	2	8	6
League Cup	5	2	2	1	5	3
Other	0	0	0	0	0	0
Total	**85**	**35**	**19**	**31**	**123**	**104**

Hillsborough

Stadium History

Sheffield Wednesday moved to Hillsborough in 1899, though it wasn't until 1914 that their new home changed its name from the Owlerton Stadium. Chesterfield were beaten 5-1 in the club's opening game at the ground, the first of 19 consecutive victories at the venue.

April 15, 1989 was the darkest day in the stadium's history, as 96 Liverpool fans lost their lives during an FA Cup semi-final. The disaster led to nationwide safety improvements, and Hillsborough went on to host several matches during Euro 96.

Seating Plan

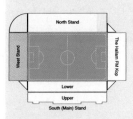

Capacity
39,859

▶ family area
▶ away fans
☐ disabled

Stadium Statistics 05/06

Highest attendance
33,439 v Sheffield United 18.02.06

Lowest attendance
20,244 v Plymouth Argyle 22.11.05

Average attendance
24,853

How to Get There

Travel Information

Car parking
Parking is available at the nearby Owlerton Greyhound Stadium.

Train
Sheffield Railway Station is in the city centre, some 3 miles from the ground.

Bus
Numbers 53, 77 and 80 run to Hillsborough from the Flat Street Bus Terminus.

Area Map

Local Map

Southampton

Nickname:	The Saints	Telephone:	0870 220 0000
Manager:	George Burley	Ticket Office:	0870 220 0150
Chairman:	Michael Wilde	Club Shop:	0870 220 0130
Website:	www.saintsfc.co.uk		

Season Review 05/06

Southampton failed to make an immediate return to the Premiership, paying the price for drawing 19 of their 46 games. Many fans were delighted to see Harry Redknapp desert his managerial post in December, particularly as George Burley took over.

Five wins from the final six games of the season represented a strong finish and further boosted morale in the camp.

Points / Position

won drawn lost H home A away

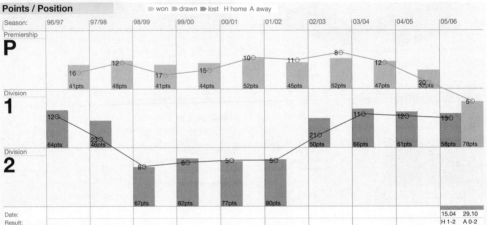

Date:	15.04	29.10
Result:	H 1-2	A 0-2

Champ. Head-to-Head

Facts	O Stoke	Southampton O
Games		
Points	0	6
Won	0	2
Drawn	0	0
Goals		
For	1	4
Clean Sheets	0	1
Shots on Target	6	18
Disciplinary		
Fouls	23	28
Yellow Cards	2	1
Red Cards	1	0

Goals by Area

O Stoke   O Southampton

0	0
0	4
1	0

Goals Scored by Period

0	0	0	0	0	1	
0	15	30	45	60	75	90
0	2	1	0	0	1	

Goals by Position

O Stoke   O Southampton

forward: 1	forward: 2
midfield: 0	midfield: 2
defence: 0	defence: 0

Average Attendance

16,501

24,095

All-Time Records

Total Championship Record	O Stoke	Southampton O
Played	92	46
Points	119	58
Won	34	13
Drawn	17	19
Lost	41	14
For	90	49
Against	101	50
Players Used	48	40

All-Time Record vs Stoke						
Competition	Played	Won	Drawn	Lost	For	Against
League	56	25	9	22	85	80
FA Cup	1	0	0	1	0	1
League Cup	0	0	0	0	0	0
Other	0	0	0	0	0	0
Total	57	25	9	23	85	81

Southampton

St Mary's Stadium

Stadium History

Following a 103-year stay at The Dell, Southampton moved to their brand new £32m stadium in time for the start of the 2001–02 season.

It took three months for a victory to arrive, leading many to believe that the venue was somehow jinxed. In truth, the poor early results were probably a consequence of visiting players feeling less intimidated than on previous visits to the South Coast. In October 2002, the stadium played host to England vs FYR Macedonia in a Euro 2004 Qualifier.

Seating Plan

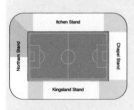

Capacity
32,251

▶ family area
▶ away fans
▷ disabled

Stadium Statistics 05/06

Highest attendance
30,173 v Leeds United 19.11.05

Lowest attendance
19,086 v Luton Town 11.12.05

Average attendance
23,613

How to Get There

Travel Information

Car parking
City centre parking is an option, due to restrictions nearer the ground.

Train
It is a 30 minute walk from Southampton Station to the stadium.

Bus
A free park and ride scheme for away supporters is in operation just off Junction 8 of the M27.

Area Map

Local Map

A roads
trunk roads
route

Southend United

Nickname:	The Shrimpers	Telephone:	01702 304 050
Manager:	Steve Tilson	Ticket Office:	08444 770 077
Chairman:	Ron Martin	Club Shop:	01702 351 117
Website:	www.southendunited.co.uk		

Season Review 05/06

Southend took to League One like ducks to water, brushing off the tag of relegation favourites to win the division. Manager Steve Tilson continued the good work of the previous campaign, leading the team to eight straight league wins in the early part of the season.

Though the team ethic was vital to the Shrimpers' success, Freddy Eastwood's goals proved crucial.

Points / Position

won drawn lost H home A away

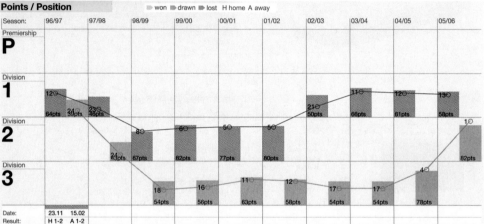

Season:	96/97	97/98	98/99	99/00	00/01	01/02	02/03	03/04	04/05	05/06
Premiership P										
Division 1	12○ 64pts	24○ 39pts	23○ 38pts				21○ 50pts	11○ 66pts	12○ 61pts	13○ 58pts
Division 2			8○	6○	5○	5○				1○ 82pts
		24○ 43pts	67pts	82pts	77pts	80pts				
Division 3			18○ 54pts	16○ 56pts	11○ 63pts	12○ 58pts	17○ 54pts	17○ 54pts	4○ 78pts	
Date:	23.11	15.02								
Result:	H 1-2	A 1-2								

Champ. Head-to-Head

Facts
	○ Stoke	Southend ○
Games		
Points	0	0
Won	0	0
Drawn	0	0
Goals		
For	0	0
Clean Sheets	0	0
Shots on Target	0	0
Disciplinary		
Fouls	0	0
Yellow Cards	0	0
Red Cards	0	0

Goals by Area
○ Stoke   ○ Southend

0 0 0 0 0

Goals by Position
○ Stoke   ○ Southend

forward:	0	forward:	0
midfield:	0	midfield:	0
defence:	0	defence:	0

Goals Scored by Period
0	0	0	0	0	0	
0	15	30	45	60	75	90
0	0	0	0	0	0	

Average Attendance

All-Time Records

Total Championship Record
	○ Stoke	Southend ○
Played	92	0
Points	119	0
Won	34	0
Drawn	17	0
Lost	41	0
For	90	0
Against	101	0
Players Used	48	0

All-Time Record vs Stoke
Competition	Played	Won	Drawn	Lost	For	Against
League	10	5	1	4	13	17
FA Cup	0	0	0	0	0	0
League Cup	2	0	0	2	1	4
Other	0	0	0	0	0	0
Total	**12**	**5**	**1**	**6**	**14**	**21**

Southend United

Roots Hall

Stadium History

Until 1988, Roots Hall was the newest ground in the Football League. Southend purchased the site in 1952 and beat Norwich 3-1 in the first game to be played there on August 20, 1955. Constructing the stands was a long process, however, and it wasn't until 1966 that building work was finally completed.

Significant further development did not take place until the 1990's, with a second tier added to the South Stand and the West Stand roof extended.

Seating Plan

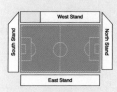

Capacity
12,392

- family area
- away fans
- disabled

Stadium Statistics 05/06

Highest attendance
11,387 v Bristol City 06.05.06

Lowest attendance
5,261 v Oldham Athletic 04.09.05

Average attendance
8,053

How to Get There

Travel Information

Car parking
The ground has a £3 car park behind the Main Stand.

Train
The nearest stations are Prittlewell (5 minute walk) and Southend Central (15 minute walk).

Bus
The main bus station is located close to Southend Central Railway Station.

Area Map

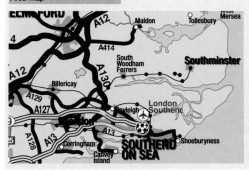

Local Map

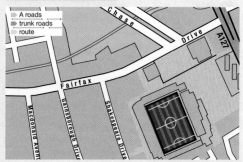

Sunderland

Nickname:	The Black Cats
Manager:	—
Chairman:	—
Website:	www.safc.com

Telephone:	0191 551 5000
Ticket Office:	0845 671 1973
Club Shop:	0191 551 5050

Season Review 05/06

The Black Cats plumbed new depths as they collected just 15 Premiership points, breaking their own unwanted record in the process. Manager Mick McCarthy paid the price for the abject failure, but caretaker replacement Kevin Ball fared no better.

Victory against Fulham in the final home game of the season at least ensured that the fans at the Stadium of Light witnessed a league win.

Points / Position

won — drawn — lost   H home A away

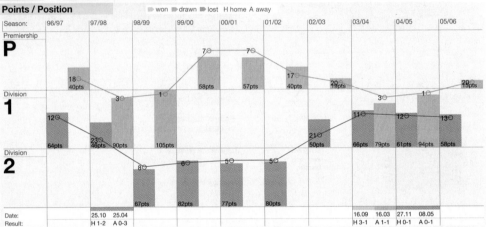

Season:	96/97	97/98	98/99	99/00	00/01	01/02	02/03	03/04	04/05	05/06

Premiership **P**

Division **1**

Division **2**

| Date: | 25.10 | 25.04 | | | | | | 16.09 | 16.03 | 27.11 | 08.05 |
| Result: | H 1-2 | A 0-3 | | | | | | H 3-1 | A 1-1 | H 0-1 | A 0-1 |

Champ. Head-to-Head

Facts

Facts	Stoke	Sunderland
Games		
Points	0	6
Won	0	2
Drawn	0	0
Goals		
For	0	2
Clean Sheets	0	2
Shots on Target	6	15
Disciplinary		
Fouls	30	26
Yellow Cards	0	0
Red Cards	0	0

Goals by Area

Stoke   Sunderland

0	1
0	1
0	0

Goals Scored by Period

0	0	0	0	0	0
0	15	30	45	60	75	90
0	0	0	1	0	1

Goals by Position

Stoke   Sunderland

forward:	0	forward:	1
midfield:	0	midfield:	1
defence:	0	defence:	0

Average Attendance

➤ **16,980**

➤ **47,350**

All-Time Records

Total Championship Record

Total Championship Record	Stoke	Sunderland
Played	92	46
Points	119	94
Won	34	29
Drawn	17	7
Lost	41	10
For	90	76
Against	101	41
Players Used	48	30

All-Time Record vs Stoke

Competition	Played	Won	Drawn	Lost	For	Against
League	118	56	27	35	174	124
FA Cup	9	2	5	2	12	10
League Cup	2	0	0	2	0	5
Other	0	0	0	0	0	0
Total	129	58	32	39	186	139

Sunderland

Stadium of Light

Stadium History

Opened in July 1997, and standing on the banks of the River Wear, the Stadium of Light is an impressive structure. Initially housing 42,000 spectators, the capacity was increased to nearer 50,000 by the extension to the North Stand and other improvements.

The ground has played host to two England internationals, a friendly against Belgium in 1999 and a Euro 2004 qualifier against Turkey in 2003. Unfortunately for the Black Cats, filling such a large arena has proved difficult.

Seating Plan

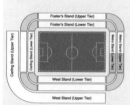

Capacity
48,300

- family area
- away fans
- disabled

Stadium Statistics 05/06

Highest attendance
44,003 v Arsenal 01.05.06

Lowest attendance
28,226 v Fulham 04.05.06

Average attendance
33,904

How to Get There

Travel Information

Car parking

The Stadium of Light provides 1,146 parking spaces for supporters as well as space for up to 24 coaches on match days.

Metro

Between Stadium of Light and St Peter's stations.

Area Map

Local Map

West Brom

Nickname:	**The Baggies**
Manager:	**Bryan Robson**
Chairman:	**Jeremy Peace**
Website:	**www.wba.co.uk**

Telephone:	**08700 668 888**
Ticket Office:	**08700 662 800**
Club Shop:	**08700 662 810**

Season Review 05/06

Bryan Robson's men were unable to repeat the "Great Escape" of twelve months earlier, suffering relegation after a two-season Premiership stay. The Baggies were unable to recover from a crushing 6-1 loss at Fulham in February, failing to win another game from then on.

On the plus side, Albion won a new fan in the shape of 2001 Wimbledon champion Goran Ivanisevic.

Points / Position

⬤ won ⬤ drawn ⬤ lost H home A away

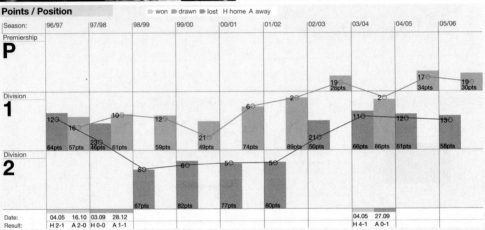

Champ. Head-to-Head

Facts	○ Stoke	West Brom ○
Games		
Points	0	0
Won	0	0
Drawn	0	0
Goals		
For	0	0
Clean Sheets	0	0
Shots on Target	0	0
Disciplinary		
Fouls	0	0
Yellow Cards	0	0
Red Cards	0	0

Goals by Area

○ Stoke ● West Brom

Goals by Position

○ Stoke ○ West Brom

▶ forward:	0	▶ forward:	0
▶ midfield:	0	▶ midfield:	0
▶ defence:	0	▶ defence:	0

Goals Scored by Period

0	0	0	0	0	0
0	15	30	45	60	75	90
0	0	0	0	0	0

Average Attendance

All-Time Records

Total Championship Record	○ Stoke	West Brom ○
Played	92	0
Points	119	0
Won	34	0
Drawn	17	0
Lost	41	0
For	90	0
Against	101	0
Players Used	48	0

All-Time Record vs Stoke

Competition	Played	Won	Drawn	Lost	For	Against
League	116	38	29	49	170	178
FA Cup	5	3	2	0	12	6
League Cup	0	0	0	0	0	0
Other	0	0	0	0	0	0
Total	**121**	**41**	**31**	**49**	**182**	**184**

The Hawthorns

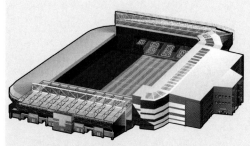

Stadium History

The home of West Bromwich Albion was the first Football League ground to be built in the 20th Century, and was opened on September 3rd 1900. Nearly 50 years later, in 1949, The Hawthorns recorded another first with the introduction of an electronic turnstile aggregator.

More recently, completion of the £7.5m East Stand in time for the start of the 2001-02 season meant that the stadium was fully enclosed. Both the ticket office and club shop are now located within this modern part of the arena.

Seating Plan

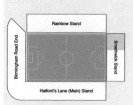

Capacity
28,003

- family area
- away fans
- disabled

Stadium Statistics 05/06

Highest attendance
27,623 v Manchester United 18.03.06

Lowest attendance
23,144 v Fulham 03.12.05

Average attendance
25,403

How to Get There

Travel Information

Car parking

The club has its own car park alongside the Tom Silk Building in Halfords Lane. The car park is stewarded, and costs £4 for the duration of the game. There are other car parks, such as along Halfords Lane, but street parking there is limited.

Train

The Hawthorns railway station is situated on Halfords Lane, 250 metres south of the stadium itself. There is also a Metro tram link which services the main route from Birmingham to Wolverhampton.

Area Map

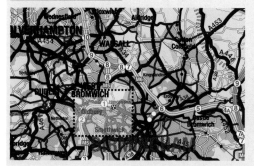

Local Map

Wolves

Nickname:	**Wolves**	Telephone:	**0870 442 0123**
Manager:	**—**	Ticket Office:	**0870 442 0123**
Chairman:	**Rick Hayward**	Club Shop:	**0870 442 0123**
Website:	**www.wolves.co.uk**		

Season Review 05/06

Wolves were perhaps the biggest disappointment of the 2005/06 Championship season, failing even to make the Playoffs. Manager Glenn Hoddle was unable to get the most out of a talented group of players and decided to leave his post during the summer.

Expensive striker Tomasz Frankowski failed to find the net, whilst fans' favourite George Ndah was forced to hang up his boots.

Points / Position

▶ won ▶ drawn ▶ lost H home A away

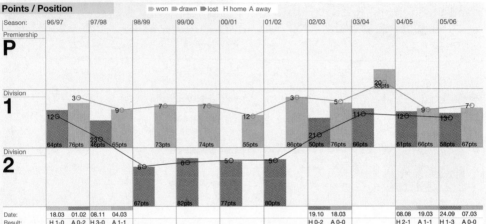

Season:	96/97	97/98	98/99	99/00	00/01	01/02	02/03	03/04	04/05	05/06
Date:	18.03	01.02 08.11 04.03					19.10 18.03		08.08 19.03 24.09 07.03	
Result:	H 1-0	A 0-2 H 3-0 A 1-1					H 0-2 A 0-0		H 2-1 A 1-1 H 1-3 A 0-0	

Champ. Head-to-Head

Facts	O Stoke	Wolves O
Games		
Points	5	5
Won	1	1
Drawn	2	2
Goals		
For	4	5
Clean Sheets	1	1
Shots on Target	21	18
Disciplinary		
Fouls	55	55
Yellow Cards	5	1
Red Cards	0	0

Goals by Area

O Stoke O Wolverhampton

	3	
3		1
1		1

Goals Scored by Period

```
 0    0    1    1    1    1
 0   15   30   45   60   75   90
 0    0    1    1    1    2
```

Goals by Position

O Stoke O Wolverhampton

	Stoke	Wolverhampton
▶ forward:	1	4
▶ midfield:	1	0
▶ defence:	2	1

Average Attendance

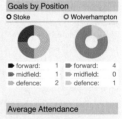

▶ **17,625**
▶ **25,271**

All-Time Records

Total Championship Record	O Stoke	Wolves O
Played	92	92
Points	119	133
Won	34	31
Drawn	17	40
Lost	41	21
For	90	122
Against	101	101
Players Used	48	39

All-Time Record vs Stoke

Competition	Played	Won	Drawn	Lost	For	Against
League	130	56	29	45	206	180
FA Cup	7	6	1	0	21	5
League Cup	0	0	0	0	0	0
Other	0	0	0	0	0	0
Total	**137**	**62**	**30**	**45**	**227**	**185**

Wolves

Molineux

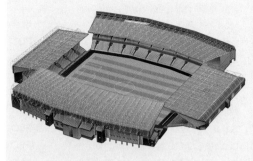

Stadium History

Wolverhampton Wanderers have called Molineux home since 1889. From humble beginnings, where spectators sat on dirt banks, the stadium has evolved into a modern football arena.

Sir Jack Hayward's money saw the transformation of an ageing venue during the 1990's, with all four sides of the ground being redeveloped. During the summer of 2003 it was decided to change the name of the John Ireland Stand to the Steve Bull Stand, thus honouring a modern Wolves hero.

Seating Plan

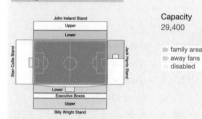

Capacity
29,400

- family area
- away fans
- disabled

Stadium Statistics 05/06

Highest attendance
27,980 v Reading 26.12.05

Lowest attendance
21,683 v Crewe Alexandra 11.02.06

Average attendance
23,624

How to Get There

Travel Information

Car parking
Parking is available in Wolverhampton city centre (5-minute walk).

Train
Wolverhampton Station is a 15 minute walk away from Molineux.

Bus
Numbers 503 and 504 run from the bus station and stop at the ground.

Area Map

Local Map

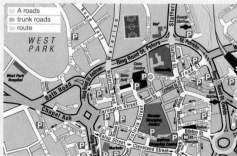

2006/07: The Fixtures

Date	KO	v	Opponent	Competition
August				
Sat 5	15:00	A	Southend	FLC
Tue 8	**19:45**	**H**	**Derby County**	**FLC**
Sat 12	**12:30**	**H**	**Birmingham**	**FLC**
Sat 19	15:00	A	Luton Town	FLC
Tue 22	**19:45**	**H**	**Darlington**	**LGCP**
Sat 26	**15:00**	**H**	**Plymouth**	**FLC**
September				
Sat 9	15:00	A	Barnsley	FLC
Tue 12	19:45	A	Sheffield Wed	FLC
Sat 16	**15:00**	**H**	**Burnley**	**FLC**
Sat 23	15:00	A	Wolves	FLC
Sat 30	**15:00**	**H**	**Preston**	**FLC**
October				
Sat 14	15:00	A	Leeds United	FLC
Tue 17	**19:45**	**H**	**Sunderland**	**FLC**
Sat 21	15:00	A	Southampton	FLC
Sat 28	**15:00**	**H**	**Norwich City**	**FLC**
Tue 31	19:45	A	Leicester City	FLC
November				
Sat 4	**15:00**	**H**	**Coventry City**	**FLC**
Sat 11	15:00	A	Crystal Palace	FLC
Sat 18	15:00	A	Hull City	FLC
Sat 25	**15:00**	**H**	**WBA**	**FLC**
Tue 28	**19:45**	**H**	**Cardiff City**	**FLC**
December				
Sat 2	15:00	A	Coventry City	FLC
Sat 9	**15:00**	**H**	**QPR**	**FLC**
Sat 16	15:00	A	Colchester	FLC
Sat 23	15:00	A	Ipswich Town	FLC
Tue 26	**15:00**	**H**	**Sheffield Wed**	**FLC**
Sat 30	**15:00**	**H**	**Leeds United**	**FLC**

Date	KO	v	Opponent	Competition
January				
Mon 1	15:00	A	Burnley	FLC
Sat 13	**15:00**	**H**	**Wolves**	**FLC**
Sat 20	15:00	A	Preston	FLC
Tue 30	**19:45**	**H**	**Ipswich Town**	**FLC**
February				
Sat 3	**15:00**	**H**	**Southend**	**FLC**
Sat 10	12:00	A	Birmingham	FLC
Sat 17	**15:00**	**H**	**Luton Town**	**FLC**
Wed 21	19:45	A	Derby County	FLC
Sat 24	**15:00**	**H**	**Barnsley**	**FLC**
March				
Sat 3	15:00	A	Plymouth	FLC
Sat 10	**15:00**	**H**	**Southampton**	**FLC**
Tue 13	19:45	A	Sunderland	FLC
Sat 17	15:00	A	Norwich City	FLC
Sat 31	**15:00**	**H**	**Leicester City**	**FLC**
April				
Sat 7	15:00	A	WBA	FLC
Mon 9	**15:00**	**H**	**Crystal Palace**	**FLC**
Sat 14	15:00	A	Cardiff City	FLC
Sat 21	**15:00**	**H**	**Hull City**	**FLC**
Sat 28	**15:00**	**H**	**Colchester**	**FLC**
May				
Sun 6	15:00	A	QPR	FLC